Y0-BCD-390

SAMUEL SEWALL

AND THE WORLD HE LIVED IN.

I Rest
your Obliged friend
Samuel Sewall.

SAMUEL SEWALL

AND

THE WORLD HE LIVED IN

BY

REV. N. H. CHAMBERLAIN

SECOND EDITION

NEW YORK / RUSSELL & RUSSELL

FIRST PUBLISHED IN 1897
REISSUED, 1967, BY RUSSELL & RUSSELL
A DIVISION OF ATHENEUM HOUSE, INC.
L. C. CATALOG CARD NO: 66-24679
PRINTED IN THE UNITED STATES OF AMERICA

TO

THE MEMORY OF THE LATE

George E. Ellis,

DOCTOR OF DIVINITY, AND GREATLY LEARNED IN THE LORE
OF THE FOREFATHERS OF NEW ENGLAND,
OF WHOSE STOCK HE WAS,

This Book,

ALAS! SO LATE, IS NOW DEDICATED BY HIS FRIEND,
THE AUTHOR.

PREFACE.

SAMUEL SEWALL, sometime business man, councillor, judge, and always Puritan, began his Diary with an entry, Dec. 3, 1673, as to what he lectured on, that day to the students of Harvard College, he himself having been there graduated in 1671. The last entry is Oct. 13, 1729. By a coincidence, significant enough to any student of this Diary, it ends with negotiations for a Puritan marriage match: "Judge Davenport comes to me, between ten and eleven o'clock in the morning, and speaks to me on behalf of Mr. Addington Davenport, his eldest son, that he might have liberty to wait upon Jane Hirst, now at my house, in the way of courtship. He told me he would deal by him as his eldest son, and more than so. Intended to build a house where his uncle Addington dwelt, for him; and that he should have his pue in the old meeting house. I gave him my hand at his going away and acknowledged his respect to me and granted his desire. He said Madam Addington would wait upon me. . . . I informed his Honor, the Lieut. Governor of what Mr. Davenport had been about. His Honor approved of it much. Commended the young man, and reckoned it a very good match."

Sewall's Diary, therefore, covers, in time, more than fifty-five years of the old New England life, and when that life was putting itself into form. The book is too late to show the details of the first planting of Massachusetts Colony under Winthrop, except by occasional back glances, more than one generation having lapsed between 1630 and 1673. Yet there were in his day many of "the renowned settlers," as he styles them, who first came; and he was near enough in time to know things from the start, the great head man, and "Fidus Achates" of New England Puritanism, John Winthrop, having died as late as March 26, 1649, or less than twenty-four years before Sewall's Diary begins.

The Diary itself, towards its opening, is broken, probably by the loss of one or more of its manuscript volumes. There is a gap from July, 1677, to March, 1684–1685. This gap has been partially filled by the able editors of the Diary, from the Diary of Sewall's father-in-law, John Hull, the Colonial treasurer of "Pine Tree Shilling" memory; so that Sewall's book, as it now stands before the public, thanks to the love and care of its editors, is substantially continuous and complete. Sewall wrote his Diary in long, thin blank books with flexible leather covers, such as business men then used, in a plain, downright hand, of which the signature attached to his portrait in this book is a fair specimen. These books, preserved with care by his descendants, have of late years been annotated and printed by the Massachusetts Historical Society in three large volumes, amounting, with the indices, to rather more than fifteen hundred pages.[1] It is perhaps needless to say that "Samuel Sewall and the World He Lived in" bases itself upon this larger publication, though the colors for its pictures have been taken, when vivid and honest, wherever found.

Diaries are about the commonest of unpublished literature, and almost every business man makes one every year. Yet, with the millions of such, only two diarists in the English tongue have as yet attained to much fame, — Samuel Pepys and John Evelyn. Of these two, Pepys is the better known to readers. John Evelyn was a gentleman, as Pepys was not, and a Christian, as Pepys only was by spasms; both lived in London, Evelyn in five reigns; and both wrote down with vivid pens such things of the great world as they saw fit; and both will last as among the makers of English literature. With these two Englishmen, in due time, by a well-weighed and just verdict, Samuel Sewall will be associated in the same lasting fame. Not that he resembles either, though more like Evelyn ethically, and like Pepys physically. The two Englishmen were Church-of-England men, and Evelyn a sincere and consistent devotee. Sewall was the very type of the Puritan, and few lives were ever more thoroughly colored by their religion than his. All had been versed in affairs, and knew their times, Pepys showing, perhaps, the most

[1] He had the habit, also, of carrying about with him a pocket almanac, in which to jot down on the spot anything which struck his fancy; and very often these entries are enlarged, and used to fortify the Diary. Several of these useful almanacs are still in existence.

dynamic ability in administration, though quite in one direction ; Sewall wrought more in a longer and more varied public career than the others ; while Evelyn, as the virtuous associate of the great and the pure in heart, was in this world's affairs an atmosphere rather than an actor who controlled. Both the Englishmen show more literary merit, better form, and Evelyn especially has vastly greater continuity and deliberation in his entries, than Sewall.

With this showing, on what ground, then, can the claim be made for Sewall's Diary, as a permanency in English literature, sure to come finally, upon its merits, to a lasting fame? First of all, because his Diary is the only one of New England, and, as to that matter, of the American nation so far, which our people, so rich in other things, can claim for its own ; and for its own, as one of its most ancient and elaborate historical monuments in its ever crescent literature. We have no other book like it ; perhaps no other storehouse of old ways and social life so abundant as it. Sewall never took the time or the pains, being too busy, to get himself a well-mannered style and fixed forms as a literary man. Perhaps the exacting, and even narrow, zeal of Puritanism, always unfavorable to art, dissuaded him. Yet there are not lacking passages in his Diary and Letter Book which show his ability to have written the strongest, well-ordered English had he willed it. Proofs of this ability will be found in this book later on. Sewall's Diary, then, will last because it is a rich mine of New England history ;

because it fulfils this cradle of so much gone into a nation's life, greater than its own, with the records and riches of its own unique and primitive life, as no other man ever has, or at this late day can. As a nation ages, it looks back, and to its monuments. When this is done, it will discover easily in the waste of its earlier days, certainly in its province of New England, that in Sewall's Diary there is more of its own history, on its human side, than in any other writing of the times, not even excepting the Winthrop literature. Indeed, by its very form, as a Diary, Sewall unconsciously was compelled, for our comfort, to ally himself with the new men in history, and not the old, in writing primarily of the people, of their dress, periwigs, funeral and wedding favors, their dinners, town meetings, personal quarrels, and the innumerable trifles, and even foibles, which make up, for most, so much of life. As a man of such social position and locality that he was almost sure to meet almost any body or thing going, and a frequent traveller through the colony; officially so connected with government here and abroad as to see the inner working of affairs; as a judge brought in contact with the tenure and rights of property in some of its more picturesque effects; now involved in the Salem witchcraft business, and for years seeing the crime of the land coming into court for trial, and perhaps sentence, — there was no other man of his age so well fitted to write a Diary like his. And, besides, he had the mind to write and persistency in writing on for fifty-five years, such as no other New England man of his age, at least, displayed. His performance in his Diary is in all ways suggestive and characteristic. It is very much as this land then was, — chaotic, migratory, rough, granite, actual, sincere. The barbaric wilderness, savage, cruel, vast, serves as the background of all his pictures, and not seldom, as an atmosphere, is often blown into them. While the Diary is rough, uncouth, and almost Gothic in its blunt, sometimes even coarse, downrightness, it is always sincere, confidential, and friendly. Sewall puts no gall in his ink, shows no malice, means to be just, with an intention that does not often fail him, and, in short, writes himself down as a strong-bodied, great-souled, honor-loving Puritan; not altogether above his age, — no genius, no saint except in intent, but withal as good "an all-round man" as New England has ever had. It is this man who has written our one great diary. Neither Evelyn nor Pepys uses more vivid colors than he. Often theirs are neither so vivid nor picturesque. Sewall's colors are, indeed, often only glimpses, flashes that reveal long vistas into old things. Put in the permanency of his Diary, and one with an eye for the inner meaning, — the searcher after the light "that never was on land or sea," — the lover of man who sees under all fashions of humanity an incarnation of the Divine which makes it reverend, holy, watches patiently and eagerly its honest pages, to meditate over the grave and almost endless problems which inhered in the old New England life of the men called Puritans. Sewall's value is not simply in what he records, but also in what he suggests. The people who never forget whose sons they are, will ever remember Sewall as the man who holds the candle to so many of the ancient secrets of the fathers.

The question whether Sewall ever expected his Diary to be published does not merit very much discussion, however we may decide it. There are certain facts which seem to answer either way. For instance, it may be said that any sane man, having written so singular a record, and intending publication, would take ample precautions to have it edited by some child or friend judicious enough to prune it sharply in the interest of his own honor. Nothing of the sort appears to have been done. Possibly so sincere a man, having written with so much Puritan sobriety, might judge that nothing of the sort needed to be done. There seems to be a twofold presumption that he intended publication. For, first, if he did not, what possible motive could have kept him at the long and exacting labor of so volu minous a record? Second, traces are not wanting in the Diary itself of the fact that Sewall regarded the New England Puritans as servants, not of themselves, but of that great Master of men whose Law revealed to Moses they endeavored to make the statute law of the Colony, and in whose hand they held themselves as clay to the potter, to take on what shape and stamp He willed so that His world through their toil and sacrifice might become more truly His.[1] That the Puritan was a man with a mission he himself firmly believed, and the fact has been often pointed out. Nor was this self-conceit, but self-surrender and self-absorption, on his part, into that Supreme Other Self who made him and all mankind. With the cross lights of heaven and history beating almost fiercely down upon the humility of him and his home in the wild, was it strange that an educated man, and a leader among his people, should try to tell to posterity how strangely and wonderfully God had dealt with His chosen? From this standpoint, at least, one is forced to conclude that Sewall, as the writing of his Diary proceeded, became aware that he was writing for posterity.

The substance of this Preface has already furnished the reasons why "Samuel Sewall and the World He Lived in" is now submitted to the public. A word or two as to its plan and purpose, and, indeed, as to its right to task the overwearied eye of conscientious

[1] There is a very striking expression of this feeling in Sewall's speech in Council after Lieutenant-Governor Dummer had taken the oaths of office Jan. 2, 1723: "When the representatives were returned to their own chamber I stood up and said, If your honor and this honorable board please to give me leave, I would speak a word or two on this solemn occasion. Although the unerring Providence of God has brought you to the chair of government in a cloudy and tempestuous time; yet you have this for your encouragement that the people you have to do with are a part of the Israel of God, and you may expect to have of the prudence and patience of Moses communicated to you for your conduct. It is evident that our almighty Savior counselled the first planters to remove hither and settle here; and they dutifully followed his advice; and therefore He will never leave nor forsake them nor theirs; so that your honor must needs be happy in sincerely seeking their interest and welfare; which your birth and education will incline you to do. *Difficilia quae pulchra.* I promise myself that they that sit at this board, will yield their faithful advice to your honor according to the duty of their place."

readers. It does not, then, pretend to original research; it avoids, with intention, the minute exactness of the antiquarian, and it uses for its groupings and pictures of the ancient Puritan life such material, from any quarter whatsoever, as could be verified and made useful. It has tried not to mutilate or mislead in its excerpts, and, in general, hopes to have succeeded. It is indebted, first of all, to the Diary itself, as given to the public by the Massachusetts Historical Society; and it is safe to say that without the aid of the publications of that Society any such book as this would be impossible. Since that Society exists to bring the treasures of American history to the American people, it is hoped, that in its own way, this book, availing itself of the Society's help, will assist in enlarging public interest in ancient things; and it hereby refers all readers, in the ten thousand historical matters which it does not handle, to the publications of the Society, which now happily are become aids in any study of our history.

Furthermore, the author is deeply indebted to the historical essays of Dr. George E. Ellis, and especially to his "Puritan Age in Massachusetts," — a philosophy of New England Puritanism which is sure to last long in honor.

THE AUTHOR.

CONTENTS.

CHAPTER		PAGE
I.	Samuel Sewall and the English South Land	3
II.	The Puritan in Old England	10
III.	The Puritan Exodus	21
IV.	Sewall and the Puritan Church	43
V.	Sewall and the Puritan Commonwealth	64
VI.	Sewall as a Business Man	86
VII.	Town and Country Life to 1700	98
VIII.	Sewall, the Indians and Negroes	110
IX.	Sewall in England	135
X.	Sewall and the Salem Witchcraft	157
XI.	Current New England Life from 1700 to 1714,	178
XII.	Sewall and the Puritan Home-Life	205
XIII.	Betty Sewall and Puritan Marriages	224
XIV.	Anne Bradstreet and Our Puritan Literature	236
XV.	Sewall and the Church of England	254
XVI.	Current New England Life from 1714 to Oct. 13, 1729	271
XVII.	Judge Sewall's Courtship of Madam Winthrop, *Aliarumque*	281
XVIII.	Sewall and Sundries	297
XIX.	A Summary	304
	Appendix	311

SAMUEL SEWALL

AND THE WORLD HE LIVED IN.

SAMUEL SEWALL

AND THE WORLD HE LIVED IN.

CHAPTER I.

SAMUEL SEWALL AND THE ENGLISH SOUTH LAND.

SAMUEL SEWALL was born at Bishopstoke, Hampshire, England, March 28, 1652, — "so that the light of the Lord's Day was the first light that my eyes saw, being born a little before daybreak. I was baptized by Mr. Rashly (sometime member of the old church in Boston, England), in Stoke Church, May 4, 1652. Mr. Rashly first preached a sermon, and then baptized me; after which an entertainment was made for him and many more." His great-grandfather, Henry Sewall, beyond whom the family cannot be traced, was a linen-draper at Coventry, where he acquired a fortune, and was several times elected mayor. His grandfather, the eldest son, a Puritan, from dislike to the English Church, sent over Sewall's father, Henry, "with neat cattle and provisions suitable for a new plantation. . . . Mr. Cotton would have had my father settle at Boston; but, in regard of his cattle, he chose to go to Newbury, where my grandfather soon followed him." In 1646 the father married, "being then about thirty-two, and my mother about nineteen years of age." The climate not agreeing with some of the elders, Henry Sewall returned with them to Hampshire, England, in 1647, where Samuel Sewall was born, and bred until 1661, when the family returned to New England by way of London.

Sewall's early years were therefore spent in the English South Land. This fact, of itself, is of no particular account; but in connection with the other fact that many of Sewall's neighbors in Boston were from there, and retained and transmitted at least the memory of its old customs, it may be as well to look a little at the civilization of the seventeenth century then extant in South England, when Sewall and so many of the old Bostonians emigrated. Indeed, he will add the next most charming page in our written history who will relate the life of Old England, with the primitive life of the New. The English South Land lies, of course, along the English Channel, which has always been an open gate for English discovery and enterprise towards the West. The sun is warmer there than in the North Land, and its gardens and orchards fuller. It is the land of the Saxon, as the North is of the Dane; a land where William the Conqueror landed; with men and women of a ruddy countenance, and of old, contented, full-fed, sunny-hearted, and inclined to the Saxon repose, in contrast with the Norseman's enterprise. Sewall's portrait shows the Saxon type. London has for long been the heart of England; but, in general, movements in English religion or politics have originated towards the North. In this South Land, so conservative of ancient habits, when Sewall was born, the civilization was narrow, rustic more than a trifle coarse, but also hearty, picturesque, and vivid, as out of warm Southron blood. It would surprise many a demure and proper family of our date if they could only know how their English ancestors fared three hundred years ago across seas.

Women scolds (and they were plenty) were then ducked, although Lord Holt gravely said of one such brought before his court, that if they ducked her she would be sure to scold on to her life's end. Women were employed to whip petty criminals in public; and a good wife, as late as 1718, earned her shilling this way. The drunkard's cloak, for punishment, was a cask with a hole in the top for his head and a hole each side for his arms. Apprentices, for the first seven years, were forbid to keep fighting-cocks or hunting-dogs. Cock-fighting was a school exercise, and the cost put in the term bills. A common village house was made of oak beams, with the interstices on the outside filled up with mortar; a deep ground cellar, entered by a flight of steps that trenched far out upon the sidewalk, the steps protected by a trap-door; while the shops were open to the streets, and without glass. Very often there were only two or three chimneys in a good-sized town, and these on the squire's or parson's house.

(The first Boston chimneys were chiefly of wood, and hence frequent fires.) Many of the old churches stand there to-day, but the rule of them in ancient days was, to say the least, peculiar. When pews first came in, in King James I.'s days, their green baize was found to harbor insects, and a regular charge was made in some parishes for "salting the fleas." Charges were also made for "mossing the church," which probably was some way of scouring it on great occasions, just as the roads were only repaired when some great person was to pass by. The old amusements in churches and churchyards have been described so often as not to need mention here. To a poor widow, asking the price of a funeral sermon for her husband, a parish clerk made answer that some were 10*s.* — one even as low as *7s. 6d.*, which no one would ever know to be a funeral sermon; but that there would not be a dry eye in the house if the guinea one was preached. Marriage notices were often accompanied by such mundane announcements as these: "Mr. Baskett to Miss Pell with £5,000," "Lord Bishop of St. Asaph to Miss Orell with £30,-000." Old Fuller saw an ancient lady being drawn to church near Lewes in her own coach by six oxen. William Blackstone, Boston's first white settler, after he went away, used to go about in a cart with one.

The social life was still more curious. All work that could be was apparently done out-doors. The women washed in the street. In some places there was a town "spit" for roasting meats, and the cooks about dinner-time were seen running around to hunt up their dogs to turn the same. In Charles II.'s time only 12,000 tons of coal were mined in contrast with 188,277,525 tons in 1894, and the common people must have used fagots. Mantelpieces got their name from the English custom of hanging up their clothes there to dry. They must have been rather coarse eaters and drinkers, though the drink was sometimes thin, as witness the indictment against Isabella Stansby (35 Henry VIII.) for brewing ale "not mighty of corn." The ale-wives — i.e., women who sold beer — were always giving the magistrates much trouble. Potatoes, first planted by an Irishman in Devon, were long objected to as breeding leprosy. Cider was much in vogue, especially in the South Land, where orchards abounded, and were usual places of family retreat, where company was entertained; and the Quaker George Fox's Journal shows that there was often preaching in such places. New England people come honestly enough by orchards and cider, and Governor Endicott tells us how at Salem he bought two hundred and fifty acres, and paid for three hundred apple-trees. Wickliffe must have known the strength of old cider; for he translates St. Luke i. 15, where in our version it is "strong drink," "He shall be great, and shall not drink wine nor cider."

All travel was slow, and to a degree dangerous, even in times of peace. The roads were mere lanes, and bad at that. Guides were often sent to show the fords and the way from one town to another. Heavy wagons with iron wheel-tires were sometimes forbidden by law as dangerous to roads and bridges.

Hackney coaches, at their introduction, were abhorred for the same reason, and because it was thought that they would raise the price of hay. That rascal Titus Oakes denounced the letter mail as a popish plot; and when the mail came to Glasgow, then a fortnight distant from London, its arrival was announced by the firing of cannon. The post coach would sometimes agree with its passengers beforehand to stop over at any town on the way where a cock-fight was proceeding. There is not wanting such public news as this: "The fly coach from London to Exeter slept at Morcomb Lake the fifth night, proceeded next morning to Axminster, where it breakfasted, and there a woman barber shaved the coach." The bells rang in Bridgewater, nineteen days after Cromwell had been made Protector. Tradesmen from the provinces going up to London made their wills, and then often walked afoot, much in the same solemn frame of mind as Sewall had when, on his return amid vivid dangers from Cambridge or Roxbury Neck, he writes "Laus Deo."

This old English life explains a great many quaint fashions and habits of mind in our forefathers. Of course the Puritans' piety often turned from the ancient ways with horror; but then they were also men of the English blood, and the cases are not infrequent in our history where the blood got the better of the piety, which is, at least, human. At any rate, many of our ancient New England ways, as well as the names of our ancient towns especially, derive themselves from the English South Land.

Sewall's account of his voyage and landing as a young emigrant nine years old at Boston is: "We were about eight weeks at sea, where we had nothing to see but water and the sky; so that I began to fear that I should never get to shore again; only I thought the captain and the mariners would not have ventured themselves, if they had not hopes of getting to land again. On the Lord's Day my mother kept aboard; but I went ashore, the boat grounded and I was carried out in arms, July 6, 1661."

CHAPTER II.

THE PURITAN IN OLD ENGLAND.

WHILE this book intends to avoid philosophies, vain or valid, it would fail to show the roots of its theme if it did not, at the start, attempt to give some account of English Puritanism, — that singular religious movement which colors Sewall's life and the New England world he lived in. Indeed, that movement has certain unwasting colors which tone and characterize Englishmen in all the empires of that dominant race, now scattered over the globe, and for ages to come determines, in a reach neither feeble nor short-armed, many things in the destiny of peoples which, for want of a more exact term, we may call the Anglo-Saxon. But Puritanism was that child of the Reformation which was born in the land of the English, and, though kin to all Protestantism, had its own special gait, genius, and conduct. Now, as to the Reformation, so called. In all the eighteen ages since the Mysterious One "was brought up at Nazareth," no movement of man is more full of subtle mystery and hidden fountains, unreachable by speculation, than this same Reformation, especially as to its beginnings. One may attribute it to the new Greek learning, to the printing-press, to the Saracens, to commerce with Oriental nations, even; to accident, to fate, — and yet there is something down below these accidents of time, inspiring and urging on this great revolution in the mind of Christendom. Agnosticism may call it kismet or destiny. The writer of this book assumes for a standpoint, and with the assent of all reformed Christianity, that the springs of this movement were in the mind of One who, for want of a wiser name, the English-speaking peoples are wont to call God. At any rate, no imperial event in civilization is, as to its origin, more entitled to have applied to it those ancient words: "The wind bloweth where it listeth, and ye hear the sound thereof, but cannot tell whence it cometh or whither it goeth. So is every one that is born of the Spirit." This is especially true of the Reformation in England. The seeds of that reform which modified the religion of the West, — the politics and economics of dominant races also, — grew, for some reason, first on English soil; and as leaves falling from the autumn trees are sometimes borne aloft of winds, and while some fall nigh at hand, others are carried across seas to lands strange to their fading beauty, so the seeds of England's mighty reform, first of all disseminated in its own soil, were borne across the channel, by what air-currents one knows not, until they infected the Continent with what some men call heresy, and John Huss died in the orchards of Constance for the new faith some generations before Martin Luther entered on his gigantic strife with ancient errors which had preoccupied Western Christendom. That John Wickliffe and the Lollards were the prereformers of Europe is apparently a fact. But they were all Englishmen. How came *they* to be first — they of a semi-civilized and not rich people, — before Venice or Paris or Madrid moved themselves? It may be argued to those who count much on heredity in men and peoples, that the race blood had something to do with all this. It may be said, perhaps, that English blood was mixed, — but it was never mixed with pliant nor servile blood,—perhaps, that, the Danish vikings, out of their Northern liberties, going forth in ships to conquer and plunder Europe, had imbibed the freedom of their ships springing as war-horses over the free waves of the sea; or on deck had watched stars at night growing innumerable to their barbaric vision, until the Norse race attained the consciousness that this world is very vast, and the Maker of it too, — too vast, indeed, to echo all His wisdom in the chants of priests, or contain all His virtue in a bit of sacramental bread; and that, in fact, in His free world He wills freedom, for men to be men, not court eunuchs of any church or kingdom, mumbling Pater Nosters and living lies; but men obedient to laws and ways as free and as exact as those by which the waves surged and swept on, or the wind filled the sails of their ships bearing them to port. The Norsemen at first killed all the English priests, and, settling down in England's North Land, gave a Norse energy to the English church, as seen in Wickliffe and the Lollards. In a measure the same facts may be true of other strains of English blood, not necessary to be stated here.

Wickliffe came in the fourteenth century, and was only a voice, like St. John the Baptist in the wilderness, demanding a reform towards decency and righteousness. But the temper of reform must have been older than he, and the crying evils of the land also. No Puritan was ever more bitter or unsparing towards false prelates or corrupt churches than he and the Lollards were. They were root and branch men against Rome, as all their fathers were, and as the Lollard tracts published by the Camden Society show. Then came Henry VIII. in the sixteenth century, with his wives and cause — whatever the last may be. But the Lollards had been already for almost three hundred years the Puritans of England, and they gave the king small thanks, going their own solitary and dangerous way, in a courage which no English king nor prelate ever quelled by axe or stake. Nothing is argued here as to what, if anything, was good or bad in the English Reformation. Whether good or bad, Lollardism, evolved into Puritanism, was the soul and flame of it, and did not quail before Henry, before Mary, before Elizabeth, — nor even before a dead headless king on the scaffold which it had built. It is the radical Protestant element of the English Reformation.

In the years between Henry VIII. and Charles I. Puritanism evolved itself into its logical form, and crystallized its own consciousness. This it was able to do because it could now educate itself at Oxford and Cambridge, and because its leaders had wider data and more exact tests to go upon in proving all matters touching the religious or political status of man, holding fast only what was found good. A great movement never explodes; it takes steps, and so long as it is living it moves on, never looking back, but always in the direction of its first infant and virgin vision. If in any age it halt and pitch tents it is to be up and about, delving lustily in the soil of its new domain. When it is quelled, or drowses, it accepts its grave, out of which, so perennial is true greatness, come perfumes gracious to the great. It does not appear that Puritanism has ever yet died at the heart, and the fragrance of its granite virtues remain as a benison upon its posterity. Oliver Cromwell and John Milton, if now on earth, would find conscience and conduct free enough in these United States to please even these foes of kings and priestcraft. Life is not a machine framed out of articulated parts, but a river whose lapse is continuous, running deep or shallow as the soil serves, and when fretted or barred by rock or dike gathering head until it overtops the obstacle, and sweeps on, generally in a white rage of ruin. Under Henry VIII. the Puritan tide, restrained so long by the barrier of the ancient ecclesiasticism, broke through and swept away the Roman bondage which had ruled in the name of God; under Charles I., and under like restraint of personal government in the place of English statute law, it swept away the throne.

But what, now, was this radical Protestantism, which we call English Puritanism, to work such dominating results? There were in it those masterful ideas which, ever looking towards both church and state, have hastened and agonized ever since in the West to establish true liberty, both in religion and politics. But how? And why? The Reformation was an attempt at a new and radical adjustment between the individual and human society. For of old, man had seemed to exist for church and state; now it was demanded that church and state should exist for man. Of old, these twin corporations of authority had seemed by their very magnitude and magnificence to abase by contrast and by conduct into littleness the worshipper and the subject. Henceforth, to a degree, every man was to be his own priest, and a king because he was a man. Protestantism at its core is the apotheosis of individualism, and the most relentless of democracies. It declares the individual to be the unit, the articulated blood globule of society upon whose health and safety the peace and thrift of all human institutions depend; that when this individual blood globule is hurt in its identity, or confused in masses with others, like, by any corporation, exactly as the cobra's poison works by confusing and compounding the blood globules of its victim in an unarticulated mass, then the common weal shrivels and tends to the dust. This enthronement and canonization of the individual, accepted gradually but infallibly by English Puritanism, rested upon a religious idea which was this, — that as an incarnate God, while wearing our flesh, had once died for every man, so no man thus redeemed could, without sacrilege, be abased by any tyranny of prelate or king from his privilege of remaining a "child of God and an inheritor of the kingdom of heaven." This point is argued with a most eager pathos by Macaulay in his Essay on John Milton, in a passage now fashionably sneered at by some of our callow critics, but which yet remains the most accurate statement of Puritanism in its ideal logic extant in the English tongue. Here is the root of English Protestantism as seen in all its ages in all its sects, — in the right of private judgment of the Scriptures, in a town meeting, in a revolution, in a civilization. Puritan politics are born of Puritan dogmatics, — and their whole history shows not otherwise. Here is the root of the French Revolution, and ours also, and the mainspring of English civilization for the last three hundred years.

Charles I. and the Church of England obstructed this Puritanism with ecclesiastical and political behaviors which the Puritan thought unjust, and offences against man. In due time the rule of both became intolerable, and Hampden protested against the ship-money demanded by the king, while a thousand Puritan parsons distressed, and were distressed by, the primate of all England, Laud. Revolution logically followed, and both king and primate, and greater than both, Strafford, died under the axe. Many men had died so long before; but for the first time in history private men, under solemn guise of law and prayers, smote so their own sovereign. The edge of the axe which smote Charles was this root idea of Puritanism, and the sound of it in falling proclaimed that the privilege of the people makes henceforth the law of the land. It is idle to say that all this sad work might have been avoided by the wisdom of the parties to the dispute. The parties to the dispute were the victims, not the criminals. The cause in issue had been framed of old by generations of prelates and statesmen long before Wickliffe and the Stuarts, and the case had to be tried upon its merits. The authorities of the English church and state were thought by their adherents to hold a venerable trust, which most Englishmen to-day would pronounce treason, to surrender without trial; and Puritanism could do no other than it did. A gentle primate, as Abbot was, would have no more availed for final peace than Laud did. A wiser and better king than Charles might have postponed, but could not have prevented, the struggle. Despite Cavalier follies or Puritan absurdities, the cause and the contention had to come. If it had come much later, England would have certainly fared much worse. The head of an Alpine stream against the barrier of a fallen avalanche grows more threatening every hour. War against Charles I. in the seventeenth century makes Queen Victoria possible in the nineteenth. The Puritan temper has never faded out of the consciousness of that England which, some ways, is the freest of all lands.

The Puritan drift, having killed a king, created an English Commonwealth of Parliament and Oliver Cromwell's sword. In the name of God Puritanism maintained itself for a few years, and failed. But while it lasted it ever appealed to the "higher law" of God as the supreme and salutary fountain of all true government. It maintained in its highest circles the duty of regicide upon due occasion. Its mouthpiece, John Milton, writes:—

> "Why not inflict justice on tyrants? To teach lawless kings and all who so much adore them that not mortal man or his imperious will but justice is the only true sovereign and supreme majesty on earth."

It analyzed human government down to its roots, and elaborated a philosophy of a nation's economic and political life which, while improved upon when seen under the new lights of human experience, must still remain as the very woof of all republics which endure. This philosophy stands forth in such ringing and subtle sentences as these of Milton:—

> "For indeed none can love freedom heartily but good men; the rest love not freedom but license which never hath more scope or more indulgence than under tyrants. Hence it is that tyrants are not oft offended nor stand much in doubt of bad men, as being all naturally servile. But in whom virtue and true worth most is eminent, them they fear in earnest, as by right their master. Against them lies all their hatred and suspicion."

Yet Puritanism failed as a governing force on Englishmen. It failed, not because its root ideas were false, but because the Puritans themselves, being men, were fallible, and, as themselves said, had their treasure in earthen vessels, not in the box of alabaster. These earthen vessels became, under the hammers of the enemies whom their fanaticism bred up, but broken potsherds; yet the very precious ointment which, as some thought, fell to the earth at their overthrow has lent a fragrance to the atmosphere of Anglo-Saxon living ever since. They failed because their environment was hopelessly against them. They appealed to the will of the people, obedient to their new faith; and the will of the vast majority of Englishmen was away from them, and towards the national church and king. This the Restoration proves. To one looking below the surface, they do not appear to have failed in Time, — only for a time. For ever since in England — in her times of danger, as when Charles II. kept unclean house with the still uncleaner gold of France, a purchased slave of Louis XIV.; when James II. tampered with England's faith and England's statute law, as his father had; when Wilberforce pleaded for free soil under the British flag for black as well as white; when the Corn Laws agitation shook the vested rights of the English aristocracy almost to overthrow, as Greville's Memoirs tell us; when again and again England has looked to her sword as she took the field against the Gaul or the Muscovite, and the thunder of her battleships quelled almost the winds to calm — the sturdy Puritan temper has vindicated its right to still live in honor, and still remains a menace to all tyranny in church or state both sides of the Atlantic.

Some people affect to laugh at English Puritanism; but they are not wise who do so. Some Americans read their prayers and almost endless sermons with a smile, but forget the prowess of their virtues. But every wise lover of the privilege of man greets their memory with the sympathy bred from the knowledge that the very and urgent problems which the English Puritans in the seventeenth century tried to solve, and failed, inhere in the history and future of this republic, and are still unsettled.

CHAPTER III.

THE PURITAN EXODUS.

If a Puritan, just come to Massachusetts Bay, had been asked what phrase would best describe his singular emigration, he might have answered, in his religious intensity and sincerity, that it should be called the New Exodus. If questioned further, he would have stoutly affirmed that the Puritans, once more in the economy of Heaven, had become a chosen people, and, on denial, would have pointed to the Covenant which they had formally made with God as proof. For indeed there was a correspondence in fortune between the Puritans and the Children of Israel. The Puritan, too, had come out of the Egypt where the Pharaohs were the archbishops and the idolatry was out of Mass Book and Prayer Book. He, too, had passed the Red Sea, which, if not divided in his behoof, had yet availed by distance to keep back his enemy from his track. He, too, had left the pyramids of an old civilization, rich in the storied monuments of palace and cathedral, for the wild, and the Promised Land which lay at the end of his travail. Above all, both Hebrews and Puritans worshipped the same Jehovah, the statute-book of whom had become the supreme authority in both theocracies. It should be added that a similarity in circumstance and religion is apt to create a resemblance in character.

Of course the Puritans were not the first white men at the Bay. When Winthrop arrived here (1630) probably three hundred whites were here; with him came about one thousand, and in the next twenty years, in some three hundred ships, there came out some twenty thousand more.

To emigrate or go a sea voyage was no novelty in the seventeenth century to Englishmen. But generally the men who expatriated themselves were young or unmarried or reckless or given to wild adventures. But the Puritans were generally in middle life, married, and with families, with roots struck deep down into the English soil, conservative and prudent in business ventures, and their emigration was a violent and sorrowful wrenching away of themselves from what most civilized men count most dear. That they emigrated at all shows that they were in deadly strife with something in England; and that something was no less than a national church, backed in its rule by the Crown. Ages of high religious excitement, curiously enough, whether in Mohammedan or Christian, tend to take a pessimistic view of this world's affairs, possibly because they measure them by those celestial grandeurs to which they believe themselves heritors, and find earthly things small and mean in contrast. Besides, ages like the Puritan age have so full faith in God's care of His own, that the best, believing that whatever is is right, come very near to being fatalists. The sharpness of the Saracen scimitar against Christendom of old was not more love of God than a sense that, if he liked, God would keep His safe in the most fatal strife. There were shades of melancholia and fatalism even in Puritans of the loftiest mind,—at least, among the early settlers in New England. Nor perhaps were these lessened by the overthrow of Cromwell's Commonwealth and the Restoration of Charles II. A high-bred Puritan writes:—

> "For the business of New England, I can say no other thing but that I believe confidently, that the whole disposition thereof, is of the Lord who disposeth all alterations, by his blessed will to his own glory and the good of his; and therefore do assure myself that all things shall work together for the best therein. As for myself, I have seen so much of the vanity of the world, that I esteem no more of the diversities of countries, than as so many inns, whereof the traveller who hath lodged in the best or in the worst, findeth no difference when he cometh to his journey's end; and I shall call that my country where I may most glorify God and enjoy the presence of my dearest friends."

But whatever be the more recondite aspects of the Puritan Exodus, one thing is plain; viz., that the emigration became very often an epic and a tragedy in the hearts of the men and women who sailed away or stayed behind. In most, of course, all this agony failed to write itself down, and went voiceless to the grave with those who suffered, as is the lot of most.

But the letters of men like Winthrop doubtless voice the common pangs, though the voice in him and them sounds like a man who will not quail. There are certain letters of his to different members of his family hardly to be outmatched in power by any like letters in the literature of the world.

As the date for embarking for New England approaches, and business in London and elsewhere multiplies, his letters preparing his wife for their separation (she was now in delicate health) multiply also. Jan. 31, 1629, he writes: —

> "I must now begin to prepare thee for our long parting which grows very near. I know not how to deal with thee by arguments; for if thou wert as wise and patient as ever woman was, yet it must needs be a great trial to thee, and the greater because I am so dear to thee. That which I must chiefly look at in thee, for a ground of contentment is thy godliness. If now the Lord be thy God, thou must show it by trusting in him and resigning thyself quietly to his good pleasure. If now Christ be thy husband thou must show what sure and sweet intercourse is between him and thy soul when it shall be no hard thing for thee to part with an earthly mortal, infirm husband for his sake. The enlargement of thy comfort in the communion of the love and sweet familiarity of thy most holy, heavenly and undefiled Lord and Husband will abundantly recompense whatsoever want or inconvenience may come by the absence of the other. The best course is to turn all our reasons and discourse into prayers; for he only can help who is Lord of sea and land and hath sole power of life and death. . . . So I kiss my sweet wife and rest,
>
> Thy frail, yet faithful husband
>
> Jo Winthrop."

Feb. 14 he writes : —

MY SWEET WIFE, —

The opportunity of so fit a messenger and my deep engagement of affection for thee, makes me write at this time, though I hope to follow soon after. The Lord our God hath oft brought us together with comfort, when we have been long absent; and if it be good for us, he will do so still. When I was in Ireland, he brought us together again. When I was sick here at London he restored us together again. How many dangers, near death, hast thou been in thyself; and yet the Lord hath granted me to enjoy thee still. If he did not watch over us, we need not go over sea to seek death or misery; we should meet it at every step, in every journey. And is not he a God abroad as well as at home? Is not his power and providence the same in New England that it hath been in Old England? If our ways please him he can command deliverance and safety in all places and can make the stones of the field and the beasts, yea the raging seas and our very enemies, to be in league with us. But if we sin against him he can raise up evil against us out of our own bowells, houses, estates &c. My good wife, trust in the Lord whom thou hast found faithful. He will be better to thee than any husband and will restore thee thy husband with advantage. But I must end with all the salutations with which I have laden this bearer, that he may be the more kindly welcome. So I kiss my sweet wife and bless thee and all ours and rest Thine ever.

Feby. 14, 1629. JO WINTHROP.

Thou must be my valentine, for none hath challenged me.

On shipboard, and preparing to set sail on the morrow, he writes this graphic and all-wise pathetic letter : —

MY FAITHFUL AND DEAR WIFE, —

It pleaseth God that thou shouldst once again hear from me before our departure, and I hope this shall come safe to thy hands. I know it will be a great refreshing to thee. And blessed be his mercy that I can write thee so good news that we are all in very good health and having tried our ships entertainment, now more than a week, we find it agree very well with us. Our boys are well and cheerful, and have no mind of home. They lie both with me and sleep as soundly in a rug (for we use no sheets here) as ever they did at Groton; and so I do myself, (I praise God). The wind hath been against us this week and more; but this day it is come fair to the north, so that we are preparing (by God's assistance) to set sail in the morning. We have only four ships ready and some two or three Hollanders go along with us. The rest of our fleet, being seven ships (the Pilgrim Mayflower being one) will not be ready this sennight. We have spent now two Sabbaths on shipboard very comfortably (God be praised) and are daily more and more encouraged to look for the Lord's presence to go along with us. Henry Kingsbury hath a child or two in the Talbot, sick of the measles, but like to do well. One of my men had them at [South] Hampton, but he was soon well again. We are, in all our eleven ships, about seven hundred persons, passengers and two hundred and forty cows and about sixty horses. The ship which went from Plimouth carried about one hundred and forty persons and the ship which goeth from Bristowe [Bristol] carrieth about eighty persons. And now, my sweet soul, I must once again take my last farewell of thee in Old England. It goeth very near to my heart to leave thee; but I know to whom I have committed thee, even to him who loves thee better than any husband can, who has taken account of the hairs of thy head and puts all thy tears in his bottle, who can and (if it be for his glory) will bring us together again with peace and comfort. O, how it refresheth my heart to think that I shall yet again see thy sweet face in the land of the living! — that lovely countenance that I have so much delighted in and beheld with so great content. I have hitherto been so taken up with business as I could seldom look back to my former happiness; but now when I shall be at some leisure I shall not avoid the remembrance of thee, nor the grief for thy absence. Thou hast thy share with me but I hope the course we have agreed upon will be some ease to us both. Mondays and Fridays at five of the clock at night we shall meet in spirit until we meet in person. Yet, if all these hopes should fail blessed be our own God that we are assured we shall meet one day, if not as husband and wife, yet in a better condition. Let that stay and comfort thy heart. Neither can the sea drown thy husband nor enemies destroy, nor any adversity deprive thee of thy husband or children. Therefore I will only take thee now and my sweet children in my arms and kiss and embrace you all, and so leave you with my God. Farewell, farewell. I bless you all in the name of the Lord Jesus. . . .

Thine wheresoever

Jo Winthrop.

From aboard the Arbella riding at the Cowes March 28 1630.

Elsewhere in the story of Sewall's voyage into England one sees how it fared with passengers crossing the Atlantic in English ships. The ships themselves were small, far below in architecture vessels of these days both in safety and convenience; the fare was meagre, enemies abounded, charts and pilots were few, shoals many, and, in short, the voyage out of Old England into New was beset with hardships and dangers.

In trying to get insight into our old New England civilization one fact should never be forgotten; to wit, that our ancestors here were emigrants, — exactly what that word implies. True, they were rare and singular emigrants, but for all that, at least for a hundred years, New England folk fared as emigrants, and as the descendants of emigrants, in a wilderness rife with fevers, labors, and foes. And the strife to conquer a civilization out of all this began with the voyage. John Winthrop in his Journal gives us very representative pictures of how it usually fared on an English ship with Puritan emigrants. By the Puritans who stayed behind such a company were regarded with all that tender interest and respect which Christians show nowadays in taking leave of those who go out to some dangerous missionary field on the Congo or in Burmah. Tuesday, April 6, 1630: "Capt. Burleigh, captain of Yarmouth Castle, a grave comely gentleman and of great age came aboard us and stayed breakfast and offering us much courtesy departed, our captain giving him four shot, out of the forecastle for his farewell. He was an old sea captain in Elizabeths time and, being taking prisoner at sea was kept prisoner in Spain three years."

Of course in those days all ships went armed, and the men as well. "Our captain called over our landmen and tried them at their muskets and such as were good shot among them, were enrolled to serve in the ship, if occasion should be." April 9, while still in the Channel, there was a warlike turmoil on board. "We saw these eight ships [mistaken for enemies] to stand towards us; having more wind than we they came up apace; whereupon we all prepared to fight with them [the English ships were only four] and took down some cabins which were in the way of our ordnance and out of every ship were thrown such bed matters as were subject to take fire and we heaved out our long boats and put up our waste cloths and drew forth our men and armed them with muskets and other weapons and instruments for fire works; and for an experiment our captain shot a ball of wild fire fastened to an arrow, out of a crossbow, which burnt in the water a good time. The lady Arbella [Johnson] and the other women and children were removed into the lower deck, that they might be out of danger. All things being thus fitted, we went to prayer upon the upper deck. It was much to see how cheerful and comfortable all the company appeared; not a woman or child that showed fear, though all did apprehend the danger to have been great, if things had proved as might well be expected, for there had been eight against four, and the least of the enemy's ships were reported to carry thirty brass pieces; but our trust was in the Lord of Hosts; and the courage of our captain and his care and diligence did much encourage us. It was now about one of the clock and the fleet seemed to be within a league of us; therefore our captain, because he would show he was not afraid of them, and that he might see the issue before night should overtake us, tacked about and stood to meet them, and when we came near we perceived them to be our friends. . . . And so (God be praised) our fear and danger was turned into mirth and friendly entertainment." Is it strange that men who would burn their bed-straw, and then go to prayer upon the upper deck, in preparation to fight two ships with one, even turning back to meet them, are found in history to be stout men to win their way to their will?

They solaced themselves, Winthrop writes, after the scare, by each ship launching out a skiff and boarding some fishermen; "and we bought of them great store of excellent fresh fish of diverse sorts."

There were prayers on board several times a day, and frequent sermons, when the weather served; fasts for head winds, and thanksgivings for fair. These ordinances were only intermitted when ministers and people were all seasick. Yet they carried the world with them, notwithstanding so much of heavenly exercise. The world, in this case, were thieves, brawlers, and people who wouldn't keep their quarters clean. Plenty of salt water under a master washed away the dirt; and as for the others, pat and homely punishments soon reduced them to their duty. "This day [April 10] two young men falling at odds and fighting contrary to the orders which we had published and set up in the ship were adjudged to walk upon the deck till night with their hands bound behind them which accordingly was executed; and another man for using contemptuous speeches in our presence, was laid in bolts until he submitted himself and promised open confession of his offence. . . . Set two fighters in the bolts till night with their hands bound behind them. . . . A maid servant in the ship being stomach-sick drank so much strong water that she was senseless and had near killed herself. We observed it a common fault in our young people that they gave themselves to drink hot waters very immoderately. . . . A servant of one of our company had bargained with a child to sell it a box worth 3*d.* for three biscuits a day all the voyage and had received about forty and had sold them and many more to some other servants. We caused his hands to be tied up to a bar and hanged a basket with stones about his neck and so he stood two hours."

The voyage lasted from March 29 to June 12. Winthrop's Journal shows all sorts of weather, much of it stormy. He speaks of "a small gale," "a good gale," "a stiff gale," and "a handsome gale." There were fogs also. Occasionally the captains came aboard to dine, or one ship waited for another ship laggard or in distress of rigging. Occasionally they borrowed meal or other edibles from each other. In some of the other ships both cattle and passengers died, while several children were born. When there was a new baby on board Winthrop's ship, and there was need of help from a consort, "we shot off a piece and lowered our topsails and then she brailed her sails and stayed for us." With the customary Winthrop taste for scientific observation, he remarks that the sun's rays are not so warm as at home. "This evening [June 1] we saw the new moon more than half an hour after sunset, being much smaller than it is at any time in England. . . . May 17. We saw a great drift; so we heaved out our skiff and it proved a fir log which seemed to have been many years in the water, for it was all overgrown with barnacles and other trash. We saw two whales."

Sometimes a strange vessel would run away from them, despite their friendly signals, or their consorts fell or sailed out of sight, to their vexation. They were now nearing land, Monday 7 (June). "About 4 in the morning we sounded and had ground at thirty fathom, and was somewhat calm ; so we put our ship a-stays and took, in less than two hours, with a few hooks, sixty seven codfish, most of them very great fish, some a yard and a half long, and a yard in compass. This came very seasonably, for our salt fish was now spent and we were taking care for victuals this day (being a fish day)." June 8 they made land at Mount Desert. Then they stood along the coast, towards Salem, catching many mackerel, and sighting vessels until Saturday 12 (June). "About 4 in the morning we were near our port. We shot off two pieces of ordnance and sent our skiff to Mr. Pierce's ship which lay in the harbour." In the afternoon Governor Endicott and the Salem pastor came on board, and the emigrants had touched their new home. "In the mean time most of our people went on shore upon the land of Cape Ann which lay very near us and gathered store of fine strawberries. An Indian came aboard us and lay there all night. . . . Lord's Day 13. In the morning the sagamore of Agawam and one of his men came aboard our ship and stayed with us all day. Thursday 17. We went to Mattachusetts to find out a place for our sitting down. Went up Mestick River about six miles." So the Exodus reached Boston.

The land they settled was strange to them. They

had to learn the climate, and to provide for it; and their experiments in crops, following English methods, had to be slowly verified by results. There was almost no cleared land for their tillage, except the Indian cornfields, which they left to their owners. Salt marshes and fresh meadows might give them hay for the mowing, but in general it was a huge forest they set themselves to subdue. This was the main business for generations. The highest in rank formed no exception. Lieutenant-Governor Stoughton, as Sewall tells us, was found by his visitors carting in his corn; Chief Justice Lynde took, occasionally, a hand at mowing; and Endicott appears to have held a sort of farm-school on his acres, with himself as teacher by example. Many of the Winthrops were practised farmers. Agriculture stood first in the general business interests of the country. The invoices of the merchants show this, — spades, scythes, and sieves for sifting meal, being the most common entries. There were no roads but Indian trails and the rivers. Men were sent out to find the best course from one place to another. These roads, at least in the shore districts, followed the highlands, to avoid rivers and creeks, which would have necessitated bridges, which they were too poor to undertake. When a miserable bridge was ordered over Eel River, every town in Plymouth Colony was taxed to pay for it. Most intercourse between towns was by a horsetrack and on horseback. Judge Lynde, who succeeded Sewall as chief justice, while on his circuit makes this entry in his Diary as late as 1726:

"1726. At landing [over the Merrimac from Newbury, north shore] we rode by a stone wall where our horses were mired and floundered and I hurt my right hand against the wall, but through God's goodness, not much; and had not God helped I might have dashed not my hand or foot, but my body and head against the rocks. God's name be praised now and ever for his preventing as well as his restoring mercies thus repeated to me."

Sewall escaped the most primitive of these hardships, coming here some thirty years after Winthrop, in 1661. But he, too, had to face the dangers of the road in his frequent journeys as a judge or business man. He writes it down in his Diary that one of his friends had a wonderful escape crossing Charlestown Ferry, and lives were sometimes lost there. After his dangerous journeys from Boston to Roxbury, Brookline, and especially Cambridge, he signifies his gratitude for his safety by pious entries in his Diary.

Such distant journeys as from Boston to Salem or Portsmouth often began and concluded with stated prayers. Private houses were, in most places, the only inns. The first houses, even at Boston, must have been very much like sheds or shanties, and this must have been even worse in the smaller places. Under oak-trees, or in the lee of some huge rock, they held their meetings, or in some storehouse. At the founding of New Haven Colony the Rev. Mr. Davenport preached in a barn, but from a lordly text (Prov. ix. 1): "Wisdom hath builded her house; she hath hewn out her seven pillars."

Rev. Mr. Wilson of Boston upon occasion could harangue a crowd from a tree, as is on record. Our fathers had "faculty," and could adapt themselves to circumstances with a tact and *finesse* not excelled by the acknowledged ability in these respects of the best class of pioneers in our West.

It took time for the Puritans to adapt themselves to their new home. That home, for those who could use it, was no desert, though a wild. Sea-food for the coast-dwellers was marvellously plentiful; and it has always been an enigma to those who know the land, why, with the sea-sands about them crammed with shellfish, any one of the Plymouth Pilgrims in health had need to die with hunger in their winter famine. Yet owing to bad crops there was sometimes want among the people.

At one time, tradition is that there was but one pint of corn in the whole settlement of Plymouth Colony, which gave to each person only five kernels. At the Pilgrim Celebration in 1820, five kernels were placed by the plate of each guest, in memory.

Yet food was sometimes very high. The authorities were charged in the Narragansett War (1675) for pork at the rate of twenty dollars a barrel. In fact, for generations New England lived on the edge of lack, and was only kept from falling into actual food want by the unremitting energy of its people. In the earlier years food was imported again and again. Nor was this limitation in physical comforts and thrift confined to the common people.

The Winthrop letters, especially those of Wait

Winthrop, give us a very vivid picture of the hardships which even the best suffered in their household life in the early years of the colony. In these letters we see able, educated men very busy, far-sighted business men of property facing a poverty and meagre diet at which the mechanics and laborers of to-day would stand aghast. It was not always so, and some of the younger Winthrops came to have comforts; yet the poverty must have lasted very long with the common people, and the toil, beyond that of serfs, has reached in the country far into this century. Nearly all of them were farmers, dreading Indians and pirates, raising cattle in the wilds or on distant islands, which seem to have been favorite places for such work, probably because the sea served as a fence, the herdsmen, whites and Indians, living there in solitary huts, and the owners going there in all sorts of weather in questionable boats, and faring on board and on horseback with their servants. Bad crops in a bad season, with no reserve of food, with their base of supplies in England or the West Indies, and these hampered by hostile Dutch or French fleets and the dangers of winter passage, not only kept the larder lean, but came often close to starvation. Their letters miscarried or came late, and their goods also. From Hartford to Boston was a long journey, before which prayers were said, and in which horses were worn out and carriage was expensive; and the coasting-vessels around Cape Cod often fell into mishap, or put back. Women waited all the season for calicoes which did not come, and went into the winter without woollens, shoes, or sugar for their household, while meat ran low; and of wheat, not to mention Indian corn, there was often actual dearth. They sent one another a shirt, a cravat, a pair of stout shoes, stockings, a little spice, a few raisins, and still fewer oranges, medicines, salves, as a great mercy. A. Winthrop had often a deal of trouble to find for himself or brother an honest leather belt, cloth for a coat, a white hat, or a periwig; and many of these letters are full of such trifles, showing the dearth. Wait Winthrop of Boston begs of his brother of Connecticut to send him tallow for candles, and on one occasion tells him that if he comes on he will be obliged to sit in the dark for lack of them. They even made tallow from the bayberry-bush, of green color and sweet odor; and in one case complaint is made that there was so much straw in their makeup that they were good for nothing. "Your candles were so intimately mixed with straw and joined together that they were good for little." "Carter has sold your punch bowl," Wait writes to Fitz-John, "and Mears has not sent your hat." Occasionally something finer goes, — a few bottles of white wine and claret, a small cask of brandy. Upon one occasion Roger Williams sends the wife of Governor Winthrop of Connecticut a basket of chestnuts, and say he will send more if she likes. Under date of June 22, 1680, Wait Winthrop writes to his brother Fitz-John from Boston: "Here is neither wash bales nor sweet powder to be had. I use starch, sprinkled with a little rose water, and so dried and beaten. As soon as I can light on some suitable ribbon and linen shall send some. I do not know where to get a miller but shall enquire. I have sent you a map of the town with Charlestown, taken by Mr. Foster the printer from Noddles Island. 'Twas sent for Amsterdam and there printed." Again he writes to the same, "I am sorry to hear from John Perry that you were not so well of your teeth, but hope you are now better. . . . I have sent you 300 of bricks and a dozen and a half of paving tiles for your oven; also a new spade and a round one which I had by me. The horse nails I thought might be useful to you when you have but bungling smiths. They cost but sixpence the pound. My wife returns thanks for the cheeses and the tallows." The rats, as repeatedly noted, take tithe of about every thing shipped by water; the cattle driven from the Connecticut come to town thin and lame, some break away into the woods and are gobbled up by Indians or bears, the drovers overcharge for driving — and, upon the whole, the times are out of joint with the best. Is it strange that in such hardship Wait Winthrop writes to Fitz-John: "I desire you would take notice that I have no thoughts of journeying after you but of resting before you. Our times are in God's hands let us endeavor to live to his glory and take no thought for the rest. . . . He has certainly made no good observation that cannot by this time of day say with Solomon all is vanity and vexation of spirit. I doubt not that you remember my father's often expression *O quantum est in rebus inanis,*"—which loosely translated may read: "Oh, how thin is everything!" There was much search after the precious and useful metals, often with high hopes and temporary success. Winthrop writes in 1648: "Mr. Endicott hath found a copper mine in his own ground. Mr. Leader hath tried it. The furnace runs 8 tons a week and their bar iron is as good as Spanish." Skilled workmen came out to mine and smelt, and valuable earths and supposed minerals were even sent to be assayed from the West Indies. Most of these expectations realized nothing.

Yet the Winthrops were gallant gentlemen, facing the times with both a prayer and a smile. Fitz-John had been one of Cromwell's Ironsides, and they all were ready to face Indians or the Devil if the war was just. Many of Fitz-John's comrades with Cromwell who came here were lifelong sufferers from rheumatism, caught by lying out in the rain or on damp ground in campaigning against King Charles. They were thrifty farmers, above all, fond of good horses, whose points they knew, always ready to improve the breed, and selling them in Boston or Barbadoes with much ado as to price, the best market, etc. They looked after the breed of dogs, stocked rabbit warrens, tried hard at raising wild turkeys on their islands, and were among the earliest scientific farmers in the land. They were Puritans, with their religion sweetened and clarified by their blood, which was Cavalier, whatever their politics might be. In their letters the reader is sensible of a warm human atmosphere which not even the wilderness can chill, and after his introduction as a stranger he is apt to remain a fast friend. Indeed, one is apt to feel, when one begins to read a Winthrop letter, especially if addressed to a lady, as if he ought to stand hat in hand before the high-bred courtesy which is sure to be therein.

The Puritan had three great enemies to contend with in his struggle for physical existence; viz., the wilderness, the Indians, backed often by the French, and wild creatures. It was the fate of the Puritan to be always in strife with something. The stress which the Indians laid on him is told elsewhere. His struggle with wild creatures, if thoroughly told, would form a very amusing as well as picturesque chapter of our history. To say that the Puritan who had not been afraid to face Prince Rupert and his Cavaliers was often in danger of being overmastered and put to flight by a flock of blackbirds or vermin that burrowed in holes, would perhaps excite surprise. But the fact is, that the loss this way to New England folk was, of old, something appalling. With their flocks never safe from wolves or bears, nor their crops from predatory birds, multiplying by aid of the very corn they plundered, it was not the least of our forefathers' tasks to destroy these enemies. This they did by town and State laws, which they and their boys enforced with traps and guns and by bounties. How much a dozen for blackbirds' heads? was a very grave question in many a town meeting, and there are those living who have seen the bounties paid. The selectmen always buried the heads, and kept strict watch over the grave, to keep back Yankee thrift from robbing the town treasury by reiterated resurrections of the same. Specific bounties for different creatures prevailed. In one place this was the tariff. A wolf's head hung on a tree by the meeting-house brought the killer 10*s*. Bounties: 1*s*. a dozen blackbirds; 2*s*. a dozen woodpeckers and jays; 3*s*. per dozen for crows.

An exception should be made in favor of the larger seaports in this delineation of the narrow and stinted life of our Puritan ancestors. Narrow, and to a degree sordid, in its circumstance that life certainly was; but the world was then *en voyage;* and as the laws against vagabonds permitted, visitors — seamen in ships, traders, and a few wayfarers of polyglot nationality — came to Boston, and fared according to the custom of the place, introducing their sins and their wines to a limited extent to the palate of human nature as they best could. Boston men traded with the West Indies, especially the Bermudas; with Bilboa in Spain, sending salt fish for fast days; with England, and with the French colonies in America, and the Southern colonies. Sewall's Diary shows that he and the leading men of his time interested themselves with the world's affairs as far East as the Turk, and grasped eagerly at even rumors that came late across seas, of changing dynasties, and the fate of wars on the seas or the Continent. But with this abatement, the fact must stand that the early days of the New England Puritans were those of emigrants. Their Exodus had brought them to a land where the heathen raged, and the ungodly imagined vain things. They realized that it was the Land of Promise, but chiefly through the eye of prophecy, while the Holy City of Jerusalem, whose foundation stones they wrought at, as they would judge if they were now on earth, is not yet built. It would be untrue to say that these emigrants were mere religious fanatics; or to say that they were knights without reproach. False history is a most expensive luxury, not only because it poisons the fountains of philosophy for posterity, but because it costs a deal of honest writing to disprove its lies. It is perhaps enough to say of them that they wrought mightily for man in that wild, aspiring drift of Protestantism, whose outcome in politics as well as religion neither they nor their posterity were able to comprehend.

What they thought of their own fortunes here is well stated (1708) by old Schoolmaster Chiever on his deathbed, referring to the Puritan hardships: "The afflictions of God's people, God did by them as a goldsmith; knock, knock, knock; knock, knock, knock to finish the plate: it was to perfect them, not to punish them."

CHAPTER IV.

SEWALL AND THE PURITAN CHURCH.

"The Puritans were the servants of posterity to endure the sowing of a nation in a wild — to break the ice that others might drink the living waters."

"New England civilization, like its soil, has a granite base, but a deep and sturdy loam on top, to last for ages."

"The entire man, so to speak, is to be seen in the cradle of the child. So it is with nations." DE TOCQUEVILLE.

"The civilization of New England has been like a beacon lit upon a hill which after it has diffused its warmth around, tinges the distant horizon with its glow." DE TOCQUEVILLE.

APOLOGY should perhaps be made for the risk which this chapter must undergo of dulness. Heretofore some things have been said of Puritanism as a mysterious evolution among Englishmen; now some things as to how it fared when it set up its own house in New England. For with its old roots it raises here old problems in their new environment.

It can hardly be reiterated too often that Puritanism was an antithesis, a protest, a revolt in time against the old religions of Romanism and Anglicanism. The key to this revolt is to be looked for among the things from which this revolt was made. It has been often said that Puritanism ran narrow but deep. All metaphors have in them the danger possibly to mislead. But if we regard truth as globular, a sphere, then certainly Puritanism moved in a tangent of the circle, with a centrifugal force which could not fail to disturb and antagonize. Any truth dislocated or distorted from its relations to Truth becomes error; and thus it happens that while the Puritan movement carried with it truths which the world will not willingly let die, it was destined to such extremes and isolation that England recoiled from its colors in disgust, and it has disappeared, in form at least, from its new home. How and why did Puritanism revolt? From what?

Not hopelessly to involve the answer in dulness, it may be stated, then, that for more than twelve centuries Christendom had held this opinion; to wit, that as God who made man had determined to save him, He had set about it in two revelations, — the Mosaic, which was temporary, and only a type and prophecy of the second; that the second, which we call Christianity, was the final and permanent economy in the salvation of the human race; that the heart of it, its stock and root, was an incarnation of the Divine in the human; that this Incarnation of God through a human virgin introduces and maintains in the circle and sphere of humanity the constant and immanent activity of God in man's behalf; that this incarnate God, — thus once and for all time, visibly come on earth, — did, by His own will and grace, elect to remain on earth, visible and forever present in His church, framed by Him, and vivified by His indwelling; that in a mystical way, but truly, this church, visibly composed of men and women, grafted in Him, but yet also a storehouse of ghostly riches, feeds its children with the bread of life, which is, in a most lofty and supernatural sense, Himself; and that this church, intended for all men, is the one church historic for men, because there cannot be two Christs or Incarnations, but only one. Whatever accretions, forms, ceremonies, or doctrines may have been had or held for twelve centuries, though in an acknowledged constant variation, this theory remained untouched and unquestioned till the Reformation. The question is not raised here as to whether this theory is true or false, nor does that question here concern the philosophy of Puritanism. But it must be noted, even by the logic of Protestantism, affirming private judgment, that what is each man's privilege must be all men's privilege, although they stand together in a corporate society of faith, and that a church of Divine origin must have a governing authority somewhere. As God, so far as the Catholic dogma went and human salvation required, dwelt in His church, that authority must also reside there. And as God apparently on earth must speak and act through His own human organism so created, human creatures and governors must be His mouthpiece.

When we consider, also, that the old faith held God to be forever the director of His own, it does not look strange that Churchmen held that a great solemn assembly of their chiefs, which they called a General Council, was the voice of God, and to be obeyed. Here is the logical development of the doctrine of church authority. From this authority, extant and enforced so long, all Protestantism revolted, and for reasons which satisfied at least itself. It was a specific revolt against a specific form of Christianity. But then there must be authority, which is government, somewhere, unless Christendom was to turn to chaos. But where? Since back of all question of authority lay the new but root Protestant idea of the dignity and privilege of the individual man, this idea added itself to the necessity of change, if change must come, and declared the individual conscience to be supreme authority in religion. It does not matter that this idea was never fully realized even among the Puritans, as Roger Williams and the Quakers show, simply because the theory was so transcendental as to be impossible. The right of private judgment was, and remains, one of the root ideas of logical Protestantism. Puritanism in England or here never revolted from much of the old theology. It believed in man's perdition or salvation, as he disobeyed or obeyed God's will; in the Mosaic Dispensation, in the Incarnation, the Atonement, the Trinity, the grace of God, the future life, very much as the old church did. Even in its dogma of the supreme authority of the Bible, it only taught what the Catholic Church has always held and holds; only that church claims to be that supreme court of judicature, to interpret the meaning of that authority, — a task which Protestantism relegates to the individual.

Again, the early Puritan found himself in at least the only visible institution in the West which called itself a church. If he left that church, there was no other to go to unless he made one. Nothing was more natural than that the man who held himself able to interpret the oracles of God should build the church of God. This, accordingly, he proceeded to do. But as before he did it that church was not, and invisible to boot, that idea of an invisible church, so rife to-day with Protestants, sprang up and throve. George Fox, the Quaker, applied the caustic to that theory when he held that, as a believer and regenerate man, he carried about the whole Christ under his waistcoat, in his heart, and fed on Him and was fed by Him there he had no need of any sacrament or outward sign to part or impart the Christ in morsels. In due time, having first been rid of Roman rule, the Puritan found himself confronting the Church of England. But that church, rightly or wrongly, has always held that it was a part of the Catholic Church; that it was not a new church of the Reformation, any more than an old house swept becomes a new or another house; that it had preserved, and intended to preserve, all those signs or notes by which the Catholic Church verifies itself, especially the three notes of orders, creeds, and sacraments; and that it never could or would conform to Rome or Geneva; and that, on the Genevan basis, it would cease to be the Catholic Church in England. True, for three hundred years and now, many in the Church of England have denied the theory and the claim. No church, perhaps, has been more rent or more betrayed; but if, at the Puritan asking, this church refused assent, and had not the reason of self-preservation to allege, it certainly committed a deadly sin against charity; and if any one mistakes incessant clamors in that church to-day as signs of any return to Puritan methods, or any one should proceed to touch its "notes" of Catholicity, the flame of its resistance would either consume itself or its foe. It should never be forgot that compliance by the Church of England with the Puritan demands would, as its dominant conscience then held and holds, have been simply suicide.

Now, then, we are in condition to understand the mooted question whether the New England Puritans were Nonconformists, as they called themselves, — i.e., people who refused merely the forms, — or Separatists, — i.e., men who had broken entirely from the Church of England, — as they denied they were. They were simply Separatists, because their root ideas touched the very vitals of the Anglican system, and, so far as they prevailed, destroyed it, root and branch. The irony of history is seldom more bitter than when it tells us that these non-conforming Puritans of New England, professing their affection for the Church of England, when that church came here with Sir Edmund Andros, treated it as outcast and felon against their civilization.

Yet one would greatly err who should say that there was any taint of hypocrisy in such men as Winthrop and Higginson when they wept over and professed their love for the Church of England. Not simply that they had been worshippers in its parish churches, where they had often heard their own beloved doctrines from men of the Puritan stamp, but because they did assent to and love much of doctrine which the Church of England held and holds in common with most Christians. What they did not love was that other part of doctrine which they asked the Church of England to give up, and which it retains till now, as necessary to its existence as a part of the historic church of God. The Puritan heart loved the Lord Jesus Christ of the Prayer Book, but its head hated the Communion office as Roman, and the office of Institution of the Priesthood as an insult to their own ministry. They honestly called themselves Nonconformists; but they were, by the resistless tide of their own logic and the assent of the root ideas of the Church of England, Separatists.

By their Charter — a very liberal and friendly one, with certain specified and guaranteed privileges — the Puritans of New England remained under English law. That this was so, at least in the judgment of English lawyers, is plain from the fact that the Charter was finally revoked on the ground that they had violated the laws of the realm; and the colonies then passed into a province, under a very different code, imposed by the Crown authorities. This, at least theoretical position, should be kept in mind when we look at the Puritan methods in establishing their church. To a degree only, their way of church establishment was logical. It was logical that each Puritan should stand upon his rights of conscience to interpret God and serve Him; it was logic for the Puritan to agree with his fellows to make common terms with God in a covenant wherein all embraced, agreed; it was logic to rest all authority in the Bible, and to interpret that Bible into laws in church and state for themselves. But it was neither logical nor Protestant then or now for them to impose their conduct as a rule for any other man's faith or behavior; to punish men by refusing them citizenship because they were not church-members; in other words, to make themselves, either by synod or any other form of clerical or lay association, church authority for dissenters when they themselves had flouted the old authority and stood against the Church of England for the free exercise of conscience by every Puritan. Very likely the Puritan here could not have done any differently. The trouble was in his premises, — which time has shown to be impossible of acceptance by the average human being. The realm of the Puritan enthusiasm lay too far above the specific gravity of mankind on its religious side, to be elsewhere than in the clouds; and by consequence, from the start the unregenerate throve in numbers, and very shortly became the majority in a commonwealth which was always alien to them.

It was people like Roger Williams, Ann Hutchinson, and the Quakers who speedily reduced the Puritan position to its logical dilemma, if not absurdity.

Roger Williams actually refused to pray with his wife, or join in grace with her at table, because she still attended the Puritan public worship; so intense was his individualism.

He and the rest at Providence made a law that no man was to be hurt for his conscience. In course of time the women and children had the habit of going to meetings, in public or private houses, every day in the week, if there were so many. A certain man forbade his wife to go. The town undertook to censure him for it. It was argued for the offender that the law was never meant to break down God's ordinance, which called for the wife's obedience to her husband; and against him, that if the townsfolk should thus restrain their wives the country would cry out on them. Now, unless the law had limit, no man was to be hurt for forbidding, upon his conscience, his wife to anything; and unless his wife was held to have no conscience, it is hard to see how the law could punish her if, upon her conscience, she refused him in everything. So hard is it for even pious people to live in the air. There is no record of the upshot of this matter, but even the timid may be bold to believe that the women went their own way, as usual.

The Puritan church developed itself along the line of this individualism until it dominated the individual with its majorities, and forced its minorities to a minute and definite obedience, compared with which the Catholic rule had been license. Nowhere on the face of the round globe have men ever been so directed, inspected, and limited in a voluntary submission to public form and the general mind as here. In the churches the rule of the congregation was in theory supreme ; but in due time church synods like those at Cambridge and Saybrook tended to mar this independency and impose their own decisions. But, however governed, logically the Puritan meeting-house from the start took precedence of the trading-house and the state house. The first meeting-houses were very like barns, and have all disappeared. Their successors were also of wood, very much like the one at Hingham, and are also mostly gone. The third crop of houses, at least in cities, was of increased dignity, as in the case of the Old South Meeting-House, Boston, still extant, and apparently of a Dutch type of architecture, while those of to-day assume multiform phases of heathen or mediæval architecture, both of which at the start the Puritans abjured. All was in sharp antithesis to most of the current ecclesiastical architecture of the times across seas, and a protest against æsthetics in religion.

But, however built, these houses, especially in the country, were the centres of affairs. In some towns people were forbid to dwell more than a mile from meeting ; the houses were often fortified with palisades, and sometimes a ditch. Here on the green auctions were held ; wolves' heads were nailed up ; publishments of intended marriages were posted ;

town meetings, in absence of any other town house, were held; and on Sunday the scattered townsfolk gathered to hear the gospel and the news. Care was taken by the authorities that a meeting-house should be built wherever white men went, and that a parson should be fed.

The Puritan parson was often the only man in the place liberally educated. According to the times he was a gentleman, of very positive character, often acting as both lawyer and physician to his flock, a man of faculty, and a general promoter of the public good. A reverence attended him which it is hard in these days to understand; and in most cases it was deserved. Town privileges and glebe lands were assigned to the clergy, and they were the chief conservators of civilization among their flock.

Rev. James Keith settled at Bridgewater, 1664, had a double house-lot, twelve acres, with a house on it, and £40 salary, one-half to be paid in Boston. In 1667 thirty cords of wood were added yearly. This gives probably a fair view of the temporalities of the clergy in those days.

The church services were long, the sermon sometimes lasting a couple of hours, and the chief prayer half as long; there were no organs or musical instruments to assist the music, which was led by a precentor, and the tune was usually one of four, York and St. David's being two. The chief persons sat in the foreseat near the pulpit, and the rest as they were ordered by "the seating committee," — boys and negroes in the galleries. At an early date tithing-men with long rods came into fashion, who kept the gallery youngsters quiet.

The custom was for all the people standing to wait till the ministers, whom they faced, passed down the aisle out of the meeting-house. Sewall notes: "The Governor Dudley turned to talk with Col. Townshend; so his back was upon the ministers as they went out."

A Plymouth deaconess sat in a convenient place in the meeting-house with a birch rod in her hand to awe little children into due propriety. The old writers say "she honored her place, and was an ornament to the congregation."

A deal has been said of the grotesque nature of some of the Puritan prayers, and the very odd things which were often prayed for. This state of things was aggravated in New England by the custom of sending up notes for the prayers of the congregation for voyages, births, sorrows, afflictions, and bereavements. When thanks were given for mercies received, the petitioner rose in his pew. The free Puritan prayers were for deliverance from Indian assaults, foreign interference, plagues, murrain, failure of crops, storms and earthquakes, and changes in the government at home. Indeed, everything that interested them they prayed over, first or last. Assuming that the Christian theory of prayer is valid, it is hard to see why all this was not logical, since there is nothing either great or small to Him who hears prayers, and a man might as properly pray for a sick horse as for the conversion of the heathen.

The Scotch, in their large declaration, 1637, begin

their petition against the Book of Common Prayer in this most democratic fashion: "We, men, women, and children and servants, having considered," etc.

Yet some of the Puritan prayers, both sides of the water, could only befit privy councillors of God, who had at all times the run of His palace. One said:—

> "O, my good Lord God I hear the king hath set up his standard at York against the Parliament and the city of London. Look thou upon them, take their cause into thine own hand; appear thou in the cause of thy saints, the cause in hand. It is thy cause, Lord. We know that the king is misled, deluded and deceived by his Popish, Arminian and temporizing, rebellious malignant faction and party."

"They would," says Dr. Echard, "in their prayers and sermons tell God that they would be willing to be at any charge and trouble for him, and do any kindness, as it were, for the Lord; the Lord might now trust them and rely upon them, they should not fail him; they should not be unmindful of his business; his works should not stand still, nor his designs be neglected. They must needs say that they had formerly received some favors from God, and have been as it were beholden to the Almighty; but they did not much question but they should find some opportunity of making some amends for the many good things and civilities which they had received from him. Indeed, as for those who are weak in the Faith and are yet but babes in Christ, it is fit that they should keep at some distance from Christ, should kneel before him and stand (as one may say) cap in hand to the Almighty; but as to those who are strong in all Gifts and grown up in all grace and are come to a fulness and ripeness in the Lord Jesus, it is comely enough to take a great chair and sit at the end of the table and with their cock'd hats on their heads to say, 'God, we thought it not amiss to call upon thee this evening and let thee know how affairs stand. We have been very watchful since we were last with thee and they are in a very hopeful condition. We hope that thou wilt not forget us; for we are very thoughtful of thy concerns. We do somewhat long to hear from thee and if thou pleasest to give us such a thing as Victory we shall be (as one may say) good to thee in something else when it lies in our way.'"

Mr. Vines, in St. Clement's Church, London, used these words: "O Lord, thou hast never given us a victory this long while for all our frequent fasting. What dost thou mean, O Lord, to fling into a ditch and there to leave us." One Robinson at Southampton (1642) prayed thus: "O God, O God, many are the hands lift up against us, but there is one God, it is thou thyself, O Father, who does us more mischief than they all." "Gather upon God," said another in a Fast sermon before the Commons, "and hold him to it as Jacob did; press him with his precepts, with his promises, with his hand, with his seal, with his oath; that is, if I may speak it reverently enough, put the Lord out of countenance; put him, as you would say, to the blush, unless we be masters of our requests."

Even Sewall shows the same temper when, writing

in 1686 to his uncle, Stephen Dummer, in England, of the attempts made to convert the Indians, he says: —

"As to the design of converting them, we in New England may sorrowfully sing the 127 Psalm: 'Except the Lord build the house they labor in vain that build it.' I am persuaded it would be a most acceptable sacrifice to God, importunately to beseech Him to put His hand to that work and not in a great measure to stand and look on."

But Sewall is prone to a more submissive and filial piety in his prayers. He writes in a time of sickness: —

"The Small Pox is in a pretty many families in town. Hath been and is also a mortal fever of which many have died. I desire your prayers that I may be fitted for the good pleasure of God who alone is able to preserve from what is mentioned and from the Indians, French or any other evil. . . . March 30 1687. We are now, blessed be God, pretty well got over a dry and cold winter. Small Pox is in town but not many die as yet."

To the Rev. John Higginson he writes (1706): —

"Let me also entreat your prayers for me and my family, that the blessing of God may rest upon the head of every one in it by reason of the good will of Him who dwelt in the Bush."

When his son Sam was leaving his business place, because, as it certainly proved, too shiftless to fill it, his good father writes, just after he had been told by a gossip that somebody had called him a knave: —

"The good Lord give me truth in the inward parts and finally give rest unto my dear son and put him into some calling wherein he will accept of him to serve Him. . . . Feb' 26. I prayed with Sam alone that God would direct our way as to a calling for him."

"Jany 13, 1696. When I came in past 7 at night my wife met me in the entry and told me Betty had surprised them. It seems Betty Sewall had given some signs of dejection and sorrow; but a little after dinner she burst out into an amazing cry which caused all the family to cry too; Her mother asked the reason; she gave none; at last said she was afraid she should go to hell — her sins were not pardoned. She was first wounded by my reading a sermon of Mr. Norton's about the 5th of Jany. Text John 7.34. Ye shall seek me and shall not find me. And those words in the sermon (John 8.21.) 'ye shall seek me and shall die in your sins' ran in her mind and terrified her greatly. And staying at home Jan' 12 she read out of Mr. Cotton Mather — 'Why hath Satan filled thy heart,' which increased her fear. Her mother asked her whether she prayed. She answered Yes — but feared her prayers were not heard because her sins [were] not pardoned. Mr. Willard [the Sewalls' minister] though sent for timelier, came not till after I came home. He discoursed with Betty who could not give a distinct account, but was confused, as his phrase was, and as he had experienced in himself. He prayed excellently."

"Feb' 22. Betty comes into me almost as soon as I was up and tells me the disquiet she had when waked; told me was afraid she should go to hell, was like Spira, not elected. Asked her what I should pray for, she said that God would pardon her sins and give her a new heart. I answered her fears as well as I could, and prayed with many tears on either part; hope God heard us. I gave her solemnly to God."

"Sabbath May 3. Betty can hardly read her chapter for weeping; tells me she is afraid she is gone back, does not taste that sweetness in reading the Word which once she did; fears that what was once upon her has worn off. I said what I could to her and in the evening prayed with her alone."

The Diary concludes its notice of Betty Sewall's religious "concern of mind" with the last entry. The reader will no doubt see in the affair the deep sincerity of the Puritan mind in what is called conversion. The picture stands for thousands of others like, from that day till now. Certainly such a state of mind no one sneers at; and however aside many may be in accounting for the mental phenomena, all must respect the earnestness of the sorrow, and wish it a to-morrow of peace. This picture of Betty Sewall's mind and her father's case certainly antagonize the vulgar theory that the Puritans were hypocrites.

"May 7, 1696. Col Shrimpton marries his son to his wive's sister's daughter, Elizabeth Richardson. All of the Council in the town were invited to the wedding and many others. Only I was not spoken to. As I was glad not to be there because the lawfulness of the intermarrying of Cousin-Germans is doubted; so it grieves me to be taken up in the lips of talkers and to be in such a condition that Col Shrimpton shall be under a temptation in defence of himself to wound me; if any should happen to say, Why was not such a one here? The Lord help me not to do or neglect anything that should prevent the dwelling of brethren together in unity. And Oh most bountiful and gracious God who givest liberally and upbraidest not, admit me humbly to bespeak an invitation to the marriage of the Lamb and let thy Grace with me and in me be sufficient for me in making myself ready. And out of thy infinite and unaccountable compassions, place me among those who shall not be left; but shall be accepted by thee here and taken into glory hereafter. Though I am beyond conception vile who may say unto thee 'What doest thou?' Thou canst justify thyself in thy proceedings. And, O Lord God forgive all my unsuitable deportment at thy table the last Sabbath day, that wedding day; and if even I be again invited (Invite me once again) help me entirely to give myself to thy Son as to my most endeared Lord and Husband. And let my dear wife and all my children partake in this privilege and that not as *umbras* [probably he means as shadows or echoes of himself] but on their own account."

There must also have been some quaint sermons listened to. A fight between a snake and a mouse having been seen at Watertown, Mr. Wilson of Boston, a very sincere and holy man, showed in a sermon how the snake was the Devil and the mouse a poor contemptible people (the Puritans) which God had brought here to overcome Satan and dispossess him of his kingdom.

Nor was there always lacking to the austerity of Puritan worship a certain grim mother-wit, which on occasion made itself heard.

A Puritan minister was preaching to a fishing congregation in Plymouth Colony. He besought them to set a good example, because they came out to convert the world to Christianity, when one of the congregation interrupted him with, "Sir, that is what the people of the Bay came out for; but we came to catch fish."

The Puritan Sabbath in all its colors was Hebraic and ascetic. It began at sunset on Saturday, and ended at sunset on Sunday. In the old religion, Sunday was a feast day; they made it a fast, probably following their usual rule to adopt the exact opposite practice from that which prevailed in alien churches. In this, excepting the Scotch, they were singular among Protestants. Even Calvin at Geneva, where he ruled with a rod of iron, allowed games and pastimes after the morning service. But the Puritans were the first and only ones to vie with the Mosaic code in causing all lightheartedness to cease from the day. All work, travel, unnecessary or avoidable, absence from public worship, was punished by fine or the whipping-post. Strict public watch was kept for delinquents. In the home, silence and Scripture prevailed. The social life, austere at the best, was clouded with the thick darkness of an imposed solemnity worse than solitary confinement in a cave or closet; and this custom of Sabbath-keeping, while so much of Puritanism has ceased, continues in a modified form in many quarters to this day. Sewall was a strict observer of this fast, and is always urgent for the strict enforcement of the Sabbath laws. He notes in his Diary when a warship fires guns coming up the harbor, or when there is a bustle of soldiers escorting a royal governor on the Sabbath; as a magistrate, he is on the alert to stop all carousing Saturday nights, and bids a cooper hammering at his barrels, a trifle late, to give over. There is a characteristic entry in his Diary, Nov. 18, 1709:—

"Capt Teat by his letter desires a license of the Governor to work on his ship on the Lords Day; the ship was on the ground and feared he should be nipped. Governor argued hard for it; Captain was judge of the necessity. I argued against it; he had time enough before, and had time enough to come before the sailing of the Mast Fleet. At last the Governor collected the voices and said it was carried by one; when I was asked I said, I am dissatisfied, he ought not to be licensed."

Feb. 5, 1703, Sewall, with other Puritans, rode out to Roxbury —

"on purpose to speak to the Governor against having illuminations, especially in the town house; that so the profanation of the Sabbath [i.e., Saturday night] might be prevented. I said twould be most for the honor of God and that would be, most for the honor and safety of Queen Anne. Governor said twould be hard for him to forbid it, considering how good the Queen was, what successes God had given her. Feby 6. between eight and nine all the bells begin to ring to celebrate Queen Anne's birthday, being the last of the week. . . . Feb 11. The Governor under his hand remits the fines of several sentenced to pay 5*s*. apiece for drinking at Mrs. Monk's on Saturday night last about 9 o'clock. I had warned Mrs. Monk an hour before."

The governor here interfered to remit the fine of men who were drinking their queen's health in an orderly manner, at a licensed inn, at a sober hour. Yet this was a part of the British realm, and supposed to be under the protection of English law, as it was certainly under the protection of the English arms. Can the anomaly of the Puritan rule here on its political side be more sharply stated than in an incident like this?

An examination of the colonial laws will show that the Puritans intended to enforce their religion with industry and exactly, and did so. For certain heresies, such as denying the immortality of the soul, the resurrection of the body, or Sabbath-keeping, or infant baptism, or the authority of magistrates, or even more subtle problems of Christianity, the penalty was banishment. They whipped, branded, banished, and hung dissenters from their dogma, and the abler of them were foremost in enforcing punishment. When Sewall came on the stage the day of the great heresies of Mrs. Hutchinson and the Quakers had mostly passed, though more were coming. Yet Sewall shows that he would have hung as well as the rest. He votes against allowing the Quakers, who petition, to fence in the graves of their fellow-Christians on Boston Common who had been hung as martyrs.

The fine gold of Puritanism had begun to grow dim before the first fathers were in their graves. Fever is neither normal nor long-lived in man. The Puritan ecstasy cooled in the chill atmosphere of that human nature which, though sometimes climbing the hills, usually abides at a lower level of religious and political mediocrity. The form which was temporal passed; the essential became an atmosphere which still abides and thrives. The sun sets, but its heat remains in its absence. The Puritan religion was impossible to man; but its root ideas of the privilege of man as against the claim and usurpation of the old ecclesiasticism will in time force acceptance from those very churches which, in the seventeenth century, refused assent. The Puritan crossed the line of his own logic; failed to see his own drift, — in fact, was in a tide which he did not and could not resist; wrought according to his light, and vanished. The Puritan long since went out, but his light remains. His box might not be of alabaster, but its treasure will last as long as the story of the woman who poured the precious ointment upon her Master's head as He sat at meat.

CHAPTER V.

SEWALL AND THE PURITAN COMMONWEALTH.

"The book of 'the Prince' is closed forever as a state manual; and the book of 'the people' — a book perhaps of darker sophistries and more pressing tyranny — is as yet unwritten."

"Men are not corrupted by the exercise of power or debased by the habit of obedience; but by the exercise of a power which they believe to be illegal, and by obedience to a rule which they believe to be usurped and illegal." DE TOCQUEVILLE.

"'Tis better to have tried and failed
Than never to have tried at all."

IN the political economy of Puritanism the state existed for the church, not the church for the state. Religion was first, not politics. The logic of all vital Protestantism is towards democracy, and only that subordination or restraint of the individual in a well-ordered state which is for the necessary good of all. Yet the Puritan rule in New England did not reach so far, but stopped short at a theocracy, — a government in which God is the distinct head and fountain of law. Now, if the Puritan had been exactly at one with God, His infallible mouthpiece and chief justice (as he was not), then the Puritan commonwealth would have been a complete and satisfactory theocracy, both in theory and practice. But exactly so far as he missed and mistook his own decisions for God's, and imposed them as law upon other men, his government became an oligarchy. Indeed, that was the real quality of government here so long as the church-members governed the majority outside their church, who had no vote. The Puritan, therefore, was never a democrat. In 1636 Rev. John Cotton wrote to Lord Say and Seal a very clear statement of what sort of government was intended. He says: "Democracy I do not conceive that ever God did ordain as a fit government either for church or commonwealth. If the people be governors, who shall be governed? As for monarchy and aristocracy, they are both of them clearly approved and directed in Scripture, yet so as referreth the sovereignty to Himself and setteth up Theocracy in both, as the best form of government in the commonwealth as in the church." The Puritans intensified classes among themselves much more than we do. Not only were ladies set in the foreseat and a carpenter's wife in the back, but the common people themselves accepted the situation.

There was a meeting of the church and congregation at the South Church, Oct. 3, 1707, their pastor, Mr. Willard, having just died; and Sewall writes: "It was very thin, several came not because Mr. Pemberton [the officiating minister] said, *Gentlemen*, of the church and congregation; .affirmed they were not gentlemen and therefore they were not warned to come." Adjourned.

The Puritans found the constitution of their alleged theocracy in the Jewish Scriptures. As to the question why they did not go to the Christian Scriptures instead, a double answer may properly be given; viz., that in the Holy Oracles of the apostles' age there were no formularies of government such as seen in the Mosaic code, and that the Old Testament in general being a history of other men's affairs in many ages, it was there other men might find the richest fund of counsel when they came to administer their own. Their general conception of the place which the Bible should occupy in human affairs is well stated in their own words: —

> "The whole Council of God, concerning all things necessary for his own glory, Man's salvation, faith and life is either expressly set down in Scripture or by good and necessary consequence may be deduced from Scripture. Unto which nothing at any time is to be added, whether by new revelations of the Spirit or traditions of men."

It was inevitable that these New England Lollards (if such a phrase may be ventured on to remind the reader that the Puritan on all sides of him — in religion, politics, and social life — was the child and offspring of a profound and ancient movement which drove him on to his destiny, and still thrives in the world) should take God's word for the constitution of his commonwealth. It is hard to see where they could have discovered any other; and in inventing one, this sacred monad and individual — this Puritan — for whom Christ died and the whole creation groaned in sympathy, might not be able to agree with his next-door neighbor, — a cobbler, may be, of old shoes on earth, but a king and priest in that nearing world in which he was to live forever as a covenanted citizen. It should be only noticed that he who had refused as against his conscience to listen to the ancient church interpreting Scripture, was now forced to interpret for himself, and imposed his interpretation on the rest, — on at least all aliens.

The first result of this attempt to establish and maintain his impossible creed was not exactly a reign of terror, but a government full of severity and hardship. The Puritan himself suffered with the rest; and the New England life became granitic, and vexed by harsh restraints and unreasonable demands. Human nature, thus challenged and irritated, revenged itself by a constant, if often silent, protest. Under harsh laws even the most unmentionable crimes and the fiercest passions revealed themselves to an extent, considering the population, hardly realized to-day. The wicked people, if not many, were very wicked, although environed with the Puritan piety. All suffered, and the saints not least.

In their unique selection of the Mosaic code for their own civil constitution lies perhaps the explanation of the actual status of the Puritan clergy in their commonwealth. For nothing was more reasonable to be believed than that if the Mosaic code was to be the common law of the land, then that class of men who were best versed in it were certainly the best interpreters of it. As a matter of fact, the Puritan clergy, not only as admirably educated, but as professional men, were best fitted to expound and apply the same to current events in the commonwealth. They were, in fact, not so much by appointment as from the nature of things, a supreme court of judicature, to decide what the laws should be or the Scripture meant. The colonial statute book abounds in Scripture texts in the nature of precedents to ratify and affirm the statute; and in inscribing these laws it was directed that wide margins should be left to insert these texts. From this point of view we may regard the mooted question whether the Puritan clergy were sinners above all who dwelt at Jerusalem; whether, in short, they were the head tyrants in their commonwealth. Certainly any law resting not on justice, but on force, if enforced, is tyranny. The Puritans had many such laws, and the logical conclusion stands against their fame. But this tyranny was not irregular, not personal, but formal and legal. It was a part of the situation; and the Puritan in general is more entitled to the sympathy of history than its blame. The clergy could not escape the necessity of expounding their theocratic code, and, in fact, were often invited by the magistrates to do so. If they had not done so, the state would have gone very close to being compelled to change its constitution. But in fact the clergy were willing to do so, as being as much a part of their duty to their religion and their government as it was to baptize a child, or pray protection from smallpox or the Indians. Human nature is seldom transfigured even in a parson; and the Puritan parson was always a man, and sometimes a very meddlesome and mischievous one. Increase and Cotton Mather, as bold men as ever filled a pulpit, and leaders in their own order, were no saints, even when they wrought the hardest for the common weal; but their New England would not have fared so well without them. But, with these limitations, there are few facts more firmly established as a part of our history than that the Puritan clergy here were no tyrants over the laity, nor pre-eminent tyrants among them. They had their power, beyond their calling, inasmuch as they represented the laity of their church. It is incredible to most students of our colonial annals, that if at any time the clergy had given a decision against the conscience of their laity, that the latter would not have stood against them and controlled them. Instances, indeed, of individuals are not wanting where this was done, as, for instance, in the case of Rev. John Cotton and the Antinomian wrangle. To hold that this handful of men, face to face with magistrates as able as Winthrop, the elder Dudley, Stoughton, and a host of others, could or did control the public will to the clerical pleasure is irrational, and can never be maintained in the forum of history.

What they actually did was to aid the land where they had come with such counsel as they had, when it was needed, and sometimes when it was even demanded by the civil authorities as a duty inherent in their pastoral office which they could not and would not avoid.

Two cardinal necessities imposed themselves upon the Puritans, involved as they were in a vast material enterprise; to wit, to subdue a wild to a field, where the wild was a continent: (1) It was necessary to maintain spiritual vitality enough to mould and saturate the material with the spiritual, and not suffer the calamity of a reverse process, as the Spaniards in South America had, since no vital civilization was ever wrought out by muscle alone, by whole men of brain and soul, with these gone into it; (2) It was necessary, inasmuch as they dwelt so far from social customs and the wonted forms of law, that on the frontier of barbarism, with all human ties working themselves loose, stringent laws should be enforced rigorously. To the first necessity the New England Puritan answered with his church; to the second, with his commonwealth.

In this way we may approach the mooted question as to whether we should praise or blame the Puritans for their treatment of such people as the Quakers, Mrs. Hutchinson, and Roger Williams. Some of these they hung, and the rest they banished; while the victims all clamored — Williams the loudest, at least in history — that they suffered for conscience' sake. Assuming that they did, what then? The Puritan suffered much toil and vexation in hanging them or driving them out for his conscience' sake. When the consciences of two sets of people are at strife, the conscience backed by the more robust physique must drive, or at least will try to drive, the other to the wall. Both sides would have done it, and one side did it. It can hardly be repeated too often that the Puritan, when we judge his behavior, is to be judged by the standards of his age, not ours, unless we insist that he ought to have been a prophet, and seen his duty with our eyes. To say that he was both fallible and peccable is merely to insist on the idle affirmation that he was not God. To pass him by with a jest, — to say, for instance, that after this age has heard so much of the blessings which have flowed from the Pilgrims landing on Plymouth Rock, it is high time to inquire what blessings would have flowed in upon us if Plymouth Rock had landed on the Pilgrims, may be a witticism, but it is surely not the philosophy nor the rectitude of history. The fact is, the Puritan, by an English charter, was put in command here, and was responsible for what went on. He held the helm, and made his voyage. The captain of a ship, by statute law, is made to a degree an autocrat on his quarter-deck, — let us say, to express the dynamics of his command, a tyrant. But if he makes his voyage, and keeps his ship in mid channel on entering port, "his sea words" to the forecastle, and, to a degree, his violence, are very reasonably condoned to his responsibility and to his proved success. Men are human, burdens are heavy, and human laws at least recognize these facts when men are brought into judgment. To take the case of Roger Williams, one of the most amiable and troublesome of mortals. He chose to come on board the Puritan ship, with the Puritan at the helm and responsible for the voyage, as Williams was not. Assume that Williams brought on board (as he did) his absolute but ideal truth that conscience is and ought to be free, and that the Puritan denied his truth (as he did), which in the abstract was certainly error, — what then? No man who knows the times but must confess that if any or all these sectaries which Williams represents had had their way, the Puritan commonwealth would have fallen into such general mutiny as would have perilled both the voyage and cargo. It was because the Puritan drove out or hung such men as Williams, with their ill-timed, abstract truths, that he managed to found a civilization which this day gives open-handed freedom of conscience to sixty millions of Americans. "He builded better than he knew" when he punished to preserve; and his works live after him.

The charter — which so far as the English Crown was the fountain of authority to New England as a part of the British realm, was the formal authority under which the Puritan set up his government in Massachusetts Colony — was granted by Charles I. in 1628 to a trading company, according to the ancient custom whereby trading guilds of all sorts had been granted special privileges from time immemorial; as James I. had granted a charter to Plymouth Colony; as a hundred years before the East India Company had been allowed to trade and rule in India; and as some twenty years later the Hudson Bay Company had gained it special rights in the North. But this trading company of Massachusetts Bay chose to transfer its government speedily out of England into the colony itself, and to color its behaviors with the peculiar religion of its members, as no other like corporation ever did. Yet on its secular side the company remained for a long time a trading company, with a monopoly of furs. To a great degree a religious mission on the part of the adventurers in this mixed undertaking was recognized by the terms of the charter itself. It is formally declared that the authority granted by the charter is on purpose that "the inhabitants there may be so religiously, peaceably and civilly governed, as their good life and orderly conversation may win and incite the natives of the country to the knowledge and obedience of the only true God and Savior of mankind and the Christian faith which in our royal intention and the adventurer's free profession is the principle end of this plantation." The emphatic phrase "in our royal intention and the adventurer's free profession" is repeated in the Provincial Charter after given by King William III.

The very fact of this charter, thus given and taken, was itself an assertion that the English Crown claimed sovereignty over the land and the people, and that the latter agreed to the claim in accepting their privileges. The New England Puritans, therefore, from the start professed themselves as subjects of the English Crown. The charter repeatedly affirms it. In the unique position in which they after found themselves so far away from the central government, and with such singular exigencies often arising, and with the generous powers granted by the charter itself, the Puritan rulers, without blame from just history, might sometimes transcend their powers, or be tempted into extravagances in lawmaking incompatible with a due respect for the rights of the Crown. But this possibility does not explain their conduct. Man, in contrast with all other animals, is liable to fits of bad logic and contradictory conduct, arising from his complex nature, which they never show. The wolf has the logic of his unvarying appetite. He has tasted lamb; he likes it; therefore, undisturbed of heart or conscience, he eats lamb every time he can. But man finds himself with a double nature, each warring against the other, and is therefore liable to perturbations and vagaries in conduct. To say that the New England Puritan was a conscious rebel from the start, is not true; to say that he was a predestinated rebel from the start, is. Men like Winthrop no doubt intended to be loyal, and were. Even men like Endicott and the elder Dudley must have intended to remain good subjects after their fashion, though the fashion was a poor one. Certainly these men in a seaport town, edged round with savages, and exposed, and even doomed if left to themselves, to Holland, France, and Spain, could never have intended to break from the Crown, even though Endicott cut the cross from the English colors, and Dudley, unlet of Winthrop, would have misled the colony into overt treason. The disturbing cause of those perturbations in the Puritan's political behavior, apart from personal traits, his constant oscillation between obedience and disrespect to his king, was the persistently on-pressing logic of that English Reformation which had made him Puritan. In England itself that Reformation did not leave

English kings at peace, nor always on their thrones. Was the Puritan of New England, urged on by his heredity of personal liberty and individual dignity, less loyal than the men who from that age till now have dethroned or changed kings, destroyed rotten boroughs, brought in the Corn Laws in a furious protest against feudalism, opened Oxford and Cambridge to dissenters, and in general insisted, according to the compact and logic of the Renaissance, that man should come by his own? It is idle to stand after the event and cry out that the men before the event foresaw it. The Puritans were not a family of prophets, but a society of fallible but able men who wrought at the work in hand, and were satisfied with a day's work that showed progress, leaving to-morrow its own. Our Revolution of 1776 was as natural and inevitable as that the crocus-bulb lifts forth its flower under the returning spring. Yet it is most improbable that the colonial Puritans foresaw that event. It was their staying power which was their real value to the future. They seldom forgot they had a king to dread, yet they ever remembered with joy that they were Puritans and men. The clouds which low down veil the face of the landscape are visible, and through their rift instant glimpses of spaces beyond are possible; but the great air currents overhead, moving resistless to command the storm, are invisible. The Puritan, even when regarding his own movement in time, very often beheld only its clouds.

In the colonial charter traces are found of that

almost universal search for the precious metals which was carried on in new lands. The only tithe or tax which the Crown reserved for itself was one-fifth of all the gold and silver mined; which apparently, and to this day, the laws of geology forbade to be very much. Otherwise, on the part of the Crown, the privileges granted were very generous. The government was placed in the hands of a governor, deputy-governor, and a court of assistants; all, after the first appointment by the king, to be elected by the citizens every year. To this compact body was committed the care of the state and the power of making laws, with the simple proviso that these should not be against the laws of the realm. Substantially by this charter the colonists were left free to manage their affairs, which might be divided into two classes; viz., the affairs of their own people, and the affairs which involved themselves with the dignity and rights of the Crown. Sometimes these rights were in both classes.

The affairs of their own people the government managed with energy and much practical common-sense. They threw off new towns from the common centres of the first ones like Boston, Salem, and Newbury, exactly as fast as their people settled in the wild; and each of these became little municipalities, emphasizing their own local interests and wishes in those town meetings which were so many cradles of independence and statesmanship, narrow in their limits, but very practical and useful to the state. Persons neglecting town meeting in some places were fined 1*s.* 6*d.*; for being late, refusing to answer the roll-call, or leaving the meeting before it closed, 9*d.* This articulation of the state into the little sovereignties of towns, with its resultant benefits, lies at the basis of American Democracy. Among no people in the world, perhaps, according to their population, have so many persons, for the last three hundred years, engaged in governing as here. Our town records show a little of this work; but the amount of human mind and energy which have gone into managing local affairs, and still continue, is something wonderful. It was the practice in politics of the individualism of Protestantism, and a good example of its capacity to mould men into good citizens. The colonial government insisted on schools and churches wherever they could be had; and nowhere, according to the population, have there been more. They were the first to enroll the militia. They set everybody to do something, while tramps and vagabonds were at a frightful discount. In short, they brought up the people to be industrious, intelligent, religious, thrifty, self-reliant, and created a citizenship more than Spartan in its energy and permanency. Social life and manners here might have been or may be lacking some tenderness or elegance to be found elsewhere, but nowhere was or is there more of the dominancy and mastership which insures economic successes than here.

At first only church-members were citizens; and until a change was made which included all really responsible people in political equality, the Puritans wrangled bitterly over the matter, which was settled in the interests of a progressive democracy. The sectaries, like the Quakers, gave them some distractions, and in Puritanism it was inevitable that each man should stand stoutly for his own; but with these exceptions it may be said in general that in the colonial period at least the government and the governed were in assent and harmony. A marked exception to harmony was the case of Sir Harry Vane, of whom Sewall says: —

"He, Henry Vane, worked hard for his election, May 17, 1637. Indeed Mr. Vane seemed to stand so hard for being chosen again, as to endeavor to confound and frustrate the whole business of the election rather than he himself should fail of being chosen" (p. 295).

"There was a great struggle, he being the principal magistrate for managing the election. My father has told me many a time that he and others went on foot from Newbury to Cambridge, Forty miles on purpose to be made free and help to strengthen Gov'r Winthrop's party. The New English planters were at this time hardly bestead; being infested by the Pequot Indians and the new opinions, at the same time."

Of course the floating population, or stray men and women of other religions, cannot be included in the statement. Where the laws of England did not include a difficulty, they made one to cover it; but in general, especially as to rights of property, the colony may be said to have lived under English law.

It must be said of the Puritans as lawmakers, that their unique blending of religion and politics together often produced singular situations, which, if there had been lawyers (as there were few or none in the earlier days) free to argue a case arising under them, would have been likely to produce awkward results. For instance, if a certain act had been declared a crime, with a certain penalty affixed to it, and the cited authority for the same had been a passage out of the Pentateuch of Moses, a sharp lawyer might have led the court, owing to the difficulties of time and space, a long journey before it was able to certify to the fact of Moses or the authenticity of his authorship. But they had no such lawyers, and so no dilemma.

The Puritan also sinned against the great natural law of proportion, both in making and enforcing his laws. This is apt to be the case with all enthusiasts, who are apt to push their ideas beyond their legitimate relations, until they border on fanaticism. For instance, their laws against extravagance in dress were as solemnly formulated and as seriously enforced as if it had happened to be a sin against the Holy Ghost. This Puritan tendency to apply what, as Hawthorne says with his customary subtlety of analysis, well "befitted a people amongst whom religion and law were almost identical, and in whose character both were so thoroughly interfused that the mildest and severest acts of public discipline were alike made venerable and awful," appears very often in the colonial statutes.

In the affairs of the Crown the colonial government was less fortunate. They had not been planted three years before bitter complaints were laid against them before the Crown. Complaints continued to be made. Visitors and enemies here reported insubordinations on all hands. Many of their complaints were groundless; but after all allowance, it remains true that the Puritans were often guilty of gross imprudence, considering that they were English subjects. In general this imprudence showed itself in their assuming supreme prerogatives; as of life and death in the doubtful case of the Quakers; in their banishment of English subjects, or forbidding them entrance to their colony; in their tampering with the English laws of trade (a matter always of sensitive interest to a commercial nation like England); in their coining money; and in assuming in public acts the title of commonwealth, though a part of a kingdom. Besides, they ever showed an even fierce desire to be let alone by England. Their agents there at court had much trouble, and did not always follow straight paths in explaining to the English government the ongoings of their principals. Finally, in simple preservation of the Crown authority (4th Charles II.), their charter was "cancelled, vacated, and annihilated," as the record runs, and a new charter, "the Province Charter" as it is called, issued in the reign of William and Mary, 1691.

The new charter, after consolidating Plymouth and Massachusetts into one, abridged the liberties heretofore enjoyed, in favor of the Crown. The election of the chief magistrates was taken from the people, and they were appointed by the Crown: —

"From henceforth forever there shall be one governor; one lieutenant or deputy governor; and one secretary of our said province or territory to be from time to time commissioned by us, our heirs and successors; and eight and twenty assistants and counsellors to be advising and assisting to the governor of our said province or territory for the time being, as by these presents is hereafter directed and appointed."

It was also ordered by the new charter that once a year a Great and General Court should be elected, two from each town, who should elect the counsellors. Together these formed the government. But the governor could dissolve or adjourn the court, veto its nominations, and, in general, as the king's servant, secure the king's interests, or at least prevent the perilling of them. There was also a very liberal right of appeal allowed from the courts to the Privy Council. An examination of this charter shows that it was intended to carefully provide against the irregularities before complained of, and it certainly seriously limited the old colonial privileges. It was a curb — put on, too, upon the fiery Puritan steed with stern phrases which show the English statesman at Whitehall resolutely bent on restraint. And this, too, in the reign of a man as liberal and Protestant as King William.

It is not intended here to explain how the new charter tended to multiply dissensions between the Crown and its colony. The story is long; and much of it, especially its details, are in Sewall's Diary. But with a rough democracy in the General Court, and a king's appointee in the governor's chair armed with large powers, it will be seen that there was opportunity at least for constant wrangle which would insure a chronic feud. That feud was, and deepened into the Revolution. There was but one governor popular from the date of the charter until it ceased to operate. Each side held its own with its best. It is shorter to say what was not, than what was, a bone of contention. It was, in fact, a struggle between the old and the new; between the privilege of the king and the privilege of the people; and the future belonged to the people.

The transition period between the old charter and the new was one of extreme anxiety to the colonists, especially in the matter of their real estate, which constituted most of their wealth. Eminent lawyers at the time, and Chief Justice Parsons later on, held that when the colonial charter fell, it carried with it all laws made under it, and all land titles as well. If this were so, no man was sure even of the house he had built, paid for, and lived in. In fact, the whole question of these early land titles from which we derive, so far as theory goes, was and is always in the air. If any one owned the lands, it must have been the Indians; but their occupation of them was peculiar and uncertain. The king claimed the land by the right of discovery and the tacit or explicit agreement of his brother kings. But what claim had an English king to own from the Atlantic to the Pacific between certain lines of latitude? To discover a watch in the street hardly gives any one but the owner a title to it. The Puritans recognized the ownership to be in the Indians, and bought of them in a fair bargain, at least so far as law could insure fair dealing. But they had asked no further title from the king who claimed ownership, and themselves as subjects. When, therefore, their charter fell, and so far the king's favor with it, it was quite possible that the English courts, had the Crown claimed it, would have declared these Indian titles void in law, and the land reverted to the king. A bad king would have probably done this; but the new charter left their ownership where it was, — untouched.

Sewall himself, especially under the Province Charter, had rare opportunities to see the inside of New England politics; and his Diary abounds in minute and rare bits of intelligence. Besides his high social standing, which brought him in contact with the leaders on both sides, he was a member of the Royal Council of the Province from 1692 to 1725 (thirty-three years), when he declined re-election; and as judge and chief justice all law matters were open to him. He was a Puritan in his politics, but a discreet one. He writes it down: "Great Britain was not habitable to our fathers because the civil government fell upon them unmercifully." In a time when the Provincial courts were changed, and justice, as he probably judged it, in jeopardy from the king, he writes: "So that old Court is like to die and sink in the midst. The Lord be our King and Lord and Law-Giver. Pardon our Court-Sins and sanctify our frequent Deaths."

All the way through, in his Diary, Sewall shows himself, so far as the Crown went, a conformist to what he judged the political necessities of the hour. Puritan he was in church and state, and he took good care (and it was easy for him) not to allow himself to lose touch with the on-marching but hampered logic of New England institutions. But he was also human, constitutionally prone to peaceful ways, — no radical, having too much sound English flesh and health about him for that, — and perhaps with a settled conviction that, as lives were or might be, he and his fellow-citizens would come by more of their own if they watched and waited an opportunity than if they forced the issue, and stolidly planted their feet in spots where there was no retreat except it cost an overthrow. He might be ready enough to jostle the king, especially when the latter nodded or was busy, but not to try issues with him when seated on the throne and reaching out his sceptre. Sewall remembered his covenant, and wished it immortal; but while he served it his best, he had one eye always open to what the Master of Englishmen at Whitehall might choose to think or command. He was also a rich man, and property is always conservative. He stands stoutly upon equity and his English rights when the old South Church is invaded by the Prayer Book; but when the charter is taken away, and the question is in all quarters whether all their land titles have not gone with it, he is found an humble petitioner to the Crown that his land may be assured to him, though this behavior is evidently regarded by many as unpatriotic and time-serving. He is out of the country when Andros is overthrown by a Boston mob, and his Diary nowhere expresses any animosity to that able servant of the king. But when the news comes out by letter to England he notes it down: "We were surprised with joy." Yet if he had said that on the London Stock Exchange he would probably have gone to the Tower, with a chance of the confiscation of his New England property. He was a good man, but also a wise one in his generation.

The political history of the Puritan commonwealth in New England shows that the American Revolution was not an explosion, but an organic growth whose roots reached back beyond Winthrop and the New England fathers. The English Cabinet in the reign of King George the Third indeed blundered, but less than is often supposed. It was their chief misfortune to be late, as it was the fault of their predecessors to be careless. The reform after the Andros *émeute* did not drive deep enough to cut up the roots of the danger and prepare peace through obedience. Or, more likely, the flame of political Puritanism in this land was too fierce to be quelled either by oil or water.

The exact net results of the Puritan church and commonwealth to this land can never be expressed in any one formula, because Puritanism in our institutions exists both as a form and as an atmosphere. Looking only at the form, however, it is safe to venture this as summary: In this nation so far, in religion Puritanism has been *diminuendo;* in politics, *crescendo.*

CHAPTER VI.

SEWALL AS A BUSINESS MAN.

SEWALL'S early education was at his father's house in Newbury, under charge of his father's minister, Rev. Mr. Parker, who, leaving the pulpit after he became blind, had the courage to support himself by private pupils in Latin, Greek, and Hebrew. It has been often noted that the per cent of college men in the colony was large. His life here was that of the wilderness, with a smack of Old English in it; and he probably took his share of the hardship. He graduated at Harvard College in 1671 in a class of eleven, most of whom remained his fast friends during life. In this class there were four Samuels, two Johns, one Isaiah, one Peter, and one Thomas, with only two secular names, William and Edward.

It would be a curious inquiry as to the origin of the Puritan names, and why so many were out of the Bible, and especially the Hebrew Scriptures. That these Hebrew proper names had generally a pious meaning might be one reason; that so, in a sense, their names would thus be written in "the Lamb's Book of Life" might be another; while names like Grace or Mercy carry their own right to be given to women. The cases are not unknown where Puritan ministers even refused to baptize unless with a Scriptural name. Three years later Sewall took his Master's degree, coming first with the significant thesis, "*An peccatum originale sit et peccatum et poena?*" which may be freely translated "Whether original sin be both sin and its punishment?" The college had now been established some thirty years; and its culture from the start, although hedged in by the general poverty, had been a white flame in the darkness of that wilderness which was with a very definite gravity trying to drag down the Englishmen here to its own level. There had been presidents already, and Rev. Charles Chauncey at Sewall's graduation was at the head. That sweet man of God, President Dunster, whose fault was to have had that charity in dealing with the acrid theological quarrels of his age without which "there is nothing worth," had already departed under a heavy load of obloquy to his Old Colony home, and had there died. Gracious hands had embalmed him in a rude way by filling his coffin with tansy and other herbs; and so he was brought to Cambridge, and buried just across the road from the college where he had so wrought and suffered. Generations after, the inscription on his gravestone having become illegible, the corporation (1845) gave him new funeral honors, and identified the body by these same herbs still retaining their fragrance, very much as when they opened the coffin of Charles V. of Spain the sprigs of thyme were almost as fragrant as when they had been gathered seven ages before in the woods of Yuste.

After graduation, as was usual, he became a Resident Fellow, taking part in teaching and discipline. He was also made keeper of the college library, which, we may be sure, was both small and Puritan. The first entry in his Diary, Dec. 3, 1673, concerns his teaching at Cambridge. Incidentally Sewall gives us little glimpses of college life,—how his hair is cut; that he sends his younger brother's clothes out to wash; borrows money, gives treats, glances at the new brides, and very like at young ladies not yet come to that estate; gets gloves and visits from young men and maids; has his brother bring him from Boston an hourglass and penknife (11*s.* 3*d.*); buys beer (4*d.*), wine (3*d.*), with 6*d.* to Onesephoros (a black slave probably), tobacco pipes (3*d.*), all in honor of the peace just come, very much as young men go on in such places always. Sewall makes no entry as to Commencement expenses. But Judge Lynde writes down these expenses of his son at graduation in 1734:—

"I paid Mrs. Frances Wardell for William's Commencement things viz a large cake, 4 gall West India Rum at 8*s.* 6*d.*, 2 neats tongues at 5*s.*; 4 gallons of Madeira wine at 10*s.*—all these came to £9. 4, 5.

"Day before Thanksgiving 1734. I bought and paid for 3 quarters of lamb and 2 quarters of mutton 20*s.* and turkey and 4 fowls 6*s.* and bread with cyder for the poor."

The students and the town boys were at loggerheads, as ever. "In the evening the townsmen of Cambridge had a meeting and Mr. Gookin and I being sent for went to them. They treated us very civilly and agreed that the school boys should sit no longer in the students' hinder seat. It was also consented to by us that some sober youths for the present might be seated there." He notes a more serious event in the college discipline, — that a young man, accused of blasphemy, after examination by the corporation and advice had from the lieutenant-governor and the leading ministers, was condemned and sentenced to diverse punishments; such as being degraded in public and private before all, and finally publicly whipped. The whipping was done in the library, the culprit on his knees, the president seeing the job well done. "Prayer was had before and after by the President." Sewall keeps his eyes open for things beyond the college. "This day two boys killed at Watertown with the tumbling of a load of brush on them, on which they rode." Sept. 7 (1674): "First frost."

He makes a home visit to Newbury, and his Diary shows in another place, April 29, how things went on sometimes on the new farms: "My father having found things out of order at the little farm, viz fences down, ground eaten and rooted up by cattle and hogs and wanting a good tenant, the season of the year now spending, resolves and goes and lives there; notwithstanding the littleness and unprettiness of the house." He returned to Boston, and entered the family of John Hull, the New England mint-master and merchant, whose daughter, Hannah Hull, he married Feb. 28, 1676. Of this wife of his youth, whom he lived with forty-two years, many things are said by Sewall, but she says nothing. A single letter which her husband preserves in his Letter Book alone remains; but that shows her a matronly, broad-hearted, sensible English woman, and she bore her husband eleven children. Sewall says, "She saw me when I took my degree, and set her affection on me, though I knew nothing of it till after our marriage." (Being a woman, very likely not.) She was an heiress, and brought her husband a powerful family connection; and as Sewall was himself well-bred, the lines from the start had fallen to him in pleasant places. He became and remained a representative Bostonian of the higher rank all his life.

Sewall would naturally seemed destined for the ministry, and had indeed preached on occasion, and was urged by the clergy to ordination and a parish. He tells us that, on one occasion, preaching for his old schoolmaster, Rev. Mr. Parker, "Being afraid to look on the glass, ignorantly and unwillingly I stood two hours and a half." An hourglass stood on the pulpit, which the sexton sometimes turned, while some probably yawned. But his marriage, with his wife's property and the care of his own, seem to have driven him into business, though all his life he shows his theological training and a bias towards the clerical profession. John Hull was now old, and he seems to have turned over his business correspondents to Sewall. Both his Diary and his Letter Book show him very soon exporting and importing with the rest. For, next to God, trade seems to have had most attraction for the thrifty Puritan, and the bias is strong on his posterity. But commerce then was in a very precarious condition. Pirates swarmed, and, when caught, had short shrift with a rope. Dutch and French enemies made ventures by sea, uncertain and often disastrous. Foreign trade was chiefly to London, Bristol, Bilboa in Spain, and, above all, to the West Indies, where at this time most of the emigrating Europeans had settled. Mackerel stood first as an export; next oil, codfish, shingles, tar, alewives, beaver, and even cranberries. The imports were such as the estate of the colonists allowed, — the usual dry goods of the age, and things which agriculture called for. There is, in Sewall's entries, a large demand for sieves, probably to sift Indian corn and other grains, milk-strainers, cod hooks and lines, salt, shot, nails, tobacco pipes, scythes, knives, needles, lead, chairs, books, oranges, sweetmeats, and chocolate. Nor is Sewall behind his neighbors in looking well to his invoice when it reaches him. "The last cod hooks you sent," he writes, "are complained of as not well seasoned and dear. Several would bend out and come straight and not hold a fish." Again: "Be sure that each bunch contains a dozen [sieve bottoms] for the party I sold the last to complains that sundry held out but eleven." He sometimes handled queer goods, as, for instance, when he writes abroad that he will take a certain legacy in thirty dozen alchemy (some sort of pinchbeck) spoons; forty brass candlesticks; big kettles, not above twenty or twenty-four gallons; and pewter platters, not exceeding eighteen inches over, basins, and porringers. He keeps an eye on the crops. "English corn usually *2s. 6d.* now *5s.* or *5s. 6d.* a bushel. The English harvest is promising though much rye blasted and good for nothing. A strange plague of flies spoils most all our pease; it breeds in them and at last flies away." In 1686 mackerel are quoted at *16s.* a barrel, and pork at the same price. Here is an order he sends to England: "6 dozen scythes of a pretty long sort with strong flat backs, narrow plates, strong heels, being hard metal; 6 dozen of rubstones [whetstones] 20 dozens of good strong servicable knives with bone, horn and wooden hafts." "Let there be no silk grass in any of these silks," he writes, "but let them be all silk. Let none of these silks exceed *6s.* pr. yard; as much under as you can." New England people had this help in commerce; they were so far away from London that they paid little attention to the Acts of Trade imposed on other Englishmen, which increased their profits. This was taken notice of to their detriment by the king's government, and after the capture of Quebec in 1759 the Acts were enforced here. There were suspicious and even criminal prosecutions of traders here for selling guns and other things contraband in war to the king's enemies; and the Puritans were sometimes smitten by the very war armaments that greedy and cruel men of their own stock had sold.

Sewall was also a general trader in lands and cattle, as the Winthrops were. Such men bought land in large blocks, and sold out in parcels. Sewall had land at Martha's Vineyard and the Narragansett country, and, indeed, all over the State; and the care and sale of it took much of his business time and energy. He also appears to have been a good judge of horses. Whether he ever hired Indians to hunt skins for him does not appear; but we know that beaver-skins in his day were almost as precious as gold.

He can also be downright in business, especially if he fears fraud, to his loss. Indeed, the Puritans had a way of playing around a subject in a preamble; but when they come to the point they bring it out with a blow, as of a sledge-hammer. Sewall had consigned goods to a Mr. Higginson, who had after died, leaving the account unsettled. Irritated at the delay, he writes: "Whatever be done with Mr. Higginson's own estate, it is utterly unreasonable that the estates of other men should be buried with him and no account given of them." Here is a letter to a man who had borrowed money of him: —

"Dec. 3d, 1700. TO MR. JN' WILLIAMS OF BARBADOES.

Sir, I presume the old verse 'If knocking thrice, no one comes go off' is not to be understood of creditors in demanding their just debts. The tenth year is now current since I lent you ten pounds, merely out of respect to you as a stranger and a scholar: you having then met with disappointment by the loss of effects sent for your support. You have written to me that you would not let my kindness rot under the clods of ingratitude. But there has been hitherto *Vox* and *praeterea nihil* [a promise and no pay]. I am come again to knock at your door to enquire if any ingenuity or honor dwell there. Not doubting but if there do I shall reap benefit by it and that you will pay to my order the money which I sent you gratis July 23d 1691, of which I have not yet received one penny."

Same date he writes to his correspondents in Barbadoes about Williams: —

"I would intreat you to deal with him effectually in my behalf. Recover the money and remit it to Mr. John Ive, merchant in London for my account."

He has also preserved two dunning letters of his to President Leverett of Harvard College, with whom he had probably ceased to be on terms because of theological differences: —

"To Mr. Leverett Dec' 4, 1718.

Revd Sir;

I have a very considerable account to make up with Mr. Simon Stoddard, Treasurer of the trustees [for evangelizing Indians] and he calls on me to do it. For this end I greatly want the hundred pounds I lent you Aug. 12 1715 which you promised to pay by the Ninth of December next following. I pray you then, that it may be paid at or before the 9th of this inst Dec' without fail."

Reverend Sir;

I have heard nothing from you since my sending to you the above written. Pray, sir, let the answer now be a speedy performance of your promise which I have under your hand. I find it too burdensome to me to have great accounts lie open and ununsettled. . . . It is necessary that they be finished in order to my obtaining an acquittance. *Non respondêre est contemnere.*

Sir; your real friend and most humble Servt,

Samuel Sewall.

Boston, Feby 17, 1718.

Besides trade abroad and visiting his plantations, Sewall was a busy man at home. He lived at Cotton Hill on Tremont Street, almost opposite King's Chapel burying-ground, on property once belonging to Sir Harry Vane, and with neighbors of his own rank. The colony records show (1684):—

"In answer of the petition of Sam' Sewall Esq, humbly showing that his house of wood in Boston, at the hill where the Revd John Cotton formerly dwelt, which house is considerably distant from other building and standeth very bleak, he humbly desiring the favor of this court to grant him liberty to build a small porch of wood, about seven foot square, to break off the wind from the fore door of said house, the court grants his request."

Here and elsewhere on his Boston lots he planted apple, walnut, and shade trees; probably had a garden and flowers; pastured sometimes his cows on the Common with his neighbors'; dug and blasted rocks there for underpinning; and, in general, was a thrifty family man in the fashion then in vogue. It is a tradition that on one state occasion no less a person than Governor Hancock had these same vagrant cows milked without leave for his guests' breakfast. Bowditch shows how some of the most valuable lots on Beacon Hill gained their boundaries from cow-paths, and their titles from less honest enclosure. Sewall was also appointed master of the public printing-press, 1681, an office he held some three years, printing public and religious documents, and especially the Assembly's Catechism, five hundred copies of which he gave away to the children of his relations. He was made a freeman in 1678, having joined the Old South Church the year before, as a prerequisite to citizenship. His name also appears as a deputy from Westfield to the General Court in 1683, as his father-in-law, John Hull, had been in 1674, it being the law then that a man might be elected from a town other than that in which he lived. As all this, however, concerns his political life, it will be treated of elsewhere. He of necessity belonged to the Boston Fire Department, the Police and Watch, was obliged to go the rounds with the rest, or hire a man, and was apparently very fond of military life, and was for long a captain in the militia. Indeed, the Puritans insisted that every citizen should take his share of the public burdens, were admirable organizers, set every man to his work, according to his station, and were before their time in making a levy *en masse* into the militia. This is why in all wars they showed such martial ability, and one reason why their colony did not perish as so many others had, especially in the French and Spanish immigrations. Sewall is a fine example of a busy Puritan business man, with an unsmirched record of success.

Yet, to show the uncertainties and vexations of commerce in those days, this incident may be noted. Sewall undertook to send a package of New England books to Sir William Ashurst, the agent of the Province in England. The vessel was taken by a French privateer, and condemned in the West Indies. The books, as of no account, were given to the captain of the vessel, who, on his return to Boston, gave them to Dr. Increase Mather, who, in turn, finding them to have been once owned by Sewall, returned them, who in a very delicate equity sent them back to Mather, with the very gravely humorous remark, " For aught I know they have had travel enough, and may now properly abide at home."

CHAPTER VII.

TOWN AND COUNTRY LIFE TO 1700.

THE above date is neither exact nor logical so far as it marks any epoch in New England history. The true epoch here is Oct. 23, 1684, when, under Charles II., the English Chancery Court vacated the original charter of Massachusetts Bay, and the colony became a Province, under a very different administration of law. The wide reach of this change will appear farther on. Besides, there had been no break in the life of the people, either for the fifty-four years the charter had lasted, nor for the newer years of our Provincial existence, terminating at the Revolution. The social change, indeed, foreran the political. The Puritan in a drift stronger than his will had wrought at his ideas; but human nature was stronger, and the logic of his position, little as he knew it, bore him on to what he thought disaster, and what we know to be a better fulfilment of himself than he had as yet attained. So the thread of this old life was continuous, though it showed many and changing dyes. The thread, however, was never broken.

Of course the colonial life now before us was one of vicissitudes, springing from all sources, — foreign and Indian wars, Cromwell's victories and the resto-

An Early Style of New England Architecture.

ration of the Stuarts, bad harvests, diseases, fires, and, above all, religious dissensions, which all helped to make up a rather motley whole. Yet the grays of Puritanism always made the picture a sober one, to a degree lacking lustre, but ever showing variety. Sewall's station forced him to see more of this than most, and he writes it down. The life of the common people in the country, as before seen, was, and remains even till now in spots, a stern and Spartan one. It must have been worse at the start. In the few large towns, especially in Boston, life had more colors and juices, always classing by themselves that body of really able men, the country Puritan clergy. Some things quoted and arranged out of Sewall's Diary ought to give us plain impressions of what is intended in the above title : —

[1675.] "A Scotchman and Frenchman kill their master, knocking him in the head as he was taking tobacco. They are taken by hue and cry and condemned. Hanged. April 5, 1676, Wednesday. Gov. Winthrop dies. Sep. 13 [same year]. There were eight Indians shot to death on the Common on Wind-mill hill. Sep. 21. Stephen Gobble of Concord was executed for murder of Indians ; three Indians for firing Eames House and murder. The weather was cloudy and rawly cold, though little or no rain. Mr. Mighill prayed ; four others sat on the gallows, two men and two impudent women, one of whom at least laughed on the gallows as several testified. Nov. 27. about 5 M. Boston's greatest fire broke forth at Mr. Moor's, through the default of a tailorss boy, who rising alone and early to work fell asleep and let his light fire the house. . . . N.B. The house of the man of God, Mr. Mather and God's House were burnt with fire. Yet God mingled mercy and sent a considerable rain which gave check in great measure to the (otherwise) masterless fire. This day, at even, went to a private meeting held at Mr. Nath. Williams'. Feby. 8, 1677. John Holiday stands in the pillory for counterfeiting a lease, making false bargains, &c."

There is a gap in Sewall's Diary from July, 1677, to March, 1685, probably due to a loss of one or more volumes.

"Monday, April 20, 1685. The King is proclaimed; 8 companies, the troop and several gentlemen on horse back assisting; three volleys and then cannon fired. Monday, June 8. Charlestown was to have had a great bustle in training on Tuesday with horse and foot, Cap. Hammond engaging some of Boston to be there; but now 'tis like to be turned into the funeral of their pastor; he dying full and corpulent. June 20. Carried my wife to Dorchester to eat Cherries, Raspberries, chiefly to ride and take the air; the time my wife and Mrs. Flint spent in the orchard, I spent in Mr. Flint's study reading Calvin on the Psalms. An Indian was branded in the court and had a piece of his ear cut off for burglary. Sep. 22. Jn° Gardiner came in last night; this morning the news he brings runs through the town viz that James, late Duke of Monmouth was beheaded on Tower Hill, on the 15th of July last. Argyle drawn, hanged and quartered. Neighbor Fifield brought me the news, who had it from the crier of fish. Nov. 26. Mary an Indian, James's squaw was frozen to death upon the neck, near Roxbury Gate, being fuddled.

Dec. 30. An Indian man is found dead on the Neck, with a bottle of rum between his legs. Jany. 22, 1686. Joseph Redknap of Lynn buried, being about 110 years old; was a wine cooper in London; was about 30 years old at the Great Frost. Jany. 24, Sabbath. Friday night and Saturday were extreme cold so that the harbor frozen up and to the Castle. This day so cold that the sacramental bread is frozen pretty hard and rattles sadly as broken into the plates. Sabbath April 18. Cap. Ephr Savage puts up a bill to have God's hand sanctified in sending the smallpox into his family."

The smallpox was frequent and fatal in the colony, the people being unskilled in managing it. Sewall's Diary abounds in references to it, and the ministers preached about it. When Sir Edmund Andros comes up in his frigate to assume the new government, this is a part of the ceremony: —

"Castle fires about 25 guns; a very considerable time after the frigate fires, then the sconce and ships, Noddles Island, Charlestown battery, frigate again, ships with their ancients out and forts their flaggs. Not many spectators on Fort Hill."

"Feby. 15, 1687. Jos. Maylem carries a cock at his back with a bell in his hand in the main street; several follow him blindfold and under pretence of striking him or his cock, with great cart whips strike passengers and make great disturbance."

This was an old English sport for Shrove Tuesday, the day before Ash Wednesday.

Andros had now come, and the old English ideas were creeping in with him, marking the change which Sewall saw and dreaded. Hence the above very emphatic entry. If Jos. Maylem had done this ten years before he would have gone to the pillory or the whipping-post. The entry March 10 following shows how the ministers faced the new danger: —

"Mr. Mather preaches the [Thursday] lecture. Speaks sharply against Health drinking, cardplaying, drunkenness, profane swearing, Sabbath breaking &c. Text Jer. 2.21."

. . . .

"Monday March 14, 1687. Cap. Thaxter of Hingham sinks down and dies as went to fodder his cattle."

There was a deal of apoplexy in the colony, as the Diary shows.

"Two persons, one arrayed in white, the other in red, go through the town with naked swords advanced, with a drum attending each of them and a quarter staff, and a great rout following as is usual. It seems 'tis a challenge to be fought at Cap. Wing's next Thursday."

More old English sports. And the redcoats who came with Andros apparently countenanced and urged on such fun. The wicked maypoles, with their festivities, also now came in. Morton's had been cut down years ago at Mount Wollaston, and he driven out. Here is a hint of those darker shades of life, which for evident reasons are quoted sparingly: —

"Nov. 3. Mrs. Anne Williams tells me that an English maid was executed last Thursday at Bristol for murdering her Indian child."

"Sabbath Jany. 22 1688. My Lady Andros was prayed for in public; who has been dangerously ill ever since the last Sabbath. One of a Dutch church in London is admitted to the Lords Supper with us. About the beginning of our afternoon exercise the Lady Andros expires. . . . Friday Feby. 10. Between 4 and 5 I went to the funeral of the Lady Andros having been invited by the Clerk of the South Company. Between 7 and 8 torches illuminating the cloudy air. The corpse was carried into the herse drawn by six horses. The soldiers making a guard from the Governor's house down the prison lane to the South meeting house, there taken out and carried in at the western door and set in the alley before the pulpit, with six mourning women by it. House made light with candles and torches. Was a great noise and clamor to keep people out of the house that might not rush in too soon. I went home, where about 9 o'clock I heard the bells toll again for the funeral. It seems Mr. Ratcliffs text was Cry, all flesh is grass. The ministers turned in at Mr. Willards. 'Twas warm thawing weather and the ways extreme dirty. No volley at placing the body in the tomb. On Saturday the mourning cloth of the pulpit is taken off and given to Mr. Willard" [the minister of that parish].

Nothing in Sewall's Diary better shows the grim and bitter aversion of the Puritans to the English church and state than this quotation. It is cold beyond ice, and most significant in its silence. Here was a high-bred English lady, wife of the king's governor, innocent of any politics, a stranger in a strange land, dead and to be buried. Sewall had no doubt often made his bow to her. At any rate, he was a man of high station, nearly always in public office, a suitor to Sir Edmund to have his land titles made valid under the new Charter; a man of undoubted heart and kindness, with a wife and children of his own at home, and many of his own kin dead — and what does he do on this occasion? He would have gone to the grave of his humblest friend from Hampshire, and stayed till the sand was shovelled; but here he goes in a while, — we do not say because absence would have brought him harsh gossip, or perhaps worse, or because he had an eye to funeral pomp in general, and would not miss the show, — and before the minister preaches his sermon, with a fit text, at least, and shorter than the two hours' discourse of Sewall's parson, which he always listens to with decorum to the end, he goes home and busies himself in some gossip about the dirty streets and what became of the mourning cloth. Not a trace of pathos, nor a single religious reflection, in which he easily abounds at other funerals, though this one might in its circumstance have moved a heart of stone, — only the Puritan heart was harder than flint against any who seemed to stand, even remotely, as this dead lady did, against their cause.

The entries grow more significant of the times and the changes they bring: —

"Feby. 29. Mr. Giles Masters, the King's attorney, dies. March 27th. Last night a cold, blustering N. W. wind. Three Indian children, being alone in a wigwam at Muddy River, the wigwam fell on fire, and burnt them so that they all died."

From November, 1688, to November, 1689, Sewall was out of the country on a visit to England. The record of that visit appears elsewhere. The Home Journal opens with the date of Nov. 22. The Indian massacres at Schenectady and Hampton, with other atrocities of a guerrilla warfare in which the savages are being gradually exterminated, are of frequent mention under date of the new year, 1690.

"May 21, 1690. Mr. Eliot [the missionary] dies about one in the morning. Sabbath July 20. When Mr. Willard was in his first prayer there was a cry of fire which made the people rush out. 'Twas said Mr. Winslow's chimney was on fire. Just about the same time the house next the old meeting house, the chimney smoked so and beat into the house that made great disturbance there."

What with their wooden chimneys, and their carrying about pans of live coals, borrowed to kindle some neighbor's fire, — for there were no matches, and flintstones and tinder were sometimes difficult, — the old-time people in Boston fared hard from fires, and the meetings were often disturbed in consequence.

"Oct. 1691. The Marshal General tells me that above fifty sheep were killed at Cambridge last night having their throats bitten and blood sucked. [Wolves!] Dec. 25. 1691. General Court passes an order for prohibiting Frenchmen being in the seaports or frontier towns except by license from the Governor and Council; and pass an order for laying a duty on things exported and imported to defray the charge of a guard ship."

All which presages war.

Letter. Mrs. Martha Oakes. Not finding opportunity to speak with you at your house, nor at my own I write to persuade you to be sensible that your striking your daughter in law before me in my house is not justifiable; though twas but a small blow, 'twas not a small fault; especially considering your promise to refrain from speech itself; or at least any that might give disturbance. As for New England it is a cleaner country than ever you were in before and therefore with disdain to call it *filthy* is a sort of blasphemy which by proceeding out of your mouth hath defiled you. I write not this to upbraid, but to admonish you with whom I sympathise under your extraordinary provocations and pressures; and pray God command you freedom from them. S. SEWALL.

Here was a woman who had lost her hot temper, and had reviled New England to boot, and Sewall admonishes her like the high-toned and plain-spoken man he was. There is another letter addressed by him (1693) to a man of birth and station in the colony, in which he remonstrates with him on his intemperance, which merits reading, as exposing the sturdy Puritan temper in such matters : —

Dicere quae puduit, scribere jussit Amor.

Sir;

Not seeing you in the assembly, to speak to you and for the reason forementioned I am put upon writing my salutations to Mr. Ward, yourself and good lady: and telling you that I have sympathised with you and your family as to the report that went of some being afflicted by a person in your shape,[1] and that I

[1] Probably some charge of witchcraft.

fully believe the letter asserting your innocence. Allow me also to intimate that I was grieved upon this day was fortnight when I heard and saw that you had drunk to excess; so that your head and hand were rendered less useful than at other times. You may remember you were sitting in the south side of the Council Chamber, on the bench. I drew near to you and enquired concerning Mr. Ward; you answered he was better which made you so merry; you also told me of the breaking up of the ice of the river Merrimac having received the açcount from your son Cotton. That is the time I intend. Let me intreat you, Sir, to break off this practice (so 'tis rumored to be) not as the river; but obstinately and perpetually to refuse the yoke. As to your being denied a judge's place by the Governor, I no ways influenced him in the matter, neither do I know who did. And I was surprised to hear any talk of the north regiment of Essex being put under any other Major. Don't furnish your enemies with arms. I mention this that you may believe, I write not of prejudice, but kindness; and out of a sense of duty as indeed I do. Take it in good part from him who desires your everlasting welfare. S. S.

The Latin motto which heads this letter should be noted. It was custom among the well-bred of those days to use such mottoes so, and this is a very happy one. Under date of March 7th Sewall writes:—

"Not having had an opportunity to send my letter I was this day surprised to see Major S—— in the Court. I came home at noon and took my letter and delivered it with my own hand just at night, desiring him to read it at his lodging; but he, being impatient, sat down in the very place mentioned and discoursed me gave me thanks and desired my prayers. God give a good effect."

Here were two able and well-bred Puritans. The picture shows that under those old skies in the wild there could be shown the most gracious colors of true knighthood.

Mercy Winthrop's Wedding Room.

"Sep. 30, 1692. The Swan brings in a rich French prize of about 300 tuns, laden with claret, white wine, brandy, salt, linen, paper &c. Go to Hog Island with Joshua Gee and sell him 3 white oaks for 30*s*. I am to cart them to the water side. Nov[r] 4. Law passes for justices and ministers marrying persons. It seems they count the respect of it too much to be left any longer with the magistrate." [As in the old church, the marriage had always been by the clergy, it being regarded as of a sacramental character, the Puritans disallowed the practice, and their marriages so far had been generally by the civil magistrate.] "And salaries" [Sewall adds] "are not spoken of; as if one sort of men might live on the air. They are treated like a kind of useless, worthless, folk." Nov. 5 [the date of the Guy Fawkes Gunpowder Plot] no disturbance at night by bonfires. Nov. 19. I drove a tree nail in the governors briganteen; and invited his excellency to drink a glass of brandy."

Sewall was used to drive a nail in a new meeting-house or private dwelling for luck, according to an old English superstition. When Governor Simon Bradstreet on his deathbed called in Sewall and other gentlemen to help him add a codicil, he "called for ale, and made us drink." May 23, 1693, Sewall laid the corner-stone of his new house, next Cotton Hill.

"The foundation of the cellar is finished by stones gotten out of the Common. . . . Cap. and Deacon Eliot is buried. He was one of the most serviceable men in Boston, condescending to his friends. One of the best and most respectful friends I had in the world. Lord awaken us. Died in the 61st year of his age. Was one of the first that was born in Boston."

In 1693 a bill forbidding representatives to be chosen except in the town where they lived was passed, against strong objections that this was against English precedent and law. Sewall voted for the bill.

"Aug. 17, 1695. A duel was fought this day upon the Common, between Peggy and one Capt Cole. June 20, 1696. Wm Veasy is bound over for plowing on the day of thanksgiving." [Probably a Church of England man.]

"Wedns', May 15, 1695. Set out for Portsmouth, have a guard of six men from Newbury. Cap. Smith of Hampton meets us with twelve, by Gov. Ushers order, long arms." "Sep. 17. Govr Bradstreet drank a glass or two of wine, eat some fruit, took a pipe of tobacco in the new hall [Sewall's new house] and wished me joy of the house and desired our prayers; came to us over the little stone bridge." "Sep. 20. The Lord Bellamont is made our governor."

"Dec. 21, 1696. Note, this morn Madam Eliza Bellingham came to our house and upbraided me with setting my hand to pass Mr. Whartons acc't to the Court where he obtained a judgment for Eustace's farm. I was wheadled and hectored into that business and have all along been uneasy in the remembrance of it; and now there is one come who will not spare to lay load. The Lord take away my filthy garments and give me change of raiment."

Evidently a case where Sewall's good-nature had led him to an act of which conscience complained. And a brave woman, having her right clad in plain words, was at his elbow to blame.

Oct. 1, 1697, there is a picnic, to Noddle's Island probably; and as his parson, Mr. Willard, and eleven other young people went there it was no doubt a jolly New England frolic of "ye olden tyme." The dinner is significant and toothsome: —

"Had first honey, butter, curds and cream. For dinner, very good roast lamb, turkey, fowls, aplpy [i.e., apple pie]. After dinner sung the 121 Psalm. Note. A glass of spirits my wife sent [was it for the judge or parson, or both?] stood upon a joint stool which Simon W. [Willard the younger] jogging, it fell down and broke all to shivers. I said it was a lively emblem of our fragility and mortality."

Elsewhere he tells of dining off boiled venison, and making a cold dinner at home, in his wife's absence, off baked pigeons and pound cake.

"Oct. 16. The fires make great havock of hay meadow, fence, timber &c. Air hath been filled with smoke for above a week."

Indeed these country fires often obscured the sky for days.

"Oct. 20. When I first saw the Lieu Governor at Dorchester [Stoughton] he was carting ears of corn from the upper barn." "Feb. 21, 1698. I ride over to Charlestown on the ice."

"July 15, 1698. Mr. Edward Taylor [his classmate?] comes to our house from Westfield. Monday July 18. I walked with him upon Cotton Hill thence to Beacon hill, the pasture along the stone wall; as came back we sat down on the great rock [nearly opposite Joy Street] and Mr. Taylor told his courting his first wife and Mr. Fitch's story of Dr. Dod's prayer to God, to bring his affection to close with a person pious but hard favored."

Samuel Sewall's prayer in like case would have probably differed as to the second term.

There must have been some queer terms used at Puritan weddings sometimes, as witness Sewall's note[1] on Mr. Willard's marrying Atherton Haugh and Mercy Winthrop, at Mr. Dean Winthrop's, Pulling Point, and this further exercise at their wedding.

"Sang a Psalm together. I set St David's tune. Sung part of two psalms concluded with the 4 last verses of the 115. Mr. Dean Winthrop lived there in his father's days and was wont to set up a bush when he saw a ship coming in. He is now 77 years old."

[1] See Appendix, Note A.

CHAPTER VIII.

SEWALL, THE INDIANS AND NEGROES.

"Some Puritans one day saw a dog and six Indians. The white men ran away, but they whistled the dog away with them."

While anxious to avoid the appearance of levity in such grave affairs, the writer has deliberately chosen to put this ancient anecdote at the head of this chapter, as a pat illustration of what has generally happened to the American Indians from the white civilization.

Here were the two races in the wild with one piece of property, to wit, a dog, between them. The property passed to the whites.

Small boys still manage somehow to associate the idea of romance with the Indians; students of our colonial history do not. Yet mystery and misery in a race almost perished at the East, the former occupants of vast domains now given over to the whites, involve the pity of every one who studies the record of the Indians in New England. Yet it is said that ten Englishmen took to the Indian life where one Indian became civilized. The birds and foxes, at least in summer, when food abounds, disport themselves with a certain largeness of freedom and content; and one can readily see that in the vagabond and careless life of the red men, free from everything but their simple physical needs, there was an attraction to even the white man on the lower side of his nature. Dr. G. E. Ellis, a chief authority, in his book on the Indians, lays his finger on the core of the matter when, explaining the fraternity which the Indians displayed for dirt, he says the Indian regarded dirt as a part of that Nature to which he himself belonged, and hence started no quarrel in his wigwam with brush or broom, — an animate part of that great wild he dwelt in, in such sense that the bear might be his grandsire, or the moose his uncle. He was of the human family, and all possible virtues might lie dormant in him, but so feebly alive that they seldom gave sign, and were oftenest thrust aside by the lower and more violent passions of the brute. Yet our earliest records show him, before contact with the whites had called out his worse elements, often hospitable, generous, and kind, at the expense of his own comfort. Conscience, and the truth-speaking that goes with it, were very rudimental in him ; and the white man, with his better standards, called him treacherous. He was simply a savage, with all that term implies. Perhaps Roger Williams is the best witness of all, as to what the Indian who confronted the Puritan really was, both because he himself was full of truth and mercy, and because in his Rhode Island banishment he had dwelt with them and they with him longer and more intimately than any other white man of equal merit. In his letters of advice to the Winthrops and the

Puritan authorities he discriminates with great caution and frankness:—

"I commonly guess shrewdly at what a native utters, and, to my remembrance, never wrote particular, but either I know the bottom of it, or else I am bold to give a hint of my suspense."

Dwelling near the great Narragansett, Mohican, and Pequot tribes, and visiting in the wigwams, he writes:—

"'Tis true there is no fear of God before their eyes, and all the cords that ever bound the barbarians to foreigners were made of self and covetousness; yet if I mistake not I observe in Miantonimo some sparks of true friendship; could it be deeply imprinted on him that the English never intended to despoil him of the country, I probably conjecture his friendship would appear in attending of us with 500 men against any foreign enemy."

He writes (1647):—

TO JOHN WINTHROP JR., NEW LONDON, CONN[T].

Sir, Concerning Indian affairs reports are various; lies are frequent. Private interests, both with Indians and English, are many; yet these things you may and must do. First, Kiss truth where you evidently, upon your soul, see it. 2. Advance justice though upon a child's eyes. 3. Seek and make peace, if possible with all men. 4. Secure your own life from a revengeful malicious arrow or hatchet. I have been in danger of them and delivered yet from them; blessed be His holy name in whom I desire to be,

Your worships, in all unfeigned respects and love

ROGER WILLIAMS.

"The report was," he says elsewhere "(as most commonly all Indian reports are), absolutely false."

A peacemaker Williams always was between the two races, and his management and advices to both often prevented violence. Yet the peace he sought was to be based on justice towards the red men. "Mercy," he writes to John Winthrop, "outshines all the works and attributes of Him who is the Father of mercies." When the Narragansetts complained that their Pequot prisoners and their booty had been taken from them by the English, he writes: —

"For though I would not fear a jar with them, yet I would fend off from being foul and deal with them wisely as with wolves endowed with men's brains."

[1637.] "Concerning Miantonimo I have not heard as yet of any unfaithfulness towards us. I know that they belie each other; and I observe our countrymen have almost quite forgotten our great pretences to King and state and all the world, concerning their souls. I shall desire to attend with my poor help to discover any perfidious dealing and shall desire the revenge of it for a common good and peace, though myself and mine should perish by it; yet I fear the Lord's quarrel is not ended for which the war began, viz., the little sense of their soul's condition and our large protestations that way. The general speech is, all must be rooted out. The body of the Pequot men yet live and are only removed from their den. The good Lord grant that the Mohawks and they and the whole, at the last, unite not."

He writes of the Pequot captives made slaves to the whites: —

"My humble desire is that all who have those poor wretches might be exhorted as to walk wisely and justly towards them, so as to make mercy eminent, for in that attribute the Father of Mercy most shines to Adam's miserable offspring."

In this same first Indian war, when every Indian of every age and sex was killed at sight, Canonicus, although the Pequots' bitter enemy, said to Roger Williams that it would be pleasing to all natives that the women and children of the Pequots should be spared.

In the same war he writes:—

"Divers of the friendly Indians were hurt by the English because they had no mark to distinguish them. You may please therefore to provide some yellow or red for their heads. The Connecticut English had yellow but not enough."

He even extends his care to the comfort of the Indian chiefs, his neighbors. He writes to John Winthrop (1637):—

"Sir, if anything be sent to the princes I find that Canonicus would gladly accept of eight or ten pounds of sugar, and indeed he told me he would thank Mr. Governor for a box full."

And again:—

"For any gratuities or tokens Canonicus desires sugar; Miantonimo powder."

The first attitude of the Puritans towards the Indians was one of justice, good-will, and a strong desire for their conversion to civilization and religion. It was expressly stated in their charter as the king's wish and their own. In fact, they regarded them as their wards, and took firm measures accordingly. Whenever and wherever else on this continent the red man suffered wrong at the hands of the white man's government, here in the first years of the colony he did not. The Puritan in his treatment of the Indians, in contrast with the Spaniard shows like an angel of light. It may go without saying that bad white men did maltreat and rob them, — men themselves dwelling on the very outskirts of civilized decencies, and, for long, emigrants from honor. But what they did was in the very teeth of plain Puritan law forbidding, with sharp penalties, the outrage. This the colonial laws prove. The first law regarding Indians is one establishing the Indian's right and title to all lands which they had improved and occupied, solemnly appealing to the Word of God as demanding the same (Gen. i. 28; ix. 1. Psalms cxv. 16). There were laws also that civilized Indians might either dwell among the English on equal terms with them, or have townships granted to them, and dwell there as citizens, exactly as the English had and did; that none should meddle with "their planting grounds and fishing places;" in 1633–1637 that no man should pretend to buy land of the Indians except by license of the General Court, under penalty of forfeiting the land so bought, with the intent, apparently, that government oversight might control private greed or craft against Indians; that their planted grounds were to be protected from the white man's cattle; and that the towns, at the public expense, were to help any Indian in their jurisdiction fence his own land, if he asked it; in short, that the Indians should have justice.

Of course these wards of the Puritans were to

a degree put under watch out of sheer necessity. All powder, shot, bullets, guns, were at first forbidden to be sold to them, as well as boats and skiffs; but as they hired Indians to hunt, and the Massachusetts Company claimed the monopoly of fur skins just as legally by their charter as the Hudson Bay Company after did, this law was repealed a few years before King Philip's War. Besides, the Dutch and French were always ready to sell these contraband goods, and did so, to the mortal hurt of Englishmen. They further prohibited the sale of every sort of strong drink (1657), "under penalty of 40*s*. for one pint, and so proportionately for greater or lesser quantities so sold, bartered, or given, directly or indirectly, as above said." For the better execution of this order, all trucking-houses erected, but not allowed by the Court were to be demolished; the Grand Jury of every shire were to inquire and present every violation of the law, the only exceptions being when, in good faith, any Indian was to be relieved in any case of sudden extremity (and then only one dram was to be given), or a physician gave an order in case of sickness, which order was to be indorsed by a magistrate.

This law repealed the preceding one of 1644, which ordered: —

"The Court apprehending that it is not fit to deprive the Indians of any lawful comfort which God alloweth to all men by the use of wine, do order that it shall be lawful for all such as are or shall be allowed license to retail wines, to sell also to the Indians so much as may be fit for their needful use or refreshing."

Yet the Puritans could not afford to forget the saying of Roger Williams that the Indians were as "wolves endowed with men's brains." In due time laws were made forbidding Indian powwows, or "the worship of the Devil," as the statute has it, fining their drunkenness with 10*s*. or ten stripes, as the offender chose, or was in funds, and insisting in a general way on Indians not offending in English settlements the Puritan Sabbath or ordinary customs of society. The severity of all such laws increased during and after King Philip's War, when the whites had felt how sharp the wolves' teeth were.

The behavior of the Indians towards the whites was both natural and consistent. They took generally from the higher civilization at their doors, as savages do, all that was worst and very little that was best. Shiftlessness was first nature to them, all the roots of their life growing thereto; and they withered before the race that built barns and filled them. Some waited on the overlords with white faces, and the rest abode in wigwams, and accepted the old dirt and want therein, every year made more acute, if possible, by the crescent fields of the white man's thrift. The great tribes in the New England South Land of Rhode Island and the Connecticut seacoast haughtily repelled intrusion upon their barbarism, and perished, tribe by tribe, and unconverted. The Cape and Island Indians of our south coast, numerous, and comfortably fed from the sea, remained in peace, and died out. The Eastern Indians of the province of Maine, recruited from the

Canadian wilds behind them and the French arms, fought long and bitterly, until their fragments hid themselves somewhere in their ruined wigwams. The great Mohawk tribes, with the same white allies, made their occasional intrusions with the tomahawk, but met their fate at other than New England hands. It was no wrong that slew them, but the Kismet or Fate of their barbarism. King Philip's War was as much destiny as is the monthly circuit of the moon or the gravity of water. It may well be questioned whether a single Indian ever comprehended the exact nature of an English title deed to which he set his mark, or more than one jot and tittle of any Puritan dogma to which he opened his ears. King Philip, with larger opportunity and observation, banded his race together to destroy the whites. That he was in no wise a great savage both his defective statesmanship and soldiership show. His complaint was that the whites had encroached on his fields, and fenced their own, and made dams to the injury of Indian fisheries. The cause which he forced to issue was, whether he knew it or not, that, as the two races could not live together, one must die, and the strife of arms must decide which.

King Philip's War marks an epoch not only in the history of our white civilization, but of the red barbarism as well. After its issue the Indian's position was never the same, nor the white man's attitude to him. For the English colonists it was the Day of Judgment, in whose fires it was to be seen whether the Puritan was a man of chaff and stubble, or a being of those more precious metals which the fire anneals only to purify from dross. The Puritans themselves understood the crisis this way. Their commissioners to the Indians were told to manage the business " with clearness and confidence, so that no panic, fear, or weakness of mind might appear; and let them know that the English were resolved to make war their work, until they enjoyed a firm peace."

Though not the first of Puritan tragedies, either in its dignity or scope, King Philip's War was perhaps the gloomiest, and, considering the numbers involved, the reddest. It was rich in dramatic elements and situation. From the time of the interview in Taunton Meeting-house, when the Puritans marched in first, and kept on one side, while the Indian warriors marched in, not with the martial tramp of armed men, but with the soft, noiseless tread of subtle savages, their long hair hanging down their shoulders, and eyes flashing latent fire, all being armed, and Philip said, "Was not my father the friend of the English? Was not my brother at peace with them? Is God angry that there should be blood on our hatchets, and that the hearth of the English should be red?" until the hour when Philip fell dead in the swamp-mud, and his only son was doomed to foreign slavery, there arose over the land a wail; but it was the wail of men and women able to conquer fate in the name of the Lord of hosts, and to transmit the treasures of the Puritan civilization, unimpaired, though, as it were, from their fireless hearthstones where they lay slain, and from where their Absaloms with golden hair had perished red-handed somewhere in the wild against the savage.

The sufferings which English women and children taken captive endured seem incredible, and the wonder is that any survived, especially women with very young children. Mrs. Rowlandson, wife of the minister of Lancaster, gives one of the most vivid pictures of how these captives fared. There must have been something very vital in that old stock when she could write of certain little children : "The children said they did not shed one tear, but prayed all the while when their mother was killed and burnt before them." Mrs. Rowlandson was brought personally in contact with Philip. She says of him :—

> "Philip spake to me to make a shirt for his boy, which I did; for which he gave me a shilling. I offered the money to my mistress but she bade me keep it, and with it I bought a piece of horseflesh. Afterwards he asked me to make a cap for his boy for which he invited me to dinner. I went and he gave me a pancake about as big as two fingers. It was made of parched wheat, beaten and fried in bear's grease; but I thought I never tasted better meat in my life.
>
> "I was with the enemy eleven weeks and five days and not one week passed without their fury and some desolation by fire and sword upon one place or other. They mourned for their own losses, yet triumphed and rejoiced in their inhuman and devilish cruelty to the English."

The statistics of King Philip's War are in all its histories. Only here, afar off, let us see its incidents. The Indian time of attack was generally after the leaves came out in the later spring and summer, since a bare forest would prevent ambuscades, their favorite mode of warfare. Having no magazines, they were always with a daily famine before them, and, being obliged to scatter to their lands to plant and gather corn, they were liable in such dispersion to be cut off coming or going and in detail. The whites had the sea and its transportation, and behind them the civilized world, as long as they had money. They strained every nerve and won, though the war dragged, Eastward, many years. There were not lacking touches of grim humor among the white combatants. Captain Mosely of Boston wore a wig, of which in battle he used to disencumber himself, acquiring among the Indians the soubriquet of "the man of two heads," very much as Captain Cook did among the Sandwich Islanders. Rev. Mr. Niles says of him, "When he came to engage the enemy, he was wont to hang his wig upon a bush and still to wear his head upon his shoulders and do great exploits among them."

But the general substances of the Indian wars in New England were cruelty and sorrow. The Pequot War was first; and the English breaking in by a night surprise into the Pequot fort, only those savages lived who managed to get out. The tribe lapsed or was scattered among the more distant Indians. Forty years after came King Philip's War; and the crisis of it was that other attack on the Narragansett fort, not far from the elder Pequot one, where on a Puritan Sabbath, in a palisaded fort, with only one entrance of a felled tree to some thirty-five hundred savages, a thousand Englishmen, marching eighteen miles in deep snow without food and on a stormy night, broke in, put to the sword all who stood, marched back all night, till two P.M., while their wounded died or froze, to Wickford, and had a crust of bread for their late dinner. The English loss was seventy killed and a hundred and fifty wounded, — more than one in five; while the martial tribe that gathered in the Kingston swamp had its mouth this day filled full with war and blood.

We have a glimpse of that day's fury in a petition of a certain Samuel Hall to the General Court for compensation for his clothes lost in "the Swamp Fight." When Captain Mason (son of the old captain against the Pequots) was shot down, Hall writes: —

> "I was just before him when he fell down and shook him by the hand I being shot down before in that very place, so that he fell very near me. But Cap. Mason got up again and went forth and I lay bleeding there in the snow and hearing the word commanded to set fire on the wigwams I considered I should be burned if I did not crawl away. It pleased God to give me strength to get up and get out, with my cutlass in my hand, notwithstanding I had received at that time, four bullets, two in each thigh, as was manifest afterwards."

There has been no armed strife in this land which better shows the toughness and mastery of the Puritan blood in battle than this of the Narragansetts' fort.

Sewall was in public life during this war, and his Diary very well expresses the daily alarm and distress.

A few excerpts will show the work that was now

going on in the New England woods almost everywhere: —

"June 6, 1676. Hatfield fight. 5 English killed and about 14 Indians. June 7. 90 Indians killed and taken by Connecticut Ferry. June 22. Two Indians, Capt Tom and another executed after lecture. Last week two killed by Taunton scouts, as they were in the river, fishing." "Note this week troopers, a party killed two men and took an Indian boy alive." "Just between the thanksgiving, June 29 and Sabbath Day July 2 Capt Bradford's expedition 20 killed and taken; almost an 100 came in; Squaws Sachem." "July 1. 9 Indians sold for £30, Capt Hincksman took a little before. The night after, James, the printer and other Indians [Christians] came into Cambridge. July 1, 1676. Mr. Hezekiah Willet slain by Narragansetts, a little more than gunshot off from his house, his head taken off, body stript. Jethro, his nigger, then taken; retaken by Capt Bradford the Thursday following. He saw the English and ran to them. He related Philip to be sound and well, about a 1000 Indians (all sorts) with him, but sickly; three died while he was there. Related that the Mt Hope Indians that knew Mr. Willet were sorry for his death, mourned, combed his head and hung peag [wampum, the Indian shell coin, their barbaric money] in his hair."

A touch of nature which shows that some of these Indians had kind hearts, though most slew so cruelly.

"July 8. 9 Indians — 2 English sallied out, slew 5 and took two alive. These Indians were killed not many miles from Dedham." "July 9, 10. This week Indians came in at Plymouth to prove themselves faithful, fetch in others by force; among those discovered are some that slew Mr. Clark's family; viz. two Indians; they accuse one of them that surrendered to the English. All three put to death."

"Note. One Englishman lost in the woods, taken and tortured to death. Medfield men with volunteers, English and Indians, kill and take Canonicus with his son and 50 more."

"July 27 Sagamore John comes in, brings Mattoonus and his son prisoner. Mattoonus shot to death the same day by John's men."

July 22, 1695, he writes: —

"We are grievously oppressed by our French and Pagan enemies by land and sea. Our blood and estates are running out apace. As several captives escaped inform us our heads are set at a certain rate by the Governor of Quebec as foreskins of the Philistines were of old. God, in his time will confound all the worshippers of graven images."

Later on he writes a letter to his cousin in England, which in one sentence expresses the current remorseless temper of the Puritan public towards the Indians: —

"It hath been generally a sick summer with us. The autumn promiseth better. As to our enemies God hath, in a great measure, given us to see our desire upon them. Most ringleaders in the late massacre have themselves had blood to drink, ending their lives by bullets and halters. Yet there is some trouble and bloodshed still in the more remote eastern parts. What is past, is so far from ushering in a famine, that all sorts of grain have been very plenty and cheap. S. S."

BOSTON, Oct. 23, 1676.

The condition of the country generally at this time and for years after is summed up in this later incisive sentence of Sewall: —

"Our husbandmen got their bread in the peril of their lives by reason of the sword of the wilderness. Every now and then we hear of some slain here and there."

A letter of Sewall's to the captive minister of Deerfield, then in the French hands in Canada, ex-

An Indian Block House.

presses, perhaps, the current religious sense of our people about these Indian sufferings: —

> "The divine poet gives us an account of God's feeding his people with the bread of tears. Well. God times things best and I endeavor of wait and hope that your merciful return will be a plain instance of it. As you prayed earnestly for those who returned last, so you will be glad to hear that they landed well here the 2d inst.
>
> S. S. TO REV^D. JOHN WILLIAMS.
> Aug. 22, 1706."

A few men both before and after King Philip's War set resolutely about the conversion of the Indians. After that war they found little sympathy from the whites, but they kept on. The most successful missions were at Cape Cod, Martha's Vineyard, Natick, and the territory forty miles around Boston. Mayhew went to the Vineyard from Watertown; Bourne, whose labors as yet have had too scant recognition from our historians, wrought up and down the Cape, with his headquarters in Sandwich; and Eliot, of course, was at Natick. The success in general was slow and checkered. The missionaries were sincere and painstaking, but they had the English prejudice; and even Eliot, when he spent the Sabbath in Natick, ate victuals which his wife cooked at home, and dwelt apart in a chamber fitted up in his meeting-house. Yet Frenchmen and gentlemen spent their lives in the dirt and smoke of Canadian wigwams alone to convert this same race to substantially the same religion. This curious antipathy of races is still preserved in this commonwealth in one of the few still extant Indian missions.

The missionaries treated the Indians very much as grown children. On their earlier visits they treated the little ones "to apples, and their elders to tobacco and what else they had at hand," before unfolding to them the riches of the gospel. They bought and imported agricultural and mechanics' tools, and tried to teach them useful arts. There were found white men who would nurse the Indians through smallpox, even when their own people had deserted them. They tried to gather them into compact settlements, where they might be less exposed to the influences of their savage countrymen, and where the civilizing influence of the whites might make itself felt. In fact, they appealed to all that was in them; but there was not much in them, or at least not much which white men actually touched. Not more than four thousand converts at the most answered their toil. There is much significance in a sentence like this: "Sagamore John near Watertown began to hearken after God and his ways but was kept down by fear of the scoffs of the Indians." For an Indian to be converted often was to be denationalized, and a traitor to boot, in the eyes of his countrymen. They were taught the Lord's Prayer and the Decalogue, and, hardest of all, were liberally treated to the Puritan theology in its full strength. One instance of the order of public worship as had by Eliot may stand for all: "Began with prayer in

English, then he preached 1¼ hours in Indian, 'running through Christianity.' The Indians were then asked if they understood all, and they answered with a multitude of voices that they understood all. Questions put and answered on both sides." There was undoubtedly some good done and actual conversions. The Indians respected the word of an Englishman. A native rebuked an Englishman for felling a tree on the Sabbath, and a chief ordered his tribe not to shoot pigeons in that holy season. Many wished to learn of the white man's God, and some actually showed the virtues of Christianity. The converts had new names given them significant of some Christian virtue.

These converts during the war behaved variously. Many joined the enemy, and were among the most cruel. Others stayed in their places, and many, for safer oversight, were put on islands in Boston and Plymouth Harbors, from whence, at peace, they went home again. Opinions were divided as to what exactly these converts in this crisis showed themselves to be, with the majority against them.

Here is one sample of the behavior: —

"James the printer was an Indian, son of a deacon of the Church of 'Praying Indians' at Grafton. He was educated at the Indian School in Cambridge, and helped in the printing of Eliot's Bible. He ran away to join Philip's warriors, but came back when mercy was promised all who would come in within 14 days. He resumed printing, and his name, with that of Green, his master, appears as printer of the Indian Psalter in 1709."

Sewall, from early manhood, as his Diary shows, took a warm interest in the conversion of the Indians, alike creditable to his head and heart. He was one of the commissioners appointed from England to overlook their interests, and he took many long journeys to Martha's Vineyard and elsewhere in their behalf. He often rewarded the best scholars among them with a Psalter or Bible, and worshipped with them. Yet withal he judged them and their religious prospects carefully, and no man's opinion of them is more entitled to respect. These opinions are expressed in his Diary and letters.

The idea was prevalent that the Indians were the lost tribes of the house of Israel.

On Martha's Vineyard.

"Sep. 16, 1706. Gave the squaw that has lost her feet 10 pounds of wool.

"Jany 30, 1708. John Neesnummin, Indian preacher, comes to me with Mr R. Cotton's letters; I shew him to Dr. Mather. Bespeak a lodging for him at Mathias Smith's; but after, they sent me word they could not do it. So I was fain to lodge him in my study. Jany 31. P.M. I sent him on his way towards Natick, with a letter to John Trowbridge, to take him in if there should be occasion."

Here is another illustration of the prevalent and constant antipathy of the whites towards the Indians. Here was an educated Indian preacher, with letters of introduction from his friend Cotton of Sandwich, himself a preacher to them. Sewall first turns him over to a tavern, which refuses to have him. Then he makes a bed for him in his library instead of his guest chamber, and, after keeping him all the next day, probably for business, sends him forth on a late January afternoon, to fare along the Indian trail to Natick, with a letter in his pocket requesting somebody to take him in if he fares late, and all at the risk of losing his way in the snow, or of being refused entertainment at any white man's house. The old American antipathy to the negro, as well as what remains of it now, is well known. Aggravate that antipathy by the negroes' frequent cruel murders and ever-present nastiness, and we have the Puritan feeling towards the Indians in 1700 A.D. Yet Sewall behaved better than most of his neighbors.

The New England Indians were preached to and perished, not because of the preaching, but of the Will or Fate which some men are not ashamed to call God.[1] They were a singular race, — singular in the mystery of their origin, their history, and the terms of their decay. The Arabs on the Nile, in the late British expedition to rescue Gordon, had nothing but contempt for the negroes around them; but in every bivouac they fraternized on terms of the most friendly equality with the Indians who came out with the Canadian boatmen. In New England as a class they never obtained respect, and at the last most were unworthy. Yet Chief Justice Lynde tells us in his diary (1732) that of the grand jury at Nantucket, out of eighteen, nine were Indians. He also tells us that one of their people was a justice there, named Corduga. In overseeing the Indians'

[1] See Appendix, Note B.

morals, if they did not tend their corn, and for "rogue tricks and being drunk," his invariable sentence was, "Ten stripes for each offence."

Here follow certain opinions of Sewall about the best way of dealing with the whole race:—

"The Indians themselves are divided in the desires upon this matter [of Christian civilization].

"Some old men wished the old ways; young men the new.

"The Indians differed in dialects. The Bible was in the Natick dialect—Nantucket could not understand N. H. . . . Their language is also continually changing; old words wearing out and new ones coming in. A discreet person lately visiting the Indian villages writes: 'There are many words of Mr. Elliotts forming which they never understood. This they say is a grief to them. Such a knowledge in their Bibles, as our English ordinarily have in ours, they seldom any of them have.'

"The best thing we can do for our Indians is to Anglicise them in all agreeable instances; and in that of language as well as others. They can scarce retain their language without a tincture of other savage inclinations, which do but ill suit, either with the honor or with the design of Christianity.

"I should think it requisite that convenient tracts of land should be set out to them; and that by plain and natural boundaries, as much as may be; as lakes, rivers, mountains, rocks; upon which for any man to encroach should be accounted a crime. Except this be done, I fear their own jealousies, and the French Friars will persuade them, that the English as they increase and think they want more room will never leave till they have crowded them quite out of all their lands. And it will be a vain attempt for us to offer heaven to them, if they take up prejudices against us as if they did grudge them a living upon their own earth."

This necessary action Sewall insists on again and again, as his Letter Book shows.

"The Savoy Confession of Faith, English on one side and Indian on the other, has been lately printed here; as also several sermons of the President's [Increase Mather] have been transcribed into Indian, and printed which I hope in God's time, will have a very good effect.

To SIR WM ASHHURST.

May 3, 1700."

Sewall did for the Indians apparently all he could. Cotton Mather sets down that Judge Sewall built the Indians a meeting-house at his own charge for one of the Indian congregations, but does not tell us where, and "gave those Indians cause to pray for him because 'he loveth our nation for he hath built us a synagogue.'" From the first volume of Sewall's Letter Book, lately published, it appears that this meeting-house was somewhere in Sandwich, Barnstable County, Cape Cod. Sewall, as his Diary shows, had often visited here in his guardianship of the Indians. He writes to the carpenter, Edward Milton, Sept. 26, 1687:—

"Capt Thomas Tupper tells me that you are to build a convenient comfortable meeting house for the natives at Sandwich 24 ft. long—18 broad with two galleries—£30. Now if it may any way forward the work, I do engage that on the finishing of the work you shall not miss of your pay."

[The next year.] "April 13, 1688. Elder Chipman visits me and tells me that the Indian Meeting House is raised."

July 9, 1688, he writes the contractor:—

"Upon Capt Tupper's sending me word that the house is ceiled as it ought to be, I will pay you five and twenty shillings in money to you or to your order. If it be not well filled between the clapboards and the ceiling, I doubt the house will be cold."

He suggests shavings for filling. Recent inquiries fairly establish the fact that this meeting-house was built at Herring River, Sandwich, near or among the Herring Pond Indians, the descendants of whom now live there, and still have their own meeting-house, not two miles from where this primitive house of worship was built.

The proofs for this locality will be found in the note.[1]

Sewall also showed himself a lite-long friend of the negro, and that very much beyond the current philanthropy of his age. Elsewhere will be found his argument, "On the Selling of Joseph," against slavery. But the slavery of the negro was in New England, as in all Christendom, and Sewall foresaw the danger and the duty. Indeed, too much praise can hardly be allotted to Sewall's memory for his stout stand all his life against wrong of any sort to these defenceless and often maltreated Africans. In this respect Sewall stands pre-eminent, and at least a hundred and fifty years before his times. Very unlike the Indians, except in misery, they both served and troubled their owners with a mild chronic medley of laziness and unreliableness.

Wait Winthrop writes of one of his brother's slaves: —

"I fear black Tom will do but little service. He used to make a show of hanging himself before folks but I believe he is

[1] See Appendix, Note C.

× Site of Sewall's Meeting House.

not very nimble about it when he is alone. 'Tis good to have an eye on him, and if you think it not worth while to keep him, either sell him or send him to Virginia or the West Indies before winter."

These poor creatures, thus bound to an inimical and masterful race, had no future of comfort, no hope of progress; and had it not been for a few men, among whom Sewall ranks first, they would have had no marriages or natural relationships respectable in law. An extract or two from the Diary will give us glimpses of the situation: —

"I essayed June 22 [1716] to prevent Indians and negroes being rated with horses and hogs; but could not prevail."

"Thursday Sep. 26, 1700. Mr. John Wait and Eunice his wife and Mrs. Debora Thayer come to speak to me about the marriage of Sebastian, negro servant of said Wait with Jane, negro servant of said Thayer. Mr. Wait desired they might be published in order to marriage. Mrs. Thayer insisted that Sebastian might have one day in six allowed him for the support of Jane, his intended wife and her children, if it should please God to give her any. Mr. Wait now wholly declined that but freely offered to allow Bastian five pounds in money p^r annum towards the support of his children by said Jane (besides Sebastian's clothing and diet.) I persuaded Jane and Mrs. Thayer to agree to it and so it was concluded; and Mrs. Thayer gave up the note of publication to Mr. Wait for him to carry it to Wm Griggs, the town clerk and to Williams in order to have them published according to law."

This closing extract from his Letter Book, referring to an old scandal of which the writer has been able to find no trace elsewhere, fitly exposes Sewall's great generous heart in his care for the downtrodden: —

"The poorest boys and girls within this province, such as are of the lowest condition, whether they be English or Indians or Ethiopians, they have the same right to religion and life, that the richest heirs have. And they who go about to deprive them of this right, they attempt the bombarding of Heaven; and the shells they throw shall fall down upon their own heads.

TO ADDINGTON DAVENPORT, ESQ., *going to Judge Smith of Sandwich for killing his negro*, 1719."

There spoke the will of Lollard, Puritan, and Protestant. The student of history, believing in the relationship of cause and effect in all the ages of time, and looking across this land to find no slave between the seas, though the white marbles marking its soldiers' stately sleep are on ten thousand hillsides, South Land, must fain confess that this Puritan judge was also prophet, and that our strain has loyally enforced, in later days, that ancient will.

CHAPTER IX.

SEWALL IN ENGLAND.

In November, 1688, Sewall undertook his only voyage back to the mother land. All the fall, as his Journal shows, he had been making ready by interviewing his relatives and collecting supplies.

"Monday Oct. 15. Speak to Gilbert Cole to bottle me a barrel of beer for the sea." "In the afternoon coming out of town I met Mr. Ratcliff [the Church of England minister], who asked me if I were going for England. He asked when; I said in Cap. Clark. He prayed God Almighty to bless me and said must wait on me." "Novr 7. Brother Stephen comes to town and brings me my letter of attorney and other writings." [Papers to authorize him to settle money affairs in England.] "I asked his Excellency [the Governor] if he has any service for me to Hampshire or Coventry. He said none in particular." "Nov. 16. Brother Stephen and I with Mr. Pole and Cap. Clark go on board the America. It rained before we got aboard and all the way as we came from the ship; had a glass of good Madeira. Brother commends the ship, dines with us and returns to Salem."

He was now a man of station and repute in Boston, and his object in going was probably to revisit the scenes of his childhood, and to renew family friendships, while at the same time he might assist Cotton Mather, now resident agent of Massachusetts in London, to make terms with the king's government in behalf of the colony, which was now substantially without a settled government, and the titles of whose citizens to their landed property were supposed to be put in jeopardy by the withdrawal of their charter. Sewall had come out when he was nine years old, and was now thirty-six years of age.

The Journal of this visit is a manuscript volume by itself, and its record of the voyage itself shows more thrift and comfort aboard than of old. Each passenger apparently laid in his own luxuries beforehand; and Sewall was always a good purveyor. His wife and friends had also assisted. We find such entries as these: —

"Novr 27. Ate my wife's pastry the remembrance of whom is ready to cut me to the heart." [Friday Dec. 7.] "Breakfast on one of my wife's plum cakes." "Dreamed much of my wife last night. Gave me a piece of cake for Hannah Hett; was in plain dress and white apron."

There are such entries as these: —

"One of the geese dies yesterday or to-day." "This day eat Simon Gates' goose;" "Killed the sheep to-day;" "Killed the shoat" [young hog].

From all which we may conclude that there was fresh meat aboard. Nor did the Puritan afloat or ashore willingly lack somewhat to drink. Yet there was little drunkenness in those days of pure liquors and much out-door exercise. Just before going into port Sewall tells us they met a pink (vessel) fourteen days from Liverpool, "who sent us some bottles of very good beer, and we him one of my bottles of brandy. We bought 3 cheeses of him."

Sewall apparently had a rough voyage of some six weeks when he landed at Dover, Jan. 13, 1689. He was not a bad sailor himself, and gives us many nautical hints of how they handled or lost sails, etc., and how things went on in the cabin:—

> "Just at night, the wind blows very hard, just in our teeth, so lie by under the Mizzen, the other sails being furled. Scarce any sleeping all night things in the cabin were so hurled to and again."

For the first week they had head winds:—

> "Nov. 30. 'Tis a very laborious day by reason of hail, snow, wind and a swollen sea all in a foaming breach." "Dec. 4th. Can't dress victuals to-day." [Again]: "wind aft, so cabin shut up and burn candles all day." "My Erasmus was quite loosened out of the binding by the breaking of the water into the cabin when it did." "The good Lord fit us for his good pleasure in this our passage."

He keeps his eyes open for all that is going on,—for a rainbow; gulls on the banks of Newfoundland; "a woodcock that flies on board of us which we drive away essaying to catch him" (Dec. 24); a storm petrel; "a flock of sparrows seen to-day" (Jan. 5). "Some say they saw a Robin Red Breast to-day" (same date). He can even lay a wager (no uncommon Puritan pastime) as to when they will see land, and sets it down that he puts up his stakes. He and the other gentlemen aboard make up a purse of between thirty and forty shillings for him who first sees land. "I gave an oblong Mexico piece of Eight."

But Sewall's main vocation on shipboard was to prayers and the reading of pious and now forgotten books of Puritan theology, and there was evidently much employ over their contents. The second day out in great discomfort of foul weather: —

> "Benny Harris reads the 21 of the Proverbs which is the first chapter I heard read on shipboard. I much heeded that verse 'He that wandereth out of the way of understanding shall remain in the congregation of the dead.'" "Mr. Clarke reads the first two chapters of Isaiah and Capt. Clark prays." [Their first Sabbath at sea, Nov. 25.] "Strong east wind. I read the 74th Psalm, being that I should have read at home in the family. Sung the 23d Psalm."

Of a Puritan book he writes: —

> "This day I finished reading Dr. Manton. Blessed be God who in my separation from my dear wife and family hath given me his apostle James with such an exposition."

Then follow Sewall's reflections, which are very keen in personal applications to himself and his fellow-Christians. "Paul's thorn in the flesh meant of some racking pain, not of a prevailing lust." Nor can he quite give over on shipboard his old pastime of dreaming, which he always regards with an awful eye: —

> "Last night I dreamed of military matters, arms and captains, and all of a sudden, Major Gookin [his ancient friend and fellow-soldier] very well clad from head to foot, and of a very fresh lively countenance . . . his coat and breeches of blood red silk beckoned me out of the room," etc.

When his ship approached land it was nigh upon wrecked on Scilly rocks; but after this narrow escape, in an easy and gossipy way among the friendly vessels making port, and yet with one eye always open for a hostile foreigner, Sewall landed at Dover, while the ship went on to London. He now found himself face to face with the social life of Old England in the seventeenth century, and seems to have enjoyed it, at least the Puritan and godly side of it, with much gusto. He went across Kent to Canterbury by way of Chatham and Rochester to London, arriving in three days from Dover, Jan. 16, 1689. The entries are as follows: —

"Sabbath Jany. 13. Through God's grace landed about 9 or 10 o'clock. Mr. Newgate and I went and heard one Mr. Goff in a kind of malt house. In afternoon all went." "Jany. 14. Rode in a coach to Canterbury. Getting there a little before night viewed the Cathedral which is a very lofty and magnificent building, but of little use. Visited Aunt Fessenden her son John and her three daughters. Cousin John supped with us at the Red Lion." "Jany. 15. Came to Rochester through Sittingburn (where dined) and Ranam [Raynham?] with other little places. No room in the inn by reason of soldiers so lodged at the coffee house."

In London he indulges in a round of sight-seeing, writing down with a brief, vivid pen sharp observations of men and things. First of all, as was Puritan, he waited on the ministry of the Word.

"Jany. 30. Heard Dr. Sharp preach before the Commons from Psalm 51." "Next day heard Mr. Chauncy [probably an ejected minister] preach." "May 31. Is a fast kept at Dr. Annesly's; they began with singing and sang 4 or 5 times.

After all, had a contribution. Five ministers exercised. Four wore their own hair." [Which was a comfort to him who hated periwigs]. June 7. "Go and hear Mr. Stretton and sit down with him at the Lord's Supper. He invites me to dinner." "Before sermon read the 32 Psalm, the 50th of Jeremiah, the 12th of Matthew. Had one plate of bread about 5 bottles of wine and two silver cups. At night about 10 aclock a great fire breaks forth in Mincing Lane." "Went to the funeral of Mr. Loves, formerly an assistant to Dr. Owens. Was buried in a grave near the Dr's. tomb. A pretty many men and women there. July 21. Went in the afternoon to Stepney and heard Mr. Lawrence. He fears the clouds returning after the rain as to Anti-Christian powers. His heart much upon the 1000 years. Something in this sermon as I perceive by them that know; few sermons without. Gives notice that Mr. Crouch, the minister is dead and will be buried tomorrow, 5 o'clock from Armourer's Hall."

So far as Sewall's rather blind reference to the above sermons are concerned, it looks as if these Puritan parsons, with due economy and care of their lives and property, were engaged in flinging at the king and the current course of English politics. There was something in these sermons undoubtedly.

"Aug. 17. Go to the new meeting-house [in Deal] 34 wide and 41 foot long; two galleries, one at each end, of 4 seats apiece. Roof is double with a gutter in the middle; built with brick covered with tile." "Sabbath Aug. 18. Heard Mr. Larner in a barn." [Quite like New England.] "Aug. 25. Mr. Mather preaches for Mr. Larner in the afternoon. Oct. 6. Go to Mr. Jacobs and in the afternoon sit down with him at the Lord's Supper; and so I go from one Pit to another to see if I can find any water to refresh me in my disappointments and discomforts."

He mentions hearing one preach from, "Have no fellowship with the works of darkness," who said that

Interior of St. Michael's Church, looking East.

erroneous worship was a work of darkness; whereby the preacher probably meant every form of worship except his own.

A description of the Lord's Supper in the then Puritan fashion may end Sewall's notes in this line.

"Sabbath May 5, 1689. Went to Dr. Annesly's [noted among the ejected ministers] in little St Helena's with Cap. Hutchinson where the Lord's Supper was administered. The Dr. went all over the meeting first, to see who was there, then spake something of the sermon, then read the words of institution, then prayed and eat and drunk himself, then gave to every one with his own hand, dropping pertinent expressions. In our pew said, 'Now our Spikenard should give its smell;' and said to me 'Remember the death of Christ.' The wine was in quart glass bottles. The deacon followed the Doctor and when his cup was empty filled it again; as at our pew all had drunk but I, he filled the cup and then gave it me; said as he gave it — must be ready in new obedience and stick at nothing for Christ."

For English churches and the Prayer Book he shows an indifferent taste; but the great schools of Cambridge and Oxford interest him very much, probably for their classical lore, and because many of his personal friends and Puritan preachers had been therein educated. He took journeys to both places.

"Wednesday June 26. Mr. Mather, his son, cousin Hull and myself set out for Cambridge 45 miles; got thither by 7 o'clock with one set [of] 4 horses. Lay at the Red Lion." "Thursday. Mr. Little of Emmanuel College shows us the gardens, walks, new chapel, gallery, library of the college, in it a Bible Mss. of Wickliffe's translation. Mr. John Cotton and Hooker had been fellows as appeared by tables hanging up. The street where it stands is called Preacher's street from Black Friars formerly resident there."

A clear case of Puritan nomenclature, which has probably long since been erased. He mentions, probably in astonishment, that this Fellow, who evidently took them round, had in his chamber pictures of Sir Roger Le Strange, Jesus Salvator, and King Charles II. hanging up together. It is clear from all we know of Sewall that he at least had no doubt that his Lord's picture was here found in very bad company.

"Saw St. Johns College which stands by the river. Hath a good library and many rarities among which was a petrified cheese. Trinity College is very large and the new case for the library very magnificent; paved with marble checkered black and white; under it a stately walk on brave stone; the square very large and in midst of it a fountain. In the hall many sparrows inhabit which is not known of any hall beside. At meal times they feed of crums and will approach very near men. Mr. Little dined with us at our inn: had leg of mutton boiled and Colley-Flowers [cauliflowers], carrets, roasted fowls and a dish of pease." "Three musicians came in, two harps and a viol and gave us music. Just before night our landlady's son had us along Bridge St. Went to the Prison and Session House, just by, which is very ordinary like a cow house, cattle having free egress and regress there. Gallows just by it in a dale, convenient for spectators to stand all round on the rising ground. In sum Cambridge is better than it shows for at first; the meanness of the town buildings and most of the colleges being brick." "June 28. Mr. Harwood and I stepped out and saw Queens College and in the garden a Dial on the ground — the hours cut in box. Over against it stands Catharine Hall, the printing room 60 foot long and 20 foot broad — six presses. Had my cousin Hull and my name printed there."

Sewall had always a bias in favor of printing-presses, using them to print his own writings and others, and his name has been printed by them, not at his expense, probably nigh ten thousand times.

"As came homewards, saw Audley Inn or End — I can't tell which is the right name. 'Tis a stately palace. Dined at Saffron Walden; went out and saw the saffron roots which are ten shillings the bushel; about an acre might yield an hundred pounds or more. Have a fair church. Went into the vault and saw the Earl of Suffolk's coffin, who died January last. Stands on tressels and may see it on the outside at the grate. Outside is black velvet and a small plate of copper telling time of his death."

In the early part of 1689 Sewall made most of his pilgrimages to his old friends and certain famous places out of London, as he has marked down thus: —

"1689. Wed^y Jany. 16. Came to London."
"Wed^y Feby. 13. Went out."
"Sat^y March 16 into London."
"Thurs^y March 28 went out."
"Monday April 15. Came into London."
"Feb. 18. Bought a bay horse at Winchester fair for which am to pay four pounds. — A pr. boots, spurs &c 15*sh.* — a letter 2*d.* — tavern 6*d.*"

On the next day he bought bridle, saddle, saddlecloth for 6*s.*, and a new girt for 6*d.* He after paid 1*s.* 6*d.* for a whip. And he appears to have gone generally on horseback.

"Feby. 20. Saw the stone of my aunt Rider's grave." "Feby. 21. Cousin Jane Holt came in the morning to invite me to dinner. Had very good bacon, veal and parsnips, very good shoulder of mutton and a fowl roasted, good currant suet pudding and the fairest dish of apples I have eat in England."

This is probably a capital menu for English country folk in that age. Sewall was always sensitive about his fare, and the insight which he gives us into the current living of well-to-do people is interesting, if not amusing. He carefully writes it all down in such entries as these: —

"Eat part of two lobsters that cost 3. 9*d.* apiece [at a state dinner apparently]. As we came home were entertained by Mr. Stephen Mason with cider, ale, oysters and a neat's tongue, being ten of us or eleven."

Occasionally there are roast ducks and cherries. He notes green pease at 6*d.* per peck.

"Went to a garden at Mile End and drank currant and raspberry wine, then to the Dog and Partridge and played ninepins. At that house a soldier was shot by his drunken companion the night before." "Had a dish of bacon with pigeons, sauce, beans and cabbage. Then roast veal-tarts. The governor came in and drank to us in a glass of ale that being the drink I chose and Mr. Brattle." "Sep. 30. Mr. Bedford invited Mr. Brattle and me to dinner to Mr. Dracots'. Had a dish of fowls and bacon with livers; a dish of salt fish and a piece of mutton, cheese and fruit; no wine." "Dined with very good beef, bacon and roast fowls." "About 6 aclock, Mr. Mather, son and I supped on two dunghill fowls." "Mr. Mather prays and we get to bed just at 9." "At the Cheker have a hog's cheek. Send for my cousins. I treat them with ale and wine but Uncle Richard will call for one pint and indeed Cousin Mercy Stork and he seem the most kind of all my relations."

Very good fare, no doubt, all this; but what with the wild fowl, venison, and fish of Massachusetts Bay, Sewall was used to fare better at home.

"Feby 25. Went to Winchester in the morning and there met with letters from my dear wife and New England friends dated Jany last. Laus Deo. Viewed Winchester College. Left my Indian Bible and Mr. Mather's letter there. Went into the Hall and Arbor to see the choice of Knights of the Shire. It came to the poll, I offered my voice but was refused because I would not lay my hand on and kiss the Book though I offered to take my oath. [Sewall undoubtedly was a landowner there, but his Puritan scruple against taking his oath as the law was, forbade.] My rapier was broken short off I suppose coming down the steps. Feby 27. Rid to Salisbury. The chancellor's clerk showed me the Cathedral, Chapter House and Cloisters. Got the organist to give us some music. Showed as a strange thing (a bishop, I think) that lay north and south [the body was generally laid before the Reformation east and west, the head to the west, that so as it was thought in the resurrection the dead might rise looking towards the east, from whence the Lord was to appear in judgment]. The cathedral is very neat and stately. Two crosses in it. Candles on the Communion Table; so at Winchester. The bells hang in a steeple distant from the church. Tell us there are 12 small chapels for prayers every hour. The Bible over the passage that leads into the chorus [choir?] that so persons may hear on both sides. The spire is excellent for height and beauty. Dined with the chancellor's clerk. His lady gone to a christening to which she was invited but could not stay, but showed us in a manner her whole house, plate, library and bedding. Her daughter of four months old I took out of the cradle and kissed though asleep."

Sewall's pen writes him down as a lover of children; and in England he seems to have played the *rôle* of my Lord Bountiful among the little men and maids related to him when he met them. He gave them buckles, gloves, spoons, primers, shillings, linen, silk stockings, etc., with a Puritan modicum of kisses thrown in to boot. This mostly appears from the items of his cash account preserved in the year's almanac. He has an honest eye for young people generally. Under date of March 7 writes :—

"Went home with Jane Kirby, Cousin Thomas Holt's mistress; but I knew it not till I met her. It being late I observed a boy run parallel with us in the grounds and asked her about it. I took him up [on horseback?] and when set him down by the mill, lent him half a crown to buy paper and quills, told him if he learned to write and read well, 'twas his; if not I must have it again with I know not how much interest and put him to a great deal of trouble." "The tenant's wife [on his farm at Lee] teaches scholars. One was reading whom I marked and gave them 6*d.* to buy apples."

Happy children with russet, or rosy, or golden apples! And peace be to the man who gave the sixpence, and wrote it down in his almanac, as a thrifty New Englander should!

"Saturday March 9. Ride to Tichfield, view the church and Oake's pulpit, removed from the pillar where it stood in his time to the other side. Sexton spoke much in his praise, and inquired after his children. Saw Miss Bromfield's monument who died in 1618. Dined with Cousin Thomas Dummer and bought the first pound of tobacco which he sold in a fair."

If Samuel Sewall smoked, it was a meditative performance in creature comforts which the statute laws of Puritans never forbade. Clay pipes were, and continued to be, imported from the very start.

The next day after Sewall's first return to London the Lord Mayor died, Sunday, March 17.

"Monday [he writes] went and saw the Jews burying place at Mile End. Some bodies were laid east and west; but now all are ordered to be laid north and south. Many tombs. Engravings are Hebrew, Latin, Spanish, English, sometimes on the same stone. Part of the ground is improved as a garden — the dead are carried through the keeper's house. First tomb is about the year 1659. Brick wall built about part. I told the keeper afterwards that I wished we might meet in heaven. He answered and we drink a glass of beer together, which we were then doing."

The Jews, as evidently that chosen people from whom the Puritans had taken the pattern of their theocratic government and their conversion, were to forerun the second appearing of that Redeemer whom the Puritans fondly hoped might come suddenly "as a thief in the night" to their waiting distress. Hence probably Sewall's interest.

According to the above schedule of travel, Sewall again went out with Mather and their two sons, each named Samuel, on a mixed business and pleasure tour, the objective point being Oxford.

[March 28.] "Sam and I went to Bray Church and writ out two epitaphs by candlelight." "Saturday March 30. Mr. Mather and we ride in the coach to Oxford, 5 miles, little ones, costs us 12*s*. of which I pay 5 and Mr. Mather the rest. At New College eat and drank ale, wine, Lent cakes full of currants, good butter and cheese, by means of Mr. Benj. Cutler, the butler to whom Dr. Woodward sent a letter on my behalf." "About 300 soldiers come to town; so the horses were pressed and we could not get out. Mr. Holland [a Fellow of Corpus Christi, Oxford] shows me his chamber, cellar, library &c. Said Holland treated me very civilly though I told him I was a New England man" [i.e., a rank Puritan].

"Warwick. April 5. St Mary's Chapel. Richard Beaucamp's statue in brass, very lively, veins and nails of his hands."

Sewall now goes to Coventry, where his family were of old and held office. Visits the churches and the town hall where his great grandfather had been mayor; also his relatives. With an eye to business he offers to confirm certain land property which had been willed them. "Lapworth [his cousin's husband] said he would not give 3*d*." Owing either to the manners of the times or some family wrangle, it certainly looks from this entry, as from other things which Sewall lets drop, as if he and his relatives, at least a part of them, did not get on well together. Sewall, of course, is fond of music, which he always sets going when he can, as he notes:—

> "Went and dined with Cousin Allen, with beans, bacon and a very good line veal roasted. Beans 5*d* a quart. Cousin Sarah played on her flute. Cousin Atwell sings well."

The musicians of his ancestral city took occasion to do him honor, and probably put money in their purse.

> "Had three of the city Waits bid me good morrow with their wind music." "About 200 soldiers I saw drawn forth to the westward of the town which had their drums, cross a horse neck [probably a white cross on their horse trappings] and a trumpet. In the Lords hall Guy's pot was filled with brandy punch; when in the field heard the volleys and huzzas, the Pope carried about."

The weeks between his country journeys, spent in London we judge from his Diary, were given up to a very vigorous course of sight-seeing and attempts to manage for the benefit of Puritan politics in New

England. They were stirring times. James II. had just gone out, and Dutch William, with James's daughter, now reigned. The old fires of religious rancor only smouldered; the Pope was acutely abhorred of most "true-born" Englishmen, and from such repeated overturns of the throne as there had been in the last forty years, there had grown up a widespread sense of uncertainty and insecurity. Soldiers were moving about, foreign spies, and perhaps home traitors, were abroad, and the future was clouded. Sewall's home was in the west, and his interests also, except as they might be affected by arbitrary power in London; and so at much of what went on about him he looked with an indifferent eye. Only he looked straight into the masquerade of life in London streets, and the genial and human part of him reached beyond his religious asceticism to fraternize with his kind at their toil or pastime. He went to the Tower, Guild Hall, St. Paul's; saw a city election, "which the sheriffs, with their gold chains, managed;" heard the Mayor's speech;

"saw [Feb. 12] the Princess [Anne] pass in her barge ancients and streamers of ships flying, bells ringing, guns roaring." "April 30. Queen's birthday. Streamers, flags, guns. Spent 4*s*. 3*d*. in going to Greenwich." "May 27. Saw the Dutch ambassadors make their public entrance. Came up through Crouched? Friars were about 50 coaches, with 6 horses apiece, besides pages on foot and youths on horseback. The main streets thwacked [packed?] with people and yet little mess of people in Fen Church and Lombard streets."

He goes off with Mr. Brattle to swim in Thames

(July 8) from the Temple stairs, and had a wherry to wait on them.

"I went in in my drawers." "Saw the Physick garden and in it among other things an olive tree, orange tree, cortex Peruvianus."

This was the garden for medical plants established at Chelsea, 1673, by the Company of Apothecaries. Sir Hans Sloane used and developed this garden in the interests of medical botany, and he it was who brought quinine into use.

He takes great interest in citizen and other soldiers, being, as we have seen, a soldier himself in Boston.

"July 16. Saw London Artillery pass by about 2 o'clock. Most had buff coats and feathers in their hats. Marched 5, 6, 7, and 8 in a rank. The pikes. Had music besides the drums." "July 23. The white regiment marches into the artillery ground of which the Lord Mayor is colonel and so they have the preeminence. Consist of eight companies, 14 or 15 hundred in the whole, perhaps. Some had silver head pieces." "Saw an ensign buried. The company was drawn up in one rank, — pikes, — next the house of mourning. When ready to go rank 6 came to funeral posture; colors covered with mourning went after pikes then captain, then parson and corps posted [or stacked] the pikes when the service was saying. Gave 3 vollies but saw not the colors open all the while."

We find him every now and then incommoded by the movement of the army, coming and going. At Plymouth, on his way home, (Sept. 23): —

"Many soldiers march away to make room for Dr. Bolton's regiment lately come hither by sea. Two sergeants go out of our house and two other soldiers come in."

He visits the pillory, the law courts, and the gallows: —

"July 12. This day two stood in the pillory before the Royal Exchange for speaking against the government. They were exceedingly pelted with dirt and eggs. Another that stood for forgery had none thrown at him that I took notice of." "Monday July 15. I rid to Tyburn and saw eighteen persons, 16 men and 2 women fall. They were unruly in the prison, which hastened their execution."

Sewall generally brings up in a graveyard, if he does not set out from one at home and abroad. He tells us, for instance, that he saw the monument of Lockier in St. Mary's Ovary (died 1672), a very successful rich quack, one couplet on his stone being this: —

"His virtues and his pills are so well known
That envy can't confine them under stone."

[July 9.] "Went to Stepney, saw Thomas Saffin's tomb [the son of a Bostonian who died and was lately buried here]. 50 shillings given for the grounds. 'Tis a very large burying place. Were to be 10 buried this night; we saw several graves open and the bones thick on the top. The Lord help me to improve my flesh, bones and spirits which are so soon to become useless and it may be exposed in one part or other of God's creation."

On Thomas Saffin's tomb, who was evidently somebody, or the son of somebody, this quaint epitaph, noted and copied in the *Spectator*, October, 1712, was inscribed: —

"Here Thomas Saffin lies interrèd, why?
Born in New England did in London die;
Was the third son of right begat upon
His mother Martha, by his father John.

Much favored by his prince he 'gan to be
But nipt by death at the age of twenty-three;
Fatal to him was that we, smallpox, name
By which his mother and two brethren came
Also to breathe their last, nine years before
And now have left their father to deplore
The loss of all his children with his wife
Who was the joy and comfort of his life."

One main purpose of Sewall's visit to England connected itself with the current politics of New England, which was to secure safe land titles, which the withdrawal of the charter had made insecure. A letter of his to an English friend under date of April 26, states the case personally and succinctly: —

"There was Capn John Hull of Boston in N.E. with whom in his lifetime you had some correspondence by way of merchandise. He died in Sep. 1683, leaving a widow and a daughter who is my wife, by whom I had an estate that might afford a comfortable subsistence according to our manner of living in New England. But since the vacating of the charter and erecting a government by commission, the title we have to our lands has been greatly defamed and undervalued; which had been greatly prejudicial to the inhabitants, because their lands, which were formerly the best part of their estate, became of very little value and consequently the owners of very little credit. Sir I am glad that you are returned again to England, to your country, possessions and dear relations and to your seat in parliament. I hope your former distresses will help you to sympathize with others in the like condition. I and several besides me are here far removed from our wives and children and have little heart to go home before some comfortable settlement obtained whereby we might be secured in the possession of our religion, liberty and property. I am informed some favorable votes have been passed in the House of Commons wherein N.E. was mentioned. I intreat your forwarding of such votes, as you have opportunity, in doing which you will be a partner with God who is wont to be concerned in relieving the oppressed. . . . My hearty service presented to you, I take leave, who am Sir your humble Servant, SAM. SEWALL."

Thomas Papillon, M.P., to whom this letter was addressed, was of a Huguenot refugee family, and undoubtedly Puritan. Sometimes Sewall and his *confrères* in patriotism were obliged to answer to written or printed pamphlets, arraigning the colonists for misbehavior, — documents likely to be well received by the government after the restoration of Charles II., and in which, from the standpoint of the laws of the realm, the accusers had often strong ground to stand on.

"May 20. Met to answer the print and in the evening another accosts us, called an abstract of our repugnant laws, full of untruths almost as the former. To comfort me when got home met with a letter from my dear brother by way of Bilboa dated the 12 March; all friends and my wife and children well but New England bleeding. May 21 writ to Mr. Flavel of our N.E. affairs. He wrote and sent N.E. documents in behalf of his cause to those who were in station and ability to aid. He writes to me, 'I find it inconvenient to be out of the way because we that are here count it our duty, if we can in anything to assist Mr. Mather. If you come to town I should be glad to see you on the N.E. walk or at my chamber.'"

From which it incidentally appears that there was a "walk" or place in London where New England merchants, sea captains, and travellers might meet and confer. What exactly Sewall and the others with him accomplished it is hard to say. King William was Protestant to the core, and in religion was their sympathizer; but the English law still stood above him and them, and no loyal man could afford to ignore the inroads which the Puritan *régime* in Boston was apparently disposed to make upon it. That the titles to their lands were made valid we know. What might have been worse we do not know. Perhaps, if it had not been for the presence of such men in London as Sewall and Mather, the colonists would have fared much worse than they did. But the fact that they never got back their old charter out of even the hands of their English Protestant friends goes very far to show that in the judgment of conservative English statesmen they were not entitled to the powers it gave them, nor were to be trusted with them.

Sewall now set about his return. In a roundabout way through Kent, and so down the Channel to Plymouth, from whence an excursion was made into Cornwall, he finally set sail out of Plymouth Sound, Oct. 11. Sewall's Journal in England is remarkable for what it leaves out. One would hardly gather from his pages that everywhere about him was a great national church, secure and dominant in the religion of the realm. Puritan as he was, he makes no mention either of John Milton or Cromwell, though their graves were there somewhere, covering the dust of the greatest of England's Puritans. Perhaps Sewall's caution made him close-mouthed. Certainly his was a judicious pen.

Sewall was always making presents to his friends, but he was also ready to save a penny when he could, as a good many men after him have pinched themselves into a fortune, and then left at death, with an open hand, thousands to some noble charity. He, while in London, always got shaved by the quarter, because it was cheaper; yet he would give four crowns to Irish Protestants. He would give silver spoons, but would buy stockings where they made them, as cheapest. One would get a very good idea of the times and the cost of living by the study of the freight bills of what men like Sewall brought out and took home. An English Testament, Oxford print, costs 1*s.* 2*d.*; quire of paper, 6*d.*; hat for self and son, £2 7*s.*; four good muffs, £2 6*s.*; twelve bottles of beer, 10*s.*; map of England, Ireland, and Scotland, 10*s.* 6*d.*

"Went and was trimmed by Cousin Harry Ward and gave his wife who sat by him in the shop ½ doz. silver spoons marked E. W. 1689. Cost 63*s.* (weighing 10 oz. 11pt.), or at the rate of more than $30 a dozen."

The grand dames of Boston, as his cash account shows, were always sending over for spoons, and were not averse to the follies of English haberdashery.

"To a bed of straw to lay under my feather bed 2*s.* 9*d.*" [this was for the voyage.] "Sep. 26. Plymouth delivered to be washed 2 shirts, 2 handkerchiefs, 5 cravats, 1 cap and 1 binder." [Did the Puritans wear as much linen as we?]

Ships in the way, "rogues," or French enemies, sometimes in sight, — for there was now war with

France, — their armed convoy leaving them some hundred and twenty miles from land, some with measles, scurvy, and his friend Mr. Brattle spitting blood, the wind often in their teeth, a rough voyage concludes itself Nov. 29 in Piscataqua River (Portsmouth).

"Saturday, Nov. 30. Ride to Newbury. Friends there exceedingly glad to see me, being surprised at my coming that way."

Let a single excerpt from Sewall's Diary conclude his visit to England : —

"Friday, Nov. 15. 9, morning. Sound and find ground in 45 or 50 fathoms. Bring the ship to and put out fishing lines. Mr. Fanuel only catches a good cod, which had several small fish in him, supposed to be anchoves. Very foggy weather. Judge are on the southermost point of the Bank. And now we have tasted afresh of American fare. Lord give me to taste more of thyself everywhere, always adequately good."

A Sewall Portrait.

Reredos, St. Michael's Church.

CHAPTER X.

SEWALL AND THE SALEM WITCHCRAFT.

"Why should I hate any man? He whom I hate is either good or bad. If he be good then am I wrong to hate him. If he be bad he will amend and so be saved, or else persevere in ill, and so everlastingly perish. If he shall be saved, why should I hate him whom eternally I must love? If he shall be damned, his pain shall be so great that rather we had cause to pity than to add affliction to affliction in hating and cursing him."

SIR THOMAS MORE.

"FIRST WITCH. Round about the cauldron go;
In the poison'd entrails throw. —
Toad, that under the cold stone
Days and nights hast thirty-one
Sweltered venom sleeping got,
Boil thou first i' the charmèd pot.
ALL. Double, double toil and trouble;
Fire, burn; and, cauldron, bubble.
. . . .
MACBETH. Infected be the air whereon they ride,
And damned all those that trust them."

Macbeth.

THE Salem witchcraft business requires careful handling by those who would be just both to the sufferers and the offenders therein. Sewall's part in the matter was a brief though sad one, as one of the judges who pronounced sentence of death upon the innocent. A man with his large heart would never forget his hand in that strange misery until his death's day. Nor is it without a certain pathos of filial love towards the dead, that shortly after Sewall's decease his son moved in the General Court (1738) that inquiry should be made as to the condition of the victims' families, looking towards some sort of restitution, poor at best. The witches' "caldron" at Salem was as purely imaginary, so far as witches went, as the one that Shakespeare makes to bubble with ill-odored and poisoned ingredients on an imaginary moor in Scotland; yet into that Salem caldron, out of the hands of that Puritan age and people, were poured some of the most mixed, unreachable, and poisonous motives of which probably the human mind, in its most occult relationship to the human body, has as yet shown itself capable of emitting. Yet, sad to say, its bubbles turned to blood, and the smoke of this witches' incense creates a great sorrow among all lovers of New England folk until now.

There is, perhaps, no more valid canon of historical criticism than this, that the people of an age are to be judged as to conduct by the ethics and environment of that age, and by no other. Ancient Rome is not to be judged by the ethics of modern Italy. In judging the Salem witchcraft catastrophe, we must start with this postulate. But at that time the peoples of Christendom devoutly believed in actual witches, the English people being as stout devotees of that delusion as any. English statute law declared witches and witchcraft to be verities by making so-called witchcraft a crime punishable with death. English judges had sentenced thousands of men and women for the offence, and European tribunals had destroyed by due process of law hundreds of thousands of accused persons for what we know to be a purely imaginary felony. Very few Englishmen in the Puritan age disbelieved in witches. Even as late as 1840, in West Dorsetshire, England, there were people who undertook to argue that a prevailing sickness there was brought about by witchcraft. It is needless to note, perhaps, what the Old Testament holds in this matter.

The Puritans held with the rest, only with a more tenacious grip. This was natural; we may well say, inevitable. This very attitude in church and state made them, more than most, doomed to the mistake. They held that they were God's chosen people in the wilderness just as actually as the Jews had been; that they had honored Him by founding institutions based on His revealed law; that they were His and He was theirs by a solemn compact; that He was therefore cognizant of their every word and deed; in minute oversight of His creatures, not even a sparrow fell to the ground unnoticed. When, therefore, an attack seemed to be in progress at Salem upon His church and people by His arch enemy the Devil, it was not simply an attack on them and their dearest aspirations, but on Him; and they were bound, on penalty of being held traitors to Him in the Judgment Day, not to stand neutral, but to fight His battle by destroying witchcraft from the land. They could logically, as New England Puritans, do nothing else. It is argued every now and then that their clergy were the chief malefactors in urging the people on to this wrong. That this point is not well taken ought to appear from the fact that in the Salem witchcraft, as indeed in everything else they put their hand to, as ought to appear in our whole colonial history, the Puritan clergy voiced and enforced with the power of an educated class the deliberate conscience and judgment of their own people, who fed them voluntarily and reverenced them greatly. If this were not so, how came it to pass that later on this same people parted from this same clergy both in politics and religion, and went their own way? With a few exceptions of the more fortunate-minded, the management at Salem was according to the consensus of the whole community. Cotton Mather is pointed to as one of the chief malefactors in inciting the Salem horrors. That Cotton Mather was a very human sort of man, and, therefore, sometimes blamable, may go without saying. But Cotton Mather actually agonized over the bewitched, or, as the ancient phrase went, "behagged," children, whom he took into his house in Boston in such a way as to remove all suspicion that he was juggling, or any way trying to do anything else than to probe to the bottom of the fact. To say that he was magnifying his office in order to hold his place in affairs, — an imputing of motives, — is not verified by the record. He, and most men about him, thought that any man who disbelieved in witches would disbelieve in the Devil; and that he who would disbelieve in the Devil would speedily come to disbelieve in God.

One thing more as a proviso. The times were ripe for such an outbreak as that at Salem. They were out of joint politically, the charter being lost, and people were sore and apprehensive of some great calamity. They were in the slough of an unknown transition. Besides, a new generation had sprung up, born here, wonted from youth to hardship and solitude, cruel from King Philip's War, less educated than their fathers, though of like faith, and actually falling backward into a barbarism bred from the wilderness. Add to this the fact that the Puritan mind, in spiritual things at least, was always high-strung, so that its vibrations were likely to be unnaturally acute, and it certainly looks as if no epoch in our history was so provocative of an honest but fierce outburst of fanaticism as the year 1692, when nineteen persons were put to death at Salem for witchcraft.

This is no place to tell the story, only to illustrate it, and narrate Judge Sewall's part in it. In brief, certain children and half-grown women at Salem, aided by a few base persons and an Indian, began the calamity by accusing some other persons — their neighbors, generally — of bewitching them. Their cries, contortions, and physical distresses and general absurdities, if stated, would seem incredible, if not impossible, to any one who had not read the record. Nothing shows like it in our history. The community rose *en masse* to inquire and to decide. It was trial by a mob, only the mob was pious. The accusations were in general, and, with a few exceptions, against respectable people, and finally reached far and wide, touching the best, — magistrates and ministers, or their wives. Then the fierce flame burned itself out, and there were graves, gallows, broken families, ruined fortunes, and misery for generations as a residuum. Here it is only intended by some extracts from the court documents to open the gates for a while upon this untold and untellable tragedy. The preliminary court of inquiry assumed from the start two things, — the honesty of the accusers and the guilt of the accused, as was natural in such a stark delusion, but very poor form in law. Children were accused; a man was charged with bewitching a dog. He barely escaped with his life. They killed the dog, — which was certainly a less expense in judgment than though it had been a cow. It was made a point against the innocence of Giles Corey's wife, one of the accused, that she was seen so often on her knees to God that she certainly must be in the service of the Devil. It was put in argument against Rev. George Burroughs, evidently a patient, sweet, but athletic clergyman, that his feats in running and handling heavy weights were beyond those of mortal man, unless assisted by the Devil. What we should say were proofs of innocence were taken for the contrary. It was a whole community acting as the prosecuting attorney in a court which judged the case against the defendants before it sat, in a court-house become an asylum for almost every one except the innocent, and with no keeper for the insane! The preliminary court of inquiry opened and closed with prayers against the accused, and when any one of the latter, in turn, wished "to go to prayer," as the phrase was, to pray God's help and justice on his side, he was denied. Those who confessed escaped; those who protested innocence were committed without bail. While in jail, awaiting trial, they were generally excommunicated by the churches to which they belonged. The citizens of Gloucester actually shut themselves up in their stockade fort, expecting an attack from the devils in force.

A few extracts from the records of the inferior court may serve to disclose the madness:—

EXAMINATION OF A CHILD WITCH.

Q. How long have you been a witch? Ever since I was six years old. How old are you now? Near eight years old; brother Richard says I shall be eight years old in November next. Who made you a witch? My mother. She made me set my hand to a book. How did you set your hand to it? I touched it with my fingers and the book was red; the paper of it was white. She said she had never seen "the Black Man,"—i.e., the Devil,—but she had touched the book, and so become the Devil's own in Andrew Foster's pasture, and that her mother, cousin, and aunt among others were there.

Q. What did they promise to give you?

A. A black dog. Did the dog ever come to you? No. But you said you saw a cat once—what did that say to you? It said it would tear me in pieces if I would not set my hand to the book. She said further, her mother baptized her, and the Devil or "black man" was not there as she saw, and her mother said when she baptized her, "Thou art mine forever and ever, Amen."

But Martha Currier defended herself with an honest woman's anger. She denied everything in every particular; that she had ever seen or dealt with the Devil, or hurt any one. She said to the magistrates, "It is a shameful thing that you should mind these folks who are out of their wits;" and turning to her accusers, now resting from their fits a little, cried, "You lie! I am wronged." Her courage threw the great crowd into uproar; and the record closes in these words: "The tortures of the afflicted were so great that there was no enduring of it, so that she was ordered away, and to be bound hand and foot with all expedition; the afflicted in the meanwhile, almost killed, to the great trouble of all spectators, magistrates, and others."

The magistrates were told by one of the witnesses, out of court, that the accused confessed to her that "she had been a witch these 40 years."

She also deposed that she afflicted persons by pinching them; that she had no images or "puppets" of these persons by her, but that she went to them, not in her body, but in her spirit, and that her mother carried her to the place of mischief. Being further asked, "How did your mother carry you when she was in prison?" she replied, "She came like a black cat." How did you know it was your mother? The cat told me so; that she was my mother. "The confession" of another infant of this same mother runs thus: Have you been in the Devil's snare? Yes. Is your brother Andrew ensnared by the Devil's snare? Yes. How long has your brother been a witch? Near a month. How long have you been a witch? Not long. She afterwards added to her last answer, "About five weeks." Rather young witches, anyway, this Sarah and Andrew also, and Simon Willard clerk writes of this ghastly nonsense "This is the substance." SIMON WILLARD.

The wife of honest shipmaster Cap. Cary of Charlestown was also accused and May (24) he went down with his Elizabeth to face the danger. They attended Court. "The prisoners Cap. Cary says were placed 7 or 8 feet from the justices and the accusers between the justices and them. The prisoners were ordered to stand right before the justices, with an officer appointed to hold each hand, lest they should therewith afflict them; and the prisoners' eyes must be constantly on the justices; for if they looked on the afflicted they would either fall into fits or cry out of being hurt by them."

Elizabeth Cary was in due form cried out on by two girls in

the court room and on arrest told the judges that she never had any knowledge of them before that day. Now comes, in that old sailor's story, touches of human love and pathos, still sweet and tender in the sympathy of those who after two hundred years read the record. "She was forced to stand with her arms stretched out. I requested that I might hold one of her hands, but it was denied me; then she desired me to wipe the tears from her eyes and the sweat from her face, which I did. Then she desired that she might lean herself on me, saying she should faint. Justice Hathorne replied that she had strength enough to torment these persons and she should have strength enough to stand. I speaking something against their cruel proceedings they commanded me to be silent or else I should be turned out of the room. The Indian, before mentioned, was also brought in to be one of her accusers; being come in he now (when before the justices) fell down and tumbled about like a hog but said nothing." This was a fellow whom just before in the tavern the Captain had treated to some cider and he had made no charge against his wife. "The justices asked the girls who afflicted the Indian; they answered she, meaning my wife. The judges ordered her to touch him in order to his cure, but her head must be turned another way, lest instead of curing she should make him worse by her looking on him, her hand being guided to take hold of his." What followed had better be left in the old records. . . . "I being troubled at their inhuman dealings, uttered a hasty speech That God would take vengeance on them and desired that God would deliver us out of the hands of unmerciful men. Then her *mittimus* was writ. I did with difficulty and charge obtain the liberty of a room, but no beds in it; if there had been," he adds naïvely, "Could have taken but little rest that night." She was committed to Boston prison; but I obtained a *habeas corpus* to remove her to Cambridge prison. Having been there one night the jailer put irons on her legs (having received such a command;) the weight of them was about 8 pounds; these irons and her other afflictions soon brought her into convulsion fits, so that I thought she would have died that night. I sent to entreat that the irons might be taken off but all entreaties were in vain. The trials at Salem coming on I went thither to see how things were managed; and finding that the spectre evidence was there received together with idle if not malicious stories against people's lives I did easily perceive which way the rest would go. I acquainted her with her danger and that if she were carried to Salem to be tried I feared she would never return. I did my utmost that she might have her trial in our own County; I with several others petitioning the judge for it; but I soon saw so much that I understood thereby it was not intended, which put me upon consulting the means of her escape which through the goodness of God was effected. She escaped first to Rhode Island and then as a safer place to New York where Gov. Fletcher was very courteous to us." "They, the accused had trials of cruel mockings, which is the more considering what a people for religion, I mean the profession of it, we have been, those that suffered being many of them church members and most of them unspotted in their conversation till their adversary the Devil took up this method for accusing them." JONATHAN CARY.

By the Provincial Charter of 1691 Sewall had been appointed one of the Council, an office to which he was annually chosen till 1725, when he was re-elected, but declined to serve, having outlived all the other councillors then appointed with him. All through March, 1692, the Salem fury had been gathering head; and on April 11, probably as a magistrate, he went down, in company with the lieutenant-governor and four others, to look into the matter.

"Went to Salem where in the meeting house the persons accused of witchcraft were examined; was a very great assembly; 'twas awful to see how the afflicted persons were agitated. Mr. Noyes prayed at the beginning and Mr. Higginson concluded."

A rather rustic event in the life of a rich man like Sewall, living in Boston, and noted down by him under date of Saturday, Feb. 27, may perhaps illustrate the abnormal excitement of men's minds, and apprehension of coming evil, running close upon a panic, before pointed out: —

"Between 4 and 5 morning we are startled at the roaring of a beast, which I conjectured to be an ox broken loose from a butcher, running along the street, but proved to be our own cow bitten by a dog, so that were forced to kill her; though calved but Jan. 4th and gives plenty of milk. Happy are they who have God for their spring and breast of supplies."

The men who could turn from a cow bit by a dog to God for mercy would be very likely to look out to Him and for Him in so strange a matter as the Salem misery.

There were now nearly one hundred accused persons in jail, and worse threatened. Governor Phipps, on his return from his Eastern expedition, found himself forced, by public opinion, to appoint a special commission of oyer and terminer to try these cases, of which Stoughton was chief-justice, with six associates, including Sewall. This court substantially was the government of the Province, so great was the solemnity thought to be. They were appointed June 13, 1692, and for the counties of Suffolk, Essex, and Middlesex. This court met at Salem in June and August, sending some nineteen persons to death. After the executions of Sept. 22, they adjourned to meet a few weeks later; but they met no more. In January, 1693, the grand jury brought in bills against some fifty persons; but all were acquitted except three, and they were reprieved. None who confessed were brought to trial. May, 1693, Governor Phipps, by proclamation, discharged all those in jail, and the delusion vanished as rapidly as it had spread.

With the exception of an entry April 11, there are no entries in Sewall's Diary for the three months of April, May, and June, when the excitement was at its height. The entries elsewhere in his journal touching this matter are few, and generally very brief. He evidently was ashamed, cast down, full of sorrow, and probably afraid of personal prosecution and loss of property at the hands of the survivors suing for damages. The court he belonged to was no doubt illegal, and its proceedings, as judged by the ethics of English law, more than questionable. From other sources, however, we can gain insight as to how things went on in court. First of all, neither he nor his associates were lawyers nor conversant with right legal procedure; although a high modern legal authority is of opinion that Sewall was the best of his associates. Indeed, as their law based itself on the Jewish Scriptures, ministers, not lawyers, were the best expounders of the same, and the common law of England was at a discount. Therefore lawyers were systematically discountenanced, and orders are not wanting by which they were to be heavily fined if their plea was over an hour in length. The prosecuting attorney at Salem was a lawyer, and the court assisted. There was very much testimony before the court, but very little evidence. One of the rulings of Chief-Justice Stoughton ought to be remembered. He told the jury "that the Devil could not appear in the form of any one who was not in league with him. It followed, therefore, as the Devil had appeared in the form of many of the accused, according to the eye-witnesses there, the defendants must be guilty." But in this Stoughton must have forgotten his Scriptures, which speak of Satan sometimes appearing as "an angel of light." It was a fatal court to every one, though Stoughton stuck to it all his life that right had been done, and resigned his place on the bench rather than even tacitly allow the opposite.

Under date of July 20, Sewall writes: "Fast at the house of Capt. Alden," etc. Alden, the son of the Plymouth Pilgrim, "the tall man in Boston," as his accusers called him, for thirty years a respected member of the South Church, a brave seaman in command of the colony's armed vessels, doing noble service in the French and Indian wars, and seventy years of age, was now in jail for witchcraft. May 31 he had gone down and met his accusers at Salem,—"a group of wenches playing their juggling tricks," as he describes them, who charged him with afflicting, after the manner of witches, people whom he had never seen nor known. The honest indignation and "sea language" which he apparently used upon them did not save him from being sent to Boston jail, where he now was while Sewall, his fellow-parishioner and judge, was holding a fast with

Revs. Cotton Mather and Willard, and a galaxy of Puritan church-members, at the captain's house for the latter's salvation. It is incredible that there should be hypocrisy of this quality on earth. But if we suppose them honest, then their Puritan behavior at Salem must at least have been honest also. After fifteen weeks in jail, Captain Alden escaped to Plymouth Colony, and probably died in his bed.

"July 30. Mrs. Cary makes her escape out of Cambridge prison who was committed for witchcraft." [That lady's story has been told before.]

"Aug. 19. This day George Burroughs, John Willard, Jno Procter, Martha Currier and George Jacobs were executed at Salem, a very great number of spectators being present. Mr. Cotton Mather was there, Mr. Sims, Hale, Noyes and Cheever, [ministers]. All of them said they were innocent, Currier and all. Mr. Mather says they all died by a righteous sentence. Mr. Burroughs by his speech, prayer, protestation of his innocence, did much move unthinking persons which occasions their speaking hardly concerning his being executed."

Most of which is no doubt true, though Cotton Mather is wrong as usual. This day the victims had been hung; men and women, drawn a long way from jail in a big wagon which "stalled" or broke down, over a rough road to the highest hill thereabouts, with its jagged rocks thrust through the thin soil, clad in the gray mosses which grow there ever since, from that eminence overlooking the summer land and sea of their wild Essex, to go asking justice from some One, if there were justice either below or above the stars, and the charity which had been denied them here. They all died stoutly, as Sewall writes. Burroughs had been his friend, and had dined with him years before, as his Diary tells. Stripped of his prison clothes in that death whose majesty the rags they clad him in could not obscure, — uncoffined body flung into the shallow grave the rocky ledge allowed him, on that gallows' plot of shame, — his right arm stiffened until it rotted or dogs tore it, was seen as if pointing to those heavens where "the wicked cease from troubling and the weary are at rest." There are no witches that we know of. But if there were, there is perhaps no spot in all this West where they should be more at home in the weird desolation of their barren and uncanny lives than that same belt of rocky moorland, south of Salem city as it remains to-day; gray, mossy, rock-crested, with its long, narrow glens creeping in among the hills, yet seeming to have gone and going nowhere, down into which the scattered cedars of funeral plumage seem to speer as sentinels on watch for something which they never find — that land at whose west gate two centuries ago Puritan sincerity in a sad mistake built the Witches' Gallows.

"Monday, Sept. 19, 1692. About noon, at Salem Giles Corey was pressed to death for standing mute."

This execution is unique in American annals. By English law, a man might be pressed to death if he refused to plead yea or nay to his indictment. In case of a recalcitrant prisoner, he was brought three times into court and told the penalty. Remaining obstinate, he was then to be laid bound hand and foot on the floor of his prison cell, with heavy iron weights on his body. The first day he was to have three morsels of the worst bread for food, and the second day three draughts of standing water found nearest the prison walls; and so weights were added until he died. Giles Corey had a somewhat unsavory reputation, well or ill earned it is hard to say, and was a downright man in his will, and, when touched, in his heart. When his wife was accused of witchcraft he was first inclined to stand against her; but her piety and sad end brought him to flout the whole business as a wrong. Very naturally he had his turn as an accused wizard. If he pleaded not guilty he knew he was sure to be condemned, and to confess that he was a wizard was not in him. There was a dilemma here. For if he had pleaded and been condemned he expected his property would be confiscated and his heirs impoverished. He made his will in prison, and held his tongue. They pressed him to death, — somewhere, tradition has it, in the rocky fields of the others' doom; and the same tradition reports that in his agony he cried out to put on more rocks, as he would never plead. There is an old saw which says that time has two ages; one in which men of oak build houses of willow, and the other when men of willow build houses of oak. Giles Corey must have been a man of oak, however housed. There was a certain grim thrift which followed the Puritan even in his dealings with accused persons. He insisted that men should pay their own. Those who were released from jail paid their own charges, — for chains, board, and court fees. Many were ruined in consequence; and their descendants, counted now among the most respected, are entitled to cherish their memories.

Sewall cherished his memories thereof. Signs multiplied of a reaction. Oct. 26, 1692, he writes: —

> "A bill is sent in about calling a fast and convocation of ministers that may be led in the right way as to the witchcrafts. The season and manner of doing it is such that the Court of Oyer and Terminer count themselves thereby dismissed, 29 noes and 33 yeas to the bill."
>
> "Dec. 24. Sam recites to me in Latin Math. 12 from the 6th to the end of the 12th. The 7th verse did awfully bring to mind the Salem Tragedy."

That verse is this: "If ye had known what this meaneth, I will have mercy, and not sacrifice, ye would not have condemned the guiltless."

There were those who would have had the Salem court and its abettors pursued and punished for their mistake. How near they were to doing so cannot now be known, nor just why they failed. Their stand was at least stout enough to compel the legislature, in what looks like a penitence somewhat late, to appoint a fast Jan. 14, 1697, for what had been done amiss "in the late tragedy raised among us by Satan and his instruments, through the awful judgment of God." Since witchcraft times, Sewall had lost several little children; and at this fast, like the brave, honest-hearted man he was, he put up the following petition in his own parish meeting-house, "standing up at the reading of it and bowing when finished:" —

"Copy of the bill I put up on the fast day, giving it to Mr. Willard as he passed by, and standing up at the reading of it and bowing when finished; in the afternoon.

"Samuel Sewall, sensible of the reiterated strokes of God upon himself and family and being sensible that as to the guilt contracted upon the opening of the late Commission of Oyer and Terminer at Salem (to which the order of this day relates,) he is upon many accounts, more concerned than any that he knows of, desires to take the blame and shame of it, asking pardon of men and especially desiring prayers that God who has an unlimited authority would pardon that sin and all other, his sins, personal and relative and according to his infinite benignity and sovereignty not visit the sin of him or of any other upon himself or any of his, nor upon the land; but that he would powerfully defend him against all temptations to sin for the future and vouchsafe him the efficacious, saving conduct of his word and Spirit."

What, then, as a study in psychology, was the Salem witchcraft? No one nor a dozen definitions can ever expose all its substances. That it was a true witches' caldron like that which Shakespeare fancies, in the strange mixture bubbling in it, compounded partly out of the base passions of "envy, hatred, and malice," and tinged with human delusions running as low as African Voodooism and Indian superstition, will be allowed by all who have looked into the matter. That the accusers — children, and Puritan children to boot — sometimes lied, showed cunning and deceit, may be also granted. Yet the limitation must be at once applied even to that admission. These very children were growing up in an atmosphere where one who did not believe in witches would be a wonder. Beginning first with some silly pastime of fortune-telling maybe, of an age and sex liable to very acute vibrations of their nervous energy, epileptic to a degree in some one of the many forms that disease assumes, brought into notoriety before a public whose credulity only heightened their physical and mental mania, perhaps growing vain of their recognition by persons in authority, testifying before crowds, and become centres of interest, — was it anything strange if they came to mistake, and even deceive themselves? that what at first in their minds was a spasm of mental aberration came to be thought by themselves to be truth, and truth which involved itself with the machinations of the Devil? If one should say in rebuttal that the accusers were often proved to be liars, the answer is that in insanity itself it is often impossible to say when the patient is or is not a responsible being, and that if these children were in any wise insane, they are not to be set down as mere impostors.

The matter certainly runs deeper. The human mind, in its relation with the body, is to-day, and always has been, the *Terra Incognita*, the "Dark Continent," even to science, as is shown in the phenomena of mesmerism, and what calls itself spiritualism. This mystery is heightened when such complex human creatures are brought together in masses under excitement such as is often seen in revivals. An excited crowd lays its stress on every one composing it, and incites to imitation. Even a mother watching her child's convulsions often finds it hard work to resist the impulse to suffer likewise. Undoubtedly a certain physical and mental atmosphere often aids in the outbreak of some kind of occult mania, such as the Salem witchcraft was. For proof of this we have only to look at certain undoubted historical facts in mediæval times; such, for instance, as the "Dancing Mania,"—a sort of epidemic disorder allied to hysteria, and evidently the result of imitative emotions acting upon susceptible subjects under the influence of a craving for sympathy or notoriety. As to this mania, there is evidence to show that there was much imposture, and also much real convulsive suffering beyond the control of the will. Such convulsions were common in Germany, Italy, and Asia, where the dancing dervishes are still a standing example of what is partly disease. They even exist in religious excitements sometimes now. In July, 1374, at Aix-la-Chapelle, there appeared assemblies of men and women who, made frantic by the wild celebration of St. John's Day, began to dance on the streets, screaming and foaming like persons possessed. This mania varied in form according to mental, local, or religious conditions. The dancers were insensible to external impressions, but had visions of blood, the Saviour, the Virgin Mary, etc., and danced in a wild delirium till they fell from exhaustion, groaning as if in death. Some dashed out their brains against the walls. The mania spread over the Low Countries, and as far south as Strasbourg; wherever the dancers went, many from contagion joining them. It was remarked that this mania spread among people kept on a low diet, or diseased, mentally distressed, and prone to religious excitements, all of which elements inhered, as we have seen, in the Salem misery. The religious rite of exorcism, as then had, proved an efficacious remedy, at least in the beginning of the mania ; and Paracelsus, the great reformer of medicine in the sixteenth century, applied immersion in cold water with great success. A tub of cold water in Salem meeting-house, well used, would have perhaps changed some of the saddest pages in our colonial history. A kindred mania showed itself in 1730 at Paris, where, around the tomb of a certain holy Francis, religious persons "threw themselves into the most violent contortions of body, rolled about on the ground, imitated birds, beasts, and fishes, and at last, when they had completely spent themselves, went off in a swoon." Even the king's order to imprison them did not completely stop the mischief, and in some French country places the mania has shown itself in this century. It is submitted from all this that the key to the Salem mania is here, and that modern science will some day relate it to these mediæval miseries.

From all which, the reasonable conclusion is, that allowing for all the evil which it wrought, and for all the baseness of any or all the originators and chief actors in it, the Salem witchcraft business, when reviewed by the judicial mind, is entitled not so much to blame as pity.

CHAPTER XI.

CURRENT NEW ENGLAND LIFE FROM 1700 TO 1714.

"WEDNS'. Feby. 28, 1700. We ship off the iron chest of gold, pearls &c. 40 bales of East India goods, 13 hogsheads, chests and case, one negro man and an East Indian born at Ceylon. I look upon it as a great mercy of God, that the store house has not been broken up, no fire has happened. Agreed in the weight of gold with our former weight and had so comfortable a day at last to finish our work. Cap. Winn would not give a receipt till he had them on board the sloop Antonio, which rid off just without the Outward Wharf. Gave a receipt for the gold at Cap. Belchar's as soon as it was weighed."

This entry, of course, was about the pirate Robert Kidd's captured treasure, now in Boston, and thus being sent away. For those times, the amount was large, especially of specie. He was arrested in Boston, and £1,000 in gold and a bag of silver were seized at the same time. On information, they sent to Mr. Gardiner of Gardiner's Island in the Sound, and obtained gold, silver, and jewels, left there by Kidd, worth £4,500, and six bales of goods, one valued at £2,000; the total value being about £14,000. Kidd said he had more hid, as he probably had, and if let go at large would recover £50,000 to £60,000, hid by himself, which no one else could recover. He was not let go, for evident reasons, and Kidd was

A New England House, about the year 1700.

hung as a pirate in London. Sewall and the rest show a curious nervousness over the handling and preserving of the property in their hands, possibly from fear that Kidd might have accomplices in Boston, or that some men in high station might interfere surreptitiously, somehow. For Kidd was not a mere vulgar pirate; besides being a sea-captain of ability, he had gone out as a privateer under the patronage of Lord Bellomont, Governor of New York. He was probably executed justly; but it should be remembered that ever since the European nations had sent discoverers and traders to the New World, there was a peculiar state of affairs on the high seas. England, before and after the Spanish Armada, had been often at war with Spain; of late, also, with France and the Dutch. Her merchant ships went armed, and often made more profit by a capture on the way than by sales in a friendly port. England had also encouraged this semi-belligerent commerce, by licensing private adventurers and privateers. These had often been of great national service. It was natural, therefore, that such adventurers, raised in such rough commerce, liable in war times or any other to be pounced upon by the ships of an alien nation, and themselves consigned to a captivity worse than death, should come to have rather dulled consciences when they sighted a ship on the seas, where a stranger, by custom, was nearly always held to be an enemy; and that few were too nice to fill their pockets, if they could do so without risking their necks. Kidd seems to have been a felon, but he was an unlucky one among a great multitude like him, who managed to die in their beds in spite of English law. There was sometimes a crowd of such lawless men on the New England coast. Sewall's Diary shows that armed vessels were sent out after them again and again; and, worst of all, some of the law-breakers seem to have been of New England and Puritan stock.

"The Selling of Joseph," Sewall's anti-slavery tract, was published June 24, 1700. Considering the age, and brutal treatment of blacks by whites current everywhere in the world about him, and that New England then bought and sold slaves to its heart's content, this tract must always stand as a monument to Sewall's foresight and magnanimity of soul. It runs thus: —

"Forasmuch as liberty is in real value next unto life; none ought to part with it themselves, or deprive others of it but upon most mature consideration. The numerousness of slaves at this day in the Province and the uneasiness of them under their slavery hath put many upon thinking whether the foundation of it be firmly and well laid; so as to sustain the vast weight that is built upon it. It is most certain that all men as they are the sons of Adam, are coheirs; and have equal right unto liberty and all other outward comforts of life. God hath given the earth (with all its commodities) unto the sons of Adam. Psalm 115. 16. [He also quotes Acts xvii. 26, 27, 29.] Now although the title given by the last Adam doth infinitely better men's estates, respecting God and themselves; and grants them a most beneficial and unviolable lease under the broad seal of Heaven, who were before only tenants at will; yet through the indulgence of God to our first parents after the fall, the outward estate of all and every of their children remains the same, as to one another. So that originally and naturally there is no such thing as slavery. Joseph was rightfully no more a slave to his brethren than they were to him; and they had no more authority to sell him than they had to slay him. And if they had nothing to do to sell him, the Ishmaelites bargaining with them and paying down twenty pieces of silver could not make a title. Neither could Potiphar have any better interest in him than the Ishmaelites had. Gen. 37. 20, 27, 28. For he that shall in this case plead alteration of property seems to have forfeited a great part of his own claim to humanity. There is no proportion between twenty pieces of silver and liberty. The commodity itself is the claimer. . . . 'Tis pity there should be more caution used in buying a horse or a little lifeless dust (gold) than there is in purchasing men and women; whereas they are the offspring of God and their liberty is '*auro pretiosior omni*' (more precious than gold). And seeing that God hath said 'He that stealeth a man and selleth him, or if he be found in his hand, he shall surely be put to death,' Exod. 21. 16. This law being of everlasting equity, wherein manstealing is ranked amongst the most atrocious of capital crimes, what louder cry can be made of that celebrated warning, '*Caveat emptor!*' (let the buyer beware!).

"And all things considered, it would conduce more to the welfare of the Province to have white servants for a term of years than to have slaves for life. Few can endure to hear of a negro's being made free; and indeed they can seldom use their freedom well; yet their continual aspiring after their forbidden liberty renders them unwilling servants. And there is such a disparity in their conditions, color and hair, that they can never embody with us and grow up into orderly families to the peopling of the land. As many negroes as there are among us, so many empty places are there in our train bands, and the places taken up of men that might make husbands for our daughters. . . . It is likewise most lamentable to think how in taking negroes out of Africa and selling of them here that which God hath joined together men do boldly rend asunder; men from their country, husbands from their wives, parents from their children. How horrible is the uncleanness, mortality if not murder, that the ships are guilty of that bring great crowds of these miserable men and women. Methinks when we are bemoaning the barbarous usage of our friends and kinsfolk in Africa [Sewall refers to Christians taken by the Algerines] it might not be unseasonable to enquire whether we are not culpable in forcing the Africans to become slaves among ourselves. And it may be a question, whether all the benefit received by negro slaves will balance the account of cash laid out upon them and for the redemption of our own enslaved friends out of Africa."

There is much more like, which can be read in the Diary (vol. ii., p. 18). This is remarkable doctrine for the age; and the logic of it made New England one hundred and fifty years later the hotbed of the anti-slavery movement which freed our slaves.

"Jany. 2, 1701. Just about break a day Jacob Amsden and 3 other trumpeters gave a blast with the trumpets on the Common near Mr. Alford's. Then went to the Green Chamber and sounded there till about sunrise. Bell man said these verses a little before break-a-day which I printed and gave them. The trumpeters cost me five pieces $\frac{8}{8}$=."

These verses Sewall calls "My Verses on the New Century," and are here given:—

1

"Once more! Our God vouchsafe to shine:
Tame thou the rigor of our clime.
Make haste with thy impartial light
And terminate this long dark night.

2

Let the transplanted English vine
Spread further still; still call it thine;
Prune it with skill: for yield it can
More fruit to thee the husbandman.

3

Give the poor Indians eyes to see
The light of life; and set them free;

That they religion may profess
Denying all ungodliness.

4

From hard'ned Jews the veil remove,
Let them their martyr'd Jesus love;
And homage unto him afford
Because he is their rightful Lord.

5

So false religions shall decay
And darkness fly before bright day;
So men shall God in Christ adore;
And worship idols vain no more.

6

So Asia and Africa
Europa with America;
All four, in concert joined, shall sing
New songs of praise to Christ our King."

"May 29, 1701. This day a burlesque comes out upon Hull street, in a travestie construing my Latin verses."

"Monday, June 2, 1701. Mr. Pemberton preaches the Artillery Sermon from Luke 3. 14. Dine at Monks. Because of the rain and mist, this day the election is made upon the town house. Sewall Capt ; Tho. Hutchinson Lieut.; Thos. Savage Jr. Ensign, &c.; Col. Pynchon gave the staves and ensign. I said was surprised to see they had mistaken a sorry pruning hook for a military spear; but paid such a deference to the company that would rather run the venture of exposing my own inability than to give any occasion to suspect I slighted their call, &c. Drew out before Mr. Usher's, gave three volleys. Drew into the town house again; sent Sergt Chauncey for Mr. Pemberton who said he was glad to see the staff in my hand; prayed with us. Had the company to my house treated them with bread, beer, wine sillabubs. They ordered Mr. Checkley and me to thank Mr. Pemberton for his sermon, which we did on Tuesday, desiring a copy."

Sewall had long served in other Boston companies. From all which it appears that on this occasion he had been popular and hospitable as usual; had made a judicious witty speech; had listened to a current Puritan sermon; and that, as usual, the Ancient and Honorable Artillery Company had neither gone hungry nor dry.

"Oct. 20, 1701. Mr. Cotton Mather came to Mr. Wilkins' shop and there talked very sharply against me as if I had used his father worse than a neger; spake so loud that people in the street might hear him. Then went and told Sam, that one pleaded much for negroes and he had used his father worse than a negro and told him that was his (Sam's) father. I had read in the morn Mr. Dod's saying 'Sanctified afflictions are good promotions.' I found it now a cordial. 'When my father and my mother forsake me then the Lord taketh me up.' Oct. 22. I with Major Walley and Capt Saml Checkley speak with Mr. Cotton Mather at Mr. Wilkins'. I expostulated with him from 1 Tim. 5. 1. Rebuke not an elder. He said he had considered that. I told him of his book of the Law of Kindness for the Tongue, whether this were correspondent with that. Whether correspondent with Christ's rule. He said having spoken to me before there was no need to speak to me again; and so justified his reviling me behind my back. Charged the council with lying hypocrisy, tricks, and I know not what all. I asked him if it were done with that meekness as it should; answered, yes. Charged the Council in general, and then showed my share, which was my speech in Council viz. If Mr. Mather [Increase, the father] should go again to Cambridge to reside there with a resolution not to read the Scriptures and expound in the Hall, I fear the example of it will do more hurt than his going thither will do good. This speech I owned. Said Mr. Corwin at Reading, upbraided him saying, This is the man you dedicate your books to. I asked him if I should suppose he had done something amiss in his church as an officer, whether it would be well for me to exclaim against him in the street for it. (Mr. Wilkins would fain have had him gone into the inner room but he would not.) I told him I conceived he had done much unbecoming a minister of the Gospel and being called by Maxwell to the Council Major Walley and I went thither, leaving Capt Checkley there.

"Oct. 23. Mr. Increase Mather said at Mr. Wilkins' If I am a servant of Jesus Christ some great judgment will fall on Capt Sewall or his family. Oct. 24. I got Mr. Moody to copy out my speech and gave it to Mr. Wilkins that all might see what was the ground of Mr. Mather's anger. I perceive Mr. Wilkins carried his to Mr. Mather's. They seem to grow calm."

The Mathers were very able men of affairs. Increase Mather had been president of Harvard College, and while in that office, and indeed after, was substantially the head of the Puritan ministers. Nor did he ever knowingly hide his talents in a napkin. The presidency was now vacant, and Increase Mather would go back only on his own terms, which were not acceptable to men like Sewall. One of his conditions were, that he should retain his parish, and reside in Boston; really, that he should do exactly as he pleased in teaching when, where, and so much as he chose. This was evidently bad policy for everybody except him, and it lost him the place. The Mathers had and gave always reasons, such as they were, for their will; but the true reason here was undoubtedly that Increase Mather was unwilling to give up the flatteries and other perquisites of a Boston parish and a residence at the centre of affairs for the seclusion of Cambridge. His son very naturally took his side, and both came to grief accordingly. Yet perhaps no other two men, father and son, have ever exercised a wider or a more mixed influence on New England affairs than they. In the present bitter quarrel, as recorded, Sewall's command of temper and the equities of his position had very much the best of the son.

"Monday, Oct. 6, 1701. Artillery trains in the afternoon. March with the company to the Elms. Go to prayer. March down and shoot at a mark. By far the most missed, as I did for the first. Were much contented with the exercise. I asked their acceptance of a half pike which they very kindly did. They would needs give me a volley in token of their respect on this occasion. The pike will, I suppose, stand me in forty shillings, being headed and shod with silver."

A Latin motto was engraved on it.

"Oct. 28, 1701. Mr. William Atwood takes the oaths &c. to qualify himself to exercise his authority here as Judge of the Admiralty. He asked for a Bible; but Mr. Cook said it was our custom to lift up the hand; then he said no more but used that ceremony. Thus a considerable part of executive authority is now gone out of the hands of New England men."

"IDEM. My wife treats. Boiled pork, beef, fowls: very good roastbeef, turkey pie, tarts."

"Feby. 21, 1702. Cap. Tim° Clark tells me that a line drawn to the Comet strikes just upon Mexico, spake of a revolution there, how great a thing it would be. This blaze had put me much in mind of Mexico. I have long prayed for Mexico and of late in those words that God would open the Mexican fountain."

Sewall was always looking to the conversion of the world, especially of the Roman world, and of course to the conversion of the Spanish colonies to the south of him.

"May 4, 1702. Artillery company trains; rainy day. Marched out and shot at a mark. Before they began I told them that I had called them to shoot in October, and had not myself hit the butt. I was willing to bring myself under a small fine, such as a single Justice might set; and it should be to him who made the best shot. I judged for Ensign Noyes and gave him a silver cup I had engraven; telling him it was in token for the value I had for that virtue in others which I myself could not attain to. Marched into the Common and concluded with prayer."

"May 28, 1702. Buffington from Newfoundland brings prints of the King's death March 8 at 8 M. Queen's speech to her Lords at St James. Then we resolved to proclaim her Majesty here, which was done accordingly below the town house. Regiment drawn up and Life Guard of horse, Council, representatives, ministers, justices, gentlemen taken within the Guard. Mr. Secretary, on foot, read the order of the Council &c. Mr. Sheriff Gookin gave it to the people. Volleys, guns. Went into the chamber to drink &c."

This entry marks the death of King William and the enthronement of Queen Anne, both events affecting the politics and administration of the Province, and that, on the whole, not favorably.

Next comes the new governor.

"June 11. Thursday before I was dressed Sam gave the word that Gov. Joseph Dudley was come. Go with Capt Crofts in his pinnace to meet the Governor and congratulate his arrival. We get aboard a little before he got within Point Alderton. Capt Heron introduced us. After all had saluted the Governor I said, Her Majesty's Council of this Province have commanded us to meet your Excellency and congratulate your safe arrival in the Massachusetts Bay, in quality of our governor; which we do very heartily, not only out of obedience to our masters who sent us, but also of our own accord. The clothes your Excellency sees us wear [they were in court mourning for King William] are a true indication of our inward grief for the departure of King William. Yet we desire to remember with thankfulness the goodness of God, who has at this time peaceably placed Queen Anne upon the throne. And as her Majesty's name imports grace so we trust God will show her Majesty favor; and her Majesty us. And we look upon your Excellency's being sent to us as a very fair first-fruit of it, for which we bless God and Queen Anne."

All of which is no doubt very graceful official courtesy, with the usual modicum of sincerity. Except as it interested the welfare of the Province, it is very doubtful whether Sewall and his associates cared a straw who reigned in England; and Dudley very soon found out of what tough fibre these men were who stood before him, whenever he crossed their policy, as he often did. But in making his bow, Sewall kept his eyes wide open for signs, good or bad, in the governor's surroundings.

"The Lt Governor a stranger sent, whom we knew nor heard anything of before. [Povey, the one referred to, made not a long stay, returning in 1705.] I saw an ancient minister, enquiring who it was, Governor said it was G—— Keith, had converted many in England [to the Church of England, of course] and now Bishop of London had sent him hither with salary of 200 guineas p^{r} annum. I looked on him as Helena [probably Helen of Troy who made so much mischief]. This man [mark the unsavory title] craved a blessing and returned thanks though there was the Chaplain of the ship and another minister on board."

There was also one other significant and distasteful observation that Sewall made:—

"Governor has a very large wigg." "Drink healths; about one and twenty guns fired as we leave the ship and cheers; then Capt Scott and another ship fired. Castle fired many guns; landed at Scarlet's wharf, where the Council and regiment waited for us; just before we came to the North Meeting house, clock strick five. Marched to the town house. There before the court, ministers and as many else as could crowd in the Governor's and Lt Governor's commissions were published; they took their oaths laying their hands on the Bible and after, kissing it. Had a great treat."

There was a Bible here, it will be observed, though the poor king's attorney, Atwood, a short time before, on his oath-taking in Boston full of Bibles, was not granted one. But then, Dudley was nearer the throne, and no man to be trifled with, being of Puritan stock himself.

"Just about dark troops guarded the Governor to Roxbury. He rode in Major Hobby's coach drawn with six horses richly harnessed." "June 28. Governor partakes of the Lord's Supper at Roxbury. In the afternoon goes to Boston to hear Mr. Myles [the Church of England minister at King's Chapel] who inveighed vehemently against schism. June 29. The governor refused to let us give our Yes and No in papers."

This last entry is significant of Dudley. He laid a firm hand on the helm, but under was a crank Puritan ship.

"Oct. 26, 1702. Billerica. Visited languishing Mr. Samo Whiting, I gave him 2 balls of chocolate and a pound of figgs which he very kindly accepted."

"Dec. 30, 1702. I was weighed in Col. Byfield's scales, 193 pounds net. Col. B weighed 63 pounds more than I: had only my close coat on. The Lord add or take away from this our corporeal weight, so as shall be most advantageous for our spiritual growth."

"Feb. 3, 1703. I carried the news to Salem that was brought by Andrew Wilson from Oporto, eight weeks, of the extraordinary success of our fleet against the Flota in the river of Vigg, which we first heard of in part by the way of Cork."

This news was the success of the Dutch and English against the Spanish treasure fleet, the 22d of October, when much booty was had.

"Tuesday, Feby. 16, 1703. 2 P.M. Town meeting at Boston to choose representatives. Mr. Colman prayed. Voters 459. This was the most unanimous election that I remember to have seen in Boston and the most voters."

"March 16, 1703. Though all things look horribly winterly by reason of a great storm of snow, hardly yet over and much on the ground; yet the robins cheerfully utter their notes this morn. So should we patiently and cheerfully sing the praises of God and hope in his mercies though stormed by the last efforts of Anti-Christ."

"April 15, 1703. I heard Mr. Sherman had run a line within mine at Kibbe's. I got Deacon Moss, Thos Holbrook, Ebenezr Leland to go with me; Fairbank was also there. Went to my bounds, asserted them, in the presence of Mr. Lynde's tenants whom I sent for, then ordered Kibbe to pull up the stakes. Told Mr. Lynde's tenants what my bounds were, and that within them was my land; forewarned them of coming there to set any stakes or cut any wood."

"July 5, 1703. Coming home from Cambridge I ordered Mr. Sheriff to take up a scurvy post out of the middle of the highway that had been a nuisance for many years. Gave his son a shilling for his pains."

"Lord's Day, April 23, 1704. There is great firing at the town, ships, Castle upon account of its being the Coronation Day, which gives offence to many, to see the Lord's Day so profaned. Down Sabbath, up St. George."

"June 30, 1704. After dinner, about 3 P.M. went to see the execution. [Pirates.] Many were the people I saw upon Broughton's Hill. But when I came to see how the river was covered with people I was amazed. Some say there were 100 boats. 150 boats and canoes saith Cousin Moody of York. He told them. Mr. Cotton Mather came with Capt Quelch and six others for execution from the prison to Scarlet's wharf, and from thence in the boat to the place of execution. [The place was on the Boston side of the Charles River flats.] Mr. Bridge [a minister] was also there. When the scaffold was hoisted to a due height the seven malefactors went up; Mr. Mather prayed for them standing upon the boat. When the scaffold was let to sink there was such a screech of the women that my wife heard it, sitting in our entry next the orchard and was much surprised at it; yet the wind was S.W. Our house is a full mile from the place."

Once for all, we may remark on the Puritan treatment of criminals condemned to death. The judges often prayed and preached on passing sentence. On Sunday preceding an execution, or at the Thursday Lecture, the doomed culprit, heavily chained, was the subject of direct and special prayer and exhortation, and often of sharp objurgation, in the meeting-house crowded with curious, excited, and morbid spectators. Then followed the public procession, with the dread ministrations of law, through the streets, the criminal being drawn in a cart, with his coffin behind him. Women, shrieking and swooning, mingled in the throng which extended from the foot of the scaffold as far as the wretched spectacle was visible; and a broadside of gallows literature was peddled about. The Boston paper of that date said: "There were sermons preached in their hearing every day. And prayers daily made with them. And they were catechised. And they had many occasional exhortations." If the criminals were hardened men, all this must have been a slow torture, and they would have much preferred to be let alone. This batch of pirates was thought to have died very obdurately and impenitently, hardened in their sin. Captain Quelch, in his dying speech, in a vein of grim humor warned the bystanders to beware "how they brought money into New England to be hanged for it." Some of these were probably of New England stock, and the captain's words may illustrate what has been before said of the sea ethics of privateers and adventurers. This account is mainly from the notes in the Diary, vol. ii., pp. 109, 110, 111.

Sewall's Diary connects him in another way with sea-robbers. He was greatly interested in the fate of New England Christians taken and made slaves by the Mohammedan pirates of the Barbary States. So, apparently, were the public; yet, except in Sewall, slight traces remain of this Christian philanthropy. Joshua Gee was one of these captives who, as the record shows, apparently was ransomed and returned to Boston, where he was a carpenter, and a man in whom Sewall always took an interest.

"I am sorry [he writes] that there is no news of honest Joshua Gee. The Turks' unjust detaining of him I believe helps to add some drops to those vials God is pouring out upon them."

"A friend of mine Mr. Joshua Gee who drank of Algier water and is good after it. He is a good man and has as considerable business as most carpenters in town."

Again he writes: —

"Twould be a very noble undertaking for the English nation for to redeem these miserable slaves; as it seems there is a report of such a thing. I pray you to use suitable applications that if there be any bounty money, ours, i.e. the New England captives, may share in it."

"March 29, 1703. By her Majesty's bounty all the captives are redeemed out of Salle."

Under date of March 29, 1699, there is an interesting record in Sewall's Letter Book of moneys collected for one Thomas Thatcher of Yarmouth, apparently a captive: —

"His relations £50.
Joshua Gee £50.
Hingham £10.
Barnstable £8. 14.
Sandwich £3. 8.
Yarmouth, Eastham Harwich £16. 5.
Judith Thatcher £9. 11.
By a friend 7sh.

From some correspondence over this fund thus raised it would seem as if "poor Thatcher," as Sewall names him, died before delivery.

"Jany. 26, 1705. Mr. Hirst and I went to Brookline to see my little granddaughter Rebecca Sewall. He and I were on horseback. Had some difficulty in going because of some deep descents between banks of snow. But went and came very well. Blessed be God. Feby. 24. Singing of birds is come."

"March 26. Set out for Barker's, a soldier from Deerfield accompanied us with his fusee."

Sewall was now probably going from Weymouth to Plymouth to hold court. The soldier for a guard shows the danger from Indians.

"March 6, 1706. At night a great ship of 370 tuns, building at Salem runs off her blocking and pitches ahead 16 foot. Her deck, not bolted off, falls in and opens at the bows; so that 'twill cost a great deal to bring her right agen; and Capt Dows thinks she will be hundreds of pounds the worse."

"Lord's Day, June 15, 1707. I felt myself dull and heavy and listless as to spiritual good; carnal, lifeless; I sighed to God that he would quicken me." "June 16. My house was broken open in two places, and about twenty pounds worth of plate stolen away, and some linen; my spoon and knife and neckcloth was taken. I said, is not this an answer to prayer? Jane came up and gave us the alarm betime in the morn. I was helped to submit to Christ's stroke and say 'Welcome Christ.'" "June 19. The measuring bason is found with Margaret Barton, just carrying it off to sea, to Hingham; said she had it of James Hews, he gave it her to sell for him. Mr. Secretary sent her to prison." "June 21. Billy Cowell's shop is entered by the chimney and a considerable quantity of plate stolen. I gave him a warrant to the constable, they find James Hews hid in the hay in Cabal's barn, on the back side of the Common; while they was seizing of him under the hay, he stripped off his pocket, which was quickly after found and Cowell's silver in it."

"Sep. 8. [He was now apparently on the South Circuit, Plymouth Colony.] Midweek sentenced a woman that whipped a man to be whipped; said a woman that had lost her modesty was like salt that had lost its savor; good for nothing but to be cast to the dunghill; — seven or eight joined together, called the man out of his bed, guilefully praying him to show them the way; then by help of a negro youth, tore off his clothes and whipped him with rods; to chastise him for carrying it harshly to his wife."

"Oct. The five stone posts are set up in our front. I went to Brookline and chose some apple trees from which my son is to send me apples."

"June, 1708. There was an enquiry by the magistrates as to 'debaucheries at North's, the Exchange tavern.' As the upshot a certain young man is fined 20s for lying; 5s curse; 10s breach of the peace for throwing the pots and scale box at the maid and bound over to keep the peace."

"Lord's Day, Aug. 29, 1708, about 4 P.M. An express brings the news, the doleful news of the surprise of Haverhill by 150

French and Indians. Mr. Rolf and his wife and family slain. About break of day these words run much in my mind, I will smite the Shepherd and the Sheep shall be scattered. What a dreadful scattering is here of poor Haverhill flock upon the very day they used to have their solemn assemblies."

"Decr 7, 1705. Went to Brookline, set out about noon, saw the Governor [Dudley] at his fence who invited me in to dinner, &c. Passed on. After dinner met the Governor upon the plain near Sol Phipps; told me of what happened on the road, being in a great passion; threatened to send those that affronted him to England."

This simple entry in the Diary stands for one of the most singular and perhaps grotesque events put on record by Sewall, which, as illustrating the sturdiness and wilfulness of the old New England stock, is worth recounting. The simple fact was that two farmers, with two carts with wood, refused in a rather narrow and snowy lane to turn out for the governor's chariot as he rode on public business; and so a ludicrous and rather dangerous fracas ensued. The affidavits on both sides have been preserved, and they show that somebody lied or had gone quite daft over the fray. The governor, undoubtedly an exceedingly choleric man, insisted that the queen's justices of her Majesty's Superior Court should make it a case of high treason; which, if assented to, would have put the two farmers in a very awkward position. Dudley swore that while he was taking his journey toward New Hampshire and the Province of Maine, for her Majesty's immediate service there, having dismissed his guards, about a mile from home he met two carts in the road, loaden with wood, the carters, he is since informed, being Winchester and Trowbridge; that his chariot had three sitters and three servants depending, with trunks and portmantles for the journey, drawn by four horses, one very unruly, and he was attended only that instant by Mr. Wm. Dudley, the governor's son; that seeing the carts approach, he directed his son to bid them give him the way, because his chariot was not fit to break the way; that his son told them this; that then the second carter came to the other's help, and one said he would not go out of the way for the governor; whereupon the latter came out of the chariot and bade Winchester give way, who said boldly, simply, "I am as good flesh and blood as you; I will not give way. You may go out of the way." Came towards the governor; that thereupon the latter drew his sword to secure himself and command the road, and went forward, yet without either saying or intending to hurt the carters, or once pointing or passing at them, and again commanded them to give way; that thereupon Winchester answered that he was a Christian, and would not give way, but advanced, and at length laid hold on the governor, and broke the sword in his hand; that very soon after came a justice of peace and sent the carters to prison. Dudley further informed the justices, as an additional and culpable insolence, that they would not give their names nor once pull off their hats. All this he averred on his honor as governor.

The other side swore to a very different story, denying substantially all the governor's averments, and making themselves out very well-behaved and innocent victims of the governor's unreasonable wrath. They claimed that they couldn't turn out; and that all the violence was on the other side. John Winchester swore that Dudley tried to stab his horse and him. "The Governor followed me with his drawn sword, and said, 'Run the dogs through,' and with his naked sword stabbed me in the back; he struck me on the head with his sword, giving me a bloody wound. I then, expecting to be killed dead on the spot, to prevent his Excellency from such a bloody act in the heat of his passion, I catcht hold on his sword and it broke; but in his furious rage he struck me divers blows with the hilt and piece of sword remaining in his hand, wounding me on the hands therewith; while I called on the byestanders to take notice that what I did was in defence of my life. Then the Governor said, 'You lie, you dog; you lie, you divil,' repeating the same words divers times. Then said I such words don't become a Christian; his Excellency replied, 'A Christian, you dog, a Christian, you divil! I was a Christian before you were born.'" Thomas Trowbridge swore that he was stabbed in the hip, and was lashed with his own cartwhip, as Winchester had been just before.

After their affidavits, one wonders that they were not all killed on the spot, or died soon of their wounds in the prison. Yet for aught we know, they died of old age in their bed. But they had good reason to rue this collision with the governor. Their fathers sued for a writ of *habeas corpus*, rather tardily granted. They could procure no counsel, probably because of the Dudley influence. Some would have had £500 and more sureties; but they were finally bound over to the Superior Court in £300 bail and three suretees, each £100. Sewall, whose son had married Dudley's daughter, was put in as a justice, — a rather delicate position in the affair, — but he evidently stood the carters' friend, and writes in his Diary: —

"I am glad that I have been instrumental to open the prison to these two young men, that they might repair to their wives and children and occasions and might have liberty to assemble with God's people on the Lord's Day."

The young men, evidently Puritans in politics, very possibly consoled themselves with the reflection that, after all, they didn't turn out for the governor's chariot. The matter passed in among the clergy and the gentry, and after nigh a year, at a session of the Superior Court, Nov. 5, 1706, four justices being present, "they were discharged by solemn proclamation."

"Novr. 1. Governor Dudley's best horse dies in his pasture at Roxbury as go to Dedham. Governor calls and smokes a pipe with my wife at night." [Hannah Sewall was now ill.]

"Jany. 6, 1709. Presently after Lecture the act of Parliament regulating coin is published by beat of drum and sound of trumpet. In Council a Spaniard's petition is read praying his freedom."

It would appear from the record here that this Spaniard was in peril of being held as a slave on the ground of his olive complexion, all men of that color, his claimant argued, being slaves. The man was probably freed, though no further mention is made of him.

> "April 7. The taking of several vessels laden with provisions on the back of the Cape over against Eastham last Wednesday makes the town very sad."
>
> "May 2. Being Artillery day and Mr. Higginson dead [their agent in London] I put on my mourning rapier; and put a black ribbon into my little cane."
>
> "Nov. 19. Very cold. Have the news of the great battle; Confederates beat the French."

This was the battle Malplaquet won by Marlborough and Prince Eugene over Marshal Villars. Thus the struggle between the Gaul and the Briton for the possession of North America was now proceeding on both continents, and Sewall's Diary makes brief but frequent mention of its epochs.

> "March 27, 1710. [He was now on a journey in Plymouth Colony.] Am much disheartened by the snow on the ground and that which was falling there being a dismal face of winter. Yet the sun breaking out I stood along about 10 M. Everything looked so wild with snow on the ground and trees that was in pain lest I should wander."

Passages like the above are rare in Sewall's Diary. Yet he had a keen vision for what he chooses to look at. He must have seen in those wild ways he travelled many wonderful sun rises and sets; and the spring woods, then as now, must have been full of flowers and beauty. Yet his Diary is bare of any record thereof. Rainbows and lightnings, eclipses of the moon and hailstorms, he knows and respects.

But did he never see the Northern Lights, or the splendid but mighty flower-garden of New England autumn forests, stretching up and along the mountain sides? He gives no mention; and indeed the reasons for the relations of the Puritan mind to what we call, for want of a better name, the Beautiful, despite John Ruskin's attempted explanation, is one of the more recondite of psychological problems.

"April 30. Last night the rudder of Capt Rose's ship was cut. The reason was Capt Belchar's sending of her away laden with wheat in this time when wheat is so dear. May 1. Forty or fifty men get together and seek somebody to head them to hale Capt Rose's ship ashore; but were dissuaded by several sober men to desist, which they did. May 2. This midweek morn Mr. Pemberton stood in his gate and occasioned my going in with him. He spake very warmly against the unlawful assembly; I said such motions ought to be suppressed; the thing should be thoroughly and effectually dealt in. I said 'twas an ill office in Capt Belchar to send away so great a quantity of wheat [about 6,000 bushels, besides bread] in this scarce time. Mr. Pemberton said I cherished those evil seditious motions by saying so. I said he unjustly charged me. He that withholds corn, the people will curse him though I did not affirm that Scripture justified the rioters. I mentioned something of God's people, that though they brought themselves into straits by their own fault yet God pitied and helped them. Mr. Pemberton said with much fierceness they were not God's people but the Devil's people that wanted corn. There was corn to be had; if they had not impoverished themselves by rum they might buy corn. I was stricken with this furious expression."

In all this, Sewall seems to show a clearer head and a warmer heart than his pastor, who appears in the Diary as a rather splenetic and wrong-headed

New England by the Sea.

man, ready to take offence and to blame. After more than a usual bitter taste of his parson's vituperations, Sewall writes: —

"These things made me pray earnestly and with great concern that God would vouchsafe to be my Shepherd and perform what is mentioned in the 23d Psalm, that he would not leave me behind in my stragglings but bring me safely to his Heavenly Fold."

The Puritan parsons had a way of fighting their battles by praying or not praying for the authorities, judges, and the like, according to their pleasure. On the Sunday following the occasion referred to, Sewall notes with regret that his pastor ordered the singing of the first five verses of the Fifty-eighth Psalm.

"I think if I had been in his place and had been kindly and tenderly affectioned I should not have done it at this time. 'Tis certain one may make libels of David's Psalms; and if a person be abused there is no remedy; I desire to leave it to God who can and will judge righteously."

If Tate and Brady's version of that Psalm was sung, this was a sample of what Judge Sewall was obliged to listen to: —

1

"Speak, O ye judges of the earth,
if just your sentence be:
Or must not innocence appeal
to Heaven from your decree?

2

Your wicked hearts and judgments are
alike by malice swayed;
Your griping hands by weighty bribes
to violence betrayed."

And much more, and worse, of the same sort. Is not here, in such clerical conduct, one reason for the decline of power in the Puritan pulpit?

"About 7 or 8 o'clock of the night between the 2d and 3d of October [1711] a dreadful fire happens in Boston; broke out in a little house belonging to Capt Ephraim Savage by reason of the drunkenness of —— Moss. Old meeting house and town house burnt. Old meeting house had stood nearly 70 years. The Lt Governor Taylor arrives. Saw the fire twenty leagues off."

"Oct. 11. Fifth day. Fast. A collection was made for sufferers by the fire; two hundred and sixty odd pounds gathered at the South Church, the oldest meeting house in town."

"Dec. 31. Major Walley has prayer at his house respecting his foot; began between 2 and 3 P.M."

"Feby. 22, 1712. Mr. Pemberton comes to see me and communicates to me the Mock Sermon and mentions my going to Mr. Secretary which I do; but 'twas night before we could concert measures."

This straw shows that the wind was already blowing against the Puritan sermons; for some ribald fellow had made and spoke a scurrilous one before a few of his boon companions, and got bound over to the next court in £50, to stand trial accordingly.

"March 26, 1713. Mr. Saml Danforth visits us in the evening. Has hopes of Mr. Jno. Williams' daughter."

This child of the Deerfield minister was captured and carried to Canada, where she joined the French Church, and married an Indian, taking up the savage life. She lived and died so. By what seems a strange anomaly in these early days, ten whites Indianized to one Indian who became Christian.

"Seventh Day, Feb. 6, 1714. I went to the town house on the occasion of the Queen's birthday. . . . My neighbor Colson knocks at my door about 9 P.M. or past to tell of the disorders at the tavern at the South End in Mr. Addington's house, kept by John Wallis. He desired me that I would accompany Mr. Bromfield and Constable Howell thither. It was 35 minutes past 9 at night before Mr. Bromfield came; then we went. I took Æneas Salter with me. Found much company. They refused to go away. Said were there to drink the Queen's health and they had many other healths to drink. Called for more drink; drank to me; I took notice of the affront, to them. Said must and would stay upon that solemn occasion. Mr. Netmaker drank the Queen's health to me. I told him I drank none; upon that he ceased. Mr. Brinley put on his hat to affront me. I made him take it off. I threatened to send some of them to prison; that did not move them. They said they could but pay their fine and doing that they might stay. I told them if they had not a care they would be guilty of a riot. Mr. Bromfield spake of raising a number of men to quell them and was in some heat, ready to run into the street. But I did not like that. Not having pen and ink I went to take their names with my pencil and not knowing how to spell their names they themselves of their own accord writ them. Mr. Netmaker, reproaching the Province, said they had not made one good law. At last I addressed myself to Mr. Banister. I told him he had been longest an inhabitant and a freeholder, I expected he would set a good example in departing thence. Upon this he invited them to his own house and away they went; and we, after them, went away. I went directly home and found it 25 minutes past 10 at night when I entered my own house."

Judge Sewall's better nature and good judgment shine here. His emotions on this occasion must have been mixed. He himself was a *bon vivant*, knew personally many of these very gentlemanly revellers; and yet they were breaking down the barriers of the ancient Puritanism by such festivity on Saturday night. They and he knew the law, and he enforced it, evidently with patience and good-humor.

The matter was not allowed to rest there. Monday, early, they were all fined five shillings. Many of them paid; some appealed, and gave bonds to prosecute their appeal. Mr. John Netmaker was the private secretary of General Nicholson, commander of her Majesty's forces. He was fined an additional five shillings for profane cursing, which he paid. Next he was bound over and required to give bonds "for contempt of her Majesty's government of this Province, and villifying the same at the house of John Wallis," etc. Finally, Netmaker and his friends lost temper, and refused to give bonds. Sewall and Bromfield promptly sent him to jail. A council was called, and after a long and bitter wrangle the governor, substantially by his own order, released Netmaker, under protest from the two magistrates, who had only executed the laws. But the trouble was that these same laws were unreasonable and unendurable to any but Puritans.

CHAPTER XII.

SEWALL AND THE PURITAN HOME-LIFE.

THE substance of the old New England domestic life was English; the coloring of it was Puritan. The homes of Old England in the seventeenth century were hearty, generous in diet (if regard be had to quantity only), homely, industrious, and full of the love of kindred. Most were religious after a fashion; had their proverbs and superstitions; were narrow, or greatly lacking in interest for almost anything that did not lie close to their narrow circle of existence, and with personal manners which were explicit, if not refined. These conditions were only modified in New England in the emigrant's lot by the inevitable differences from those in the mother land; but the white men here were Englishmen in families. Puritanism quickened and enlarged the mental movements of its votaries, and even the Sunday's sermon and the endless annex of lectures and private meetings quickened and vitalized thought. The Puritan sermons, before the quicker pulse of these new days, may seem endless and barren; but they would never have been listened to by other than keen and intelligent auditors. The story has been already told of the privations of the earlier emigrants; these continued, especially in country places, a long time. Indeed, our climate and soil at the best devote our agricultural people to a narrow and Spartan thrift. It was so in Sewall's day. There was affluence among the few in a few places, but the great body of the people wrought hard in the field. Women drudged for a lifetime at home; girls followed their mother's steps till marriage, and then they doubled their toil, if possible; boys early became of age in their privilege to fare with the hardiest apprentices; and slaves knew no holiday except the Sabbath, when "their works of necessity" multiplied according to the greed or cruelty of their masters, while a day's work by custom lasted as long as the sun, and in winter exceeded his shining. For labor, it was the Iron Age. Of course industry was a prime social virtue. Vagabonds had short shrift; the idle were put out of countenance by the public blame, while "dudes" did not then grow in this soil. No people were ever more busy. In 1655 the court passed a law that "all hands not necessarily employed on other occasions, as women, girls and boys, shall and hereby are enjoyned to spin according to their skill and ability," and that the selectmen overlook and assess the spinning. Each spinner was to spin every year for thirty weeks three pounds a week of linen, cotton, or woollen, under penalty of twelvepence for every pound short. So resolute were the authorities to enforce this law that, by one of its provisions, each town was divided into districts, and an inspector appointed over each, to report any delinquency. There was spinning in Sewall's house, and this domestic trade throve till nigh the middle of this century.

The house appointments of most people were simple, and like to those in Old England. Indeed, except in the matter of religion and its cognate affairs, the Puritan was wont to cultivate the domestic methods of the fatherland. Even casement windows with leaded panes, as in English cottages, were common until the lead was used for Revolutionary bullets, and a new style of American house-building came in. A few strong chairs, a big oak table, chests, pewter plates and platters, a few bedsteads, and a Saxon settle in the chimney-corner, and a brass kettle or two, all in old English fashion, made up the major part of the furniture. They even brought, with great care, English flower and garden seeds, and planted them. The same was true of their orchards, and their farm stock also, although the cows and horses sometimes reached here by the roundabout way of the West Indies.

Indoors, the social life was demure and ascetic, — prayer and work only in abundance. Dancing was out of the question, and cards also; musical instruments were rare, and looked at askance by Puritan prejudice, while as to books at hand, their dulness was hardly outmatched by the dulness of a conversation with a cow. Public balls were forbidden.

In May, 1651, it is ordered: —

"Whereas it is observed that there are many abuses and disorders by dancing in ordinaries [taverns] whether mixed or unmixed, upon marriage of some persons, this Court doth order that henceforward there shall be no dancing upon such occasion, or at other times in ordinaries, upon the pain of five shilling for every person that shall so dance in ordinaries."

Dancing-masters were not in vogue; and when one Stepney was brought over, and found such lions in his way as to make his calling unprofitable, Judge Sewall writes down, apparently with some glee, that the dancing-master had run away in debt.

The fare varied; was usually in plenty, but was never rich. The elders said that brown bread and the gospel were good fare enough for them; and their posterity were never stinted in such nourishments. Sewall's account of his diverse dinners when travelling (and he had the best) shows that substantial, good dining was possible in most places, but luxury was not. Grace said, and the children stood at table while the parents sat, in token of respect, speaking only when spoken to. The dress was also Puritan; ample, simple, and useful. There was a deal of leather worn by the men, and very little silk by the women. The silk-dress of Roger Williams's wife is set down at forty shillings, which, assuming that money was worth five or six times more then than now, would make it a trifle costly. The girls no doubt longed after ribbons, which came late, if at all, and human nature soon found means to bedeck itself in what that age counted fashion. Laws were passed by the court against extravagance in dress.

In October, 1651, "It is therefore ordered by this Court and the authority thereof that no person within this jurisdiction, or any of their relations depending upon them, whose visible estates, real and personal, shall not exceed the true and indifferent value of two hundred pounds, shall wear any gold or silver lace or gold or silver buttons or any bone lace above two shillings per yard or silk hoods or scarfs, upon the penalty of ten shillings for every such offence; and every such delinquent to be presented by the Grand Jury."

As late as 1675, and the distresses of the Indian war, the court seeking for causes why the hand of God lay so heavy on them, make this deliverance: —

"Whereas there is manifest pride openly appearing amongst us in that long hair, like woman's hair, is worn by some men, either their own or other's hair made into periwigs, and by some women wearing borders of hair, and their cutting, curling, and immodest laying out their hair, especially amongst the younger sort, this Court doth declare, this ill custom as offensive to them. The evil of pride in apparel, both for costliness in the poorer sort, and vain new strange fashions both in poor and rich, with naked breasts and arms, or as it were, pinioned with the addition of superstitious ribbons, &c., the County Courts are charged to attend to this grievance."

In the richer circles of Boston, and from a very early date, there is visible a restiveness under these sumptuary laws such as boded ill for their maintenance; and, as a matter of fact, they slowly fell into disuse, and a few went down at once before the fashion as it was had the other side of the water. There was a great strife over periwigs, and Sewall nearly all his life was in a rage against them, as his Diary shows. Uncouth as the fashion seems to us, it was affected by the gentility of those days, and even Puritan laws were not strong enough to keep them off men's heads. Sewall, in his baldness and cold rooms, wore a velvet cap; and one reason why his courtship of Madam Winthrop came to naught, was that he would not promise her to wear a wig. The Puritans often remind one of a grist-mill, where, when there is no other grist to grind, the upper and nether millstones grind one another.

This is the way Sewall goes for a young parson in his favorite foray against periwigs:—

"Tuesday, June 10, 1701. Having last night heard that Josiah Willard had cut off his hair (a very full head of hair) and put on a wig I went to him this morning. Told his mother what I came about and she called him. I enquired of him what extremity had forced him to put off his own hair and put on a wig? He answered none at all. But said that his hair was straight and that it parted behind. Seemed to argue that men might as well shave their hair off their head as off their face. [Sewall himself wore no beard.] I answered men were men before they had hair on their faces, half of mankind have never any. God seems to have ordained our hair as a test, to see whether we can bring our minds to be content to be at his finding; or whether we would be our own Carvers, Lords, and come no more at him. Your calling is to teach men self denial. 'Twill be displeasing and burdensome to good men; and they that care not what men think of them care not what God thinks of them. Allow me so far to be a *censor morum* for this end of the town. Prayed him to read the tenth chapter of the third book of Calvin's *Institutions*. [The subject of this chapter is, "How One Ought to Use the Present Life and Its Aids."] Told him that it was condemned by a meeting of ministers at Northampton in Mr. Stoddard's house, when the said Josiah was there. Told him of the solemnity of the Covenant which he and I had lately entered into, which put me upon discoursing to him. He seemed to say would leave off his wig when his hair was grown. I spake to his father of it a day or two after.

He thanked me and told me when his hair was grown to cover his ears he promised to leave off his wig. If he had known it would have forbidden him. His mother heard him talk of it; but was afraid positively to forbid him lest he should do it and so be more faulty."

Here is poor parson Josiah Willard and his periwig again: —

"Nov. 30. I spent this Sabbath at Mr. Colman's, partly out of dislike to Mr. Josiah Willard's cutting off his hair and wearing a wig. He that contemns the law of nature is not fit to be a publisher of the law of grace. Partly to give an example of my holding Communion with that Church who renounce the Cross in baptism, human holydays &c. as other New-English churches do. I perceive by several, that Mr. Colman's people were much gratified by my giving them my company. Several considerable persons expressed themselves so. The Lord cleanse me from all my iniquity."

Sewall does not exactly shine in these passages, either as a student of history or as a large-minded man. Wigs he undoubtedly hated to the end, and loved those who hated with him. But he might have read how that that same mediæval church which could force a German emperor on his knees in the snow as a penitent, miserably failed when it undertook to deal with the women's headdresses of that era; and, besides, he stood against the fashion, which is apt to be a blunder in a public man careful of his popularity, as Sewall was. The wigs throve in spite of his misery, until fashion bade them disappear. Yet Sewall held out against fate, and hated the Devil and periwigs all his days. Even Madam

Winthrop, in the very heyday of his winter love, could not persuade him to wear one. He told her: —

"As to a periwig, my best and greatest friend, I could not possibly have a greater, began to find me with hair before I was born and had continued to do so ever since; and I could not find it in my heart to go to another."

There was, indeed, a certain sweetness, perhaps one should fairly say much sweetness, in the family circle, though it must be confessed by the candid student of those times that it was very often the sweetness of violets on the edge of an April snow-drift. There was also a stately courtesy among the best, veiling often a very tender regard, which was yet tough enough to reach beyond the grave. This Sewall shows in his frequent lamentations for his fallen friends: —

"July 4, 1701. The Court understanding the Lt Governor's growing illness [Stoughton] were loath to press him with business and sent Mr. Secretary, Mr. Speaker and Mr. White to discourse his honor and propound an adjournment. He agreed to it very freely. I said the Court was afflicted with a sense of his honor's indisposition; at which he raised himself up on his couch. When coming away, he reached out his hand; I gave him mine and kissed his. He said before, 'Pray for me.' This was the last time I ever saw his honor."

Here we observe a high ritual of friendship and respect, coupled with a free use of titles. Yet Sewall seldom gives the title of "reverend" to a minister, and objected stoutly to the sign of the cross in baptism. In such unintended ways he many times shows the radical antagonism of Puritanism to the

Joseph Sewall,
(son)
A Pastor of the Old South Church.

old church ways, and that the root of the coming to New England was to have a free church and a state for that church.

"July 15. Funeral day of Lt Governor."

Sewall's own domestic life must have been one of the most charming expressions of Puritan housekeeping. He was from the start rich, and with a tender heart he brought up his children with a gentle but, if necessary, an unsparing hand. Here is a case in point: —

"Nov. 6, 1692. Joseph threw a knob of brass and hit his sister Betty on the forehead so as to make it bleed and swell; upon which and for playing at prayer time and eating when return thanks I whipped him pretty smartly. When I first went in (called by his grandmother) he sought to shadow and hide himself from me behind the head of the cradle; which gave me the sorrowful remembrance of Adam's carriage."

His wife (*née* Hannah Hull) must have been a gracious and stately matron, busy, like Martha, about the many things of a large family. Sewall often refers to her in his Diary, and after her death utters this plaintive cry in a letter to his friend, "I have lost a most constant lover and a most laborious nurse for 42 years together."

Only one letter of hers is extant, and that was written to her cousin in Bermuda, who had evidently tried to send her a present of some sort, which had been confiscated by some one of that horde of petty thieves which the Puritan shipmasters of those days knew so well, before it reached Hannah Sewall's hands.

The letter follows:—

HANNAH SEWALL TO LOVE FOWLE.

BOSTON, N.E., *July* 25, 1686.

GOOD COUSIN;

My husband wrote to Mr. Fowle the 28 of May last after which, viz. on June the 10, I received your kind letter dated the 4th of May upon which I made enquiry after the loving token you sent me, and the account I had was that they were half stolen before they came on board and the rest delivered to Mr. Prout, who told us he received so few, would but in a manner pay the freight, and knew not but they were for himself, and had eaten them up or near eaten them. I am sorry for the frustration of your intended kindness to me; but your desire is kindness and that I have received and gratefully accepted and would entreat you to prevent the inconvenience of being so deceived for the future, by forbearing to give yourself the trouble of sending. . . .

I am glad to hear of God's blessing you with children. I buried two sons lately. . . . I have one son and two daughters living. The Lord do me good by his various ways of Providence towards me. My service to yourself and Mr. Fowle, with my husband's, I take leave, who am your loving, obliged cousin

HANNAH SEWALL.

The Puritan respect for parents, and their social relations, are vividly expressed in Sewall's Diary, where he tells of his parents' death:—

"May 14, 1700. Get to Newbury a little before sunset, visit my sick father in bed, call in the Major General whom father salutes. Kissed my hand and I, his, again. Mr. Tappan came in and prayed with him and us." "May 15. Walks into the west end of the house with his staff, breakfasts there. I read the 17th Luke and went to prayer. My father would have stood

Newbury.

up, but I persuaded him to sit still in his chair. Took leave and went on to Portsmouth." [He was now on circuit and in a press of legal business.] "May 17. Benj. Moss Jr. is sent to acquaint me that my dear father died the evening before. It rains hard. Holds up about 5 P.M. I ride to Hampton [from Portsmouth] lodge at Mr. Cotton's where am very kindly entertained. May 18. Ride to Newbury in the rain. Bury my father. Sabbath, May 19. Mr. Tappan in the afternoon preached a funeral sermon from Prov. 19. 20. Said my father was a true Nathaniel [i.e., a man in whom there was no guile.] It seems about a fortnight before, upon discourse of going to meeting my father said he could not go, but hoped to go shortly to a Greater Assembly. The Lord pardon all my sins of omission and commission towards him and help me to prepare to die. Accept of any little labor of love towards my dear parents. I had just sent four pounds of raisins, which with the canary were very refreshing to him. Worthy Mr. Hale of Beverly [he also had a hand in the Salem witchcraft business] was buried the day before my father. So was Mr. John Wadsworth of Duxbury who died May 15th 1700. I used to be much refreshed with his company when I went to Plymouth; and was so this last time."

"Jany. 14, 1701. Having been certified last night about 10 o'clock of the death of my dear mother at Newbury, Sam and I set out with John Sewall, the messenger, for that place. Hired horses at Charlestown; set out about 10 o'clock in a great fog. I followed the bier single. Went about 4 P.M. Nathl. Bricket taking in hand to fill the grave I said Forbear a little and suffer me to say that amidst our bereaving sorrows we have the comfort of beholding this saint put into the rightful possession of that happiness, of living desired and dying lamented. She lived commendably four and fifty years with her dear husband and my dear father. And she could not well brook the being divided from him at her death; which is the cause of our taking leave of her in this place. She was a true and constant lover of God's word, worship and saints; and she always with a patient cheerfulness submitted to the divine decree of providing bread for herself and others in the sweat of her brows. And now her infinitely gracious and bountiful master has promoted her to the honor of higher employments, fully and absolutely discharged from all manner of toil and sweat. My honored and beloved friends and neighbors! My dear mother never thought much of doing the most frequent and homely offices of love for me; and lavished away many thousands of words upon me before I could return one word in answer; and therefore I ask and hope that none will be offended that I have now ventured to speak one word in her behalf; when she herself is become speechless. Made a motion with my hand for the filling of the grave. Note, I could hardly speak for passion and tears. Mr. Tappan prayed with us in the evening. Jan. 16. The two brothers and four sisters being together, we took leave by singing of the 90 Psalm from the 8th to the 15th verse inclusively."

"My mother being dead [he writes], almost all my memory is dead with her."

In his letter to Governor Dudley (Aug. 10, 1702), speaking of his sister's (Mrs. Moodey) death, at Newbury, his Puritan quality of mind shows more distinctly: —

"She lived desired and dies lamented by her neighbors. Certainly I have lost a noble spring of love and respect. Though she was a very ingenuous, tender hearted, pious creature; yet but a little crazy cistern and the breaking of it so soon (37 years 3 mo.) is a rebuke directing me to the *Fountain* of living waters. I ask your Excellency's pardon that I have wept these tears in your presence. Griefs disclosed, divide.

I am your Excellency's most humble Serv[t].

S. S.

When his sister Hannah Tappan dies, in 1699, he writes: —

"We have lived, eight of us together, thirty years and were wont to speak of it (it may be too vainly). But now God begins to part us apace. Two are taken away in about a quarter of a year's time. And methinks, now my dear brother and sister are laid in the grave I am as it were laid there in proxy. The Lord help me to carry it more suitably, more fruitfully, toward the five remaining; and put me in a preparedness for my own dissolution. And help me to live upon him alone."

As a close to these memorials of Puritan family affection, this picture of the last days of the Apostle Eliot may be added. Three years before his death, his wife died, in 1687. As he stood by her coffin, with tears streaming down his old face, he said, "Here lies my dear, faithful, pious, prudent, prayerful wife. I shall go to her, but she shall not return to me." He sat waiting for death. When Minister Watton visited him, he said, "Brother, you are welcome; but retire to your study and pray that I may be gone." He said, "My memory, my utterance, fail me, but I thank God my charity holds out." His last words were, "Welcome joy!"

Here are some letters of the Winthrops which show the Puritan social life in some of its best aspects: —

Letter of John Winthrop to His Sister.

My Good Sister;

I have been too long silent to you, considering mine own consciousness of that great debt which I owe you for your love and much kindness to me and mine. . . .

I partake with you in that affliction [her husband's last sickness] which it pleaseth the Lord to still exercise you and my good brother in. I know God hath so fitted and disposed your mind to bear troubles, as your friends may take the less care for you in them. He shews you more love, in enabling you to bear them comfortably, than you could apprehend in the freedom from them. Go on cheerfully, my good sister, let experience add more confidence still to your patience. Peace shall come

There will be a bed to rest in, large and easy enough for you both. It is preparing in the lodging appointed for you in your Father's house. He that vouchsafeth to wipe the sweat from his disciples' feet will not disdain to wipe the tears from those tender affectionate eyes. Because you have been one of his mourners in the house of tribulation you shall drink of the cup of joy and be clothed with the garment of gladness in the Kingdom of his glory. The former things, and evil will soon be passed; but the good to come shall neither end nor change. Never man saw heaven but would have passed through hell to come at it.

Your loving brother,

Jo. Winthrop.

March 25, 1628.

In the absence of his son John, a student at Trinity College, Dublin, John Winthrop writes: —

[1623.] "We all think long to see you, and, it is like, myself shall (if it please God) go over to you, before I shall be willing you should take so great a journey and be so long withdrawn from your happy studies to come to us. It satisfieth me to know you are well and can want nothing and that (I believe) God blesses you. I shall continue to pray for you and will not be wanting, to my power to further your good in everything, and know this, that no distance of place or length of absence, can abate the affection of a loving father towards a dutiful well deserving child. . : . And so in haste I end; and beseeching daily the Lord Jesus Christ to be with thee and bless thee I rest

"Your loving father

"Jo. Winthrop."

There spoke a right royal gentleman!

To the same son, gone on some naval enterprise in the king's fleet, Winthrop writes: —

[1627.] "Only be careful to seek the Lord in the first place and with all earnestness, as he who is only able to keep you in all perils and give you favor in the sight of those, who may be instruments of your welfare; and account it a great point of wisdom, to keep diligent watch over yourself that you may neither be infected by the evil conversation of any that you may be forced to converse with, neither that your own speech and behavior be any just occasion to hurt or ensnare you. Be not rash, upon ostentation of valor, to adventure yourself to unnecessary dangers; but if you be lawfully called, let it appear that you hold your life for him who gave it you and will preserve it unto the farthest period of his own holy decree. For you may be resolved, that while you keep in your way, all the cannons and enemies in the world shall not be able to shorten your days one minute. For my part, as a father, who desires your welfare as mine own, I cease not daily to commend you to God, beseeching him to preserve, prosper and bless you, that I may receive you again in peace and have assurance of enjoying you in a better life when your course here shall be finished."

He writes to his son Henry (1628), who later was drowned in Salem Harbor, and who appears to have been a son very much needing guidance: —

"It is my daily care to commend you to the Lord that he would please to put his true fear in your heart and the faith of the Lord Jesus Christ, that you may be saved and that your ways may be pleasing in his sight. I wish also your outward prosperity, so far as may be for your good."

MARGARET WINTHROP'S LETTER TO HER HUSBAND.

MY MOST SWEET HUSBAND;

How dearly welcome thy kind letter was to me I am not able to express. The sweetness of it did much refresh me. What can be more pleasing to a wife than to hear of the welfare of her best beloved and how he is pleased with her poor endeavors! I blush to hear myself commended, knowing my own wants. But it is your love that conceives the best and makes all things seem better than they are. I wish that I may be always pleasing to thee and that those comforts we have in each other may daily be increased, as far as they be pleasing to God. I will use that speech to thee, that Abigail did to David, 'I will be a servant to wash the feet of my lord.' I will do any service wherein I may please my good husband. I confess I cannot do enough for thee; but thou art pleased to accept the will for the deed and rest contented.

I have many reasons to make me love thee whereof I will name two; First because thou lovest God; and secondly because that thou lovest me. If these two were wanting, all the rest would be eclipsed. But I must leave this discourse and go about my household affairs. I am a bad housewife to be so long from them; but I must needs borrow a little time to talk with thee, my sweetheart. The term is more than half done. I hope thy business draws to an end. It will be but two or three weeks before I see thee, though they be long ones. God will bring us together in his good time; for which time I shall pray.

I thank the Lord we are all in health. We are very glad to hear so good news of our son Henry. The Lord make us thankful for all his mercies to us and ours. And thus with my mother's and my own best love to yourself and all the rest I shall leave scribbling. The weather being cold makes me make haste. Farewell my good husband; the Lord keep thee.

Your obedient wife

MARGARET WINTHROP.

GROTON, Nov. 22, 1628.

SAMUEL WINTHROP TO HIS FATHER.

TENERIFFE, April 5, 1646.

HONORED FATHER. *Sir:* By Mr. Peter Bickford, by way of the Barbadoes I presented you my duties and tidings of my health and welfare which God is pleased to continue unto me even at this present time, blessed be his name for it. This conveyance is in like manner by the Barbadoes, by Cap. Peter Strong which the remembrance of my duty and near alliance would not suffer me to pretermit without expressing my filial obedience and craving your paternal blessing upon me your unworthy son, who hopes it is not in anger but in judgment and mercy that God hath distanced not only from kindred and father's house but also from the precious means of grace, which God knows, to my helpless grief, I am deprived of which though sore at the present yet I hope will prove sweet in the end and a tedious absence now will produce a more convenient presence for the enjoyment of them hereafter. Concerning the outward man, here is as great a likelihood for the raising my outward estate as in any place, considering the troubles of this age and that with a little stock which I trust God will provide for me by some means or other in his due time. The gentlemen with whom I reside are very loving unto me and seem desirous of my company which my present resolution is to grant and your pleasure manifested to the purpose shall confirm. In the mean time I request your prayers to God for me that he may help me so to demean myself in the time of my stay that I may do what may be pleasing to himself and to those to whom I do belong. What spare time I have, which in the summer time is indifferent, I spend in reading God's word and in other good studies so that the theory of my learning may not be diminished, however the practice be lost. I submissively crave your blessing and prayers, desire the prolonging of your many comfortable years and desist. Your obedient son,

SAMUEL WINTHROP.

One often meets in Sewall and other Puritan authors references and glances at some of the old-time domestic tragedies now stilled in the grave of time, which repeat themselves so long as men mismate and husband and wife repent at leisure. For instance, there is Mrs. Usher. Sewall was her business agent, and his Diary refers to her. She was the daughter of that Lady Alice Lisle who was tried before Jeffreys and beheaded for alleged complicity in the Duke of Monmouth's rebellion, 1685. Her husband was the legal adviser of the High Court of Justice which condemned Charles I. and perished by assassination at Lausanne, a refugee. Her daughter Bridget became the wife of Dr. Hoar, the third president of Harvard College. After his death she married (1676) Mr. Hezekiah Usher, a Boston merchant. Her story is not told, but Mr. Usher's is, in this extract from his will: —

"In the first place I desire that all my due debts should be paid as soon as possibly may be, and unto my dear wife whom I may count very dear by her love to what I had but not a real love to me who should accounted it more worth than any other outward enjoyment; and for her covetousness and overreaching and cunning impression that has almost ruinated me by a gentle behavior, having only words but as sharp swords to me, whose cunning is to be like an angel of light to others but wanting love and charity to me and like Sir Edmund [Andros] to oppress the people and his hand not to be seen in it and done by his Council.

"And therefore I do cut her off from the benefit of all my estate and do not bestow anything upon her but what the law doth allow. Because I look upon her as deceivable in going over for England, getting and grasping all her estate to be in her hand and of mine whatever was done for her by me to be ungrateful; and her staying away to be an implicit divorce and gives it into the hands of women to usurp the power out of the hands of their husbands, rather than in a way of humility to seek their husband's good. If they can live comfortably abroad without them they regard not the troubles or temptations of their husbands at home and so become separate; which is far worse than the doctrine of devils which forbid to marry. . . . And this my will I make to be a warning to those women who have no love for their husbands but to what they have; which one had better had a wife that had not been worth a groat than to have one that hath no love for him."

He furthermore directs that all his papers writ on bad wives such as he has met, be overlooked and

GRAVESTONE OF SEWALL'S FATHER AND MOTHER.

edited by some judicious person, "one that is for men to rule in their own house, that it may be a matter of benefit to some that may follow after me;" and that the editor shall have £30 or £40 for his trouble.

The conclusion of these two lives was that he died (1697) when she was abroad, and on her return she lived single until her demise in 1723.

She directed by her will that she should be buried in her first husband's (Dr. Hoar) grave at Braintree, which was at least the expression of her hope that in the Judgment Day she should not rise very near to Mr. Usher. The latter's "papers" have never been edited.

CHAPTER XIII.

BETTY SEWALL AND PURITAN MARRIAGES.

UPON occasion, Judge Sewall makes this entry : —

"Pray for good matches for my children as they grow up; that they may be equally yoked."

It was the Puritan habit to marry, not once, but several times, if death came to separate. It was not reputable not to marry; and as the human instincts agreed with custom, there was much marrying in the Puritan commonwealth. Instances of old maids and bachelors, especially the latter, were rare; though Sewall's eldest daughter, Hannah, died in middle age unmarried, a life-long invalid, in her father's house. The custom was held to be derived from the explicit directions of Scripture, and was for these several reasons well observed. In a matter of so much importance, strict laws were passed and enforced; and very careful and sensible laws they were. It was made law in 1641: —

"If any person shall wilfully and unreasonably deny any child timely or convenient marriage or shall exercise any unnatural severity towards them; such children shall have liberty to complain to authority for redress in such cases."

It was ordered in 1646 that no orphan, during her minority, should be given in marriage by any one except with the approbation of the major part of the selectmen of the town where the party resided. It was ordered in 1639 that no person shall be joined in marriage before the intention of both parties has been three times published at some public lecture or town meeting, in both towns where the parties reside, or be set up in writing upon some post of their meeting-house door in public view, there to stand, so as it may easily be read by the space of fourteen days. The publishing of marriages on the meeting-house door continued into the present generation. The laws also required a strict registry of marriages, births, and deaths.

In 1647 a very important law with a preamble, concerning marriages, was passed: —

"And whereas God hath committed the care and power into the hands of parents for the disposing of their children in marriage, so that it is against rule to seek to draw away the affections of young maidens, under pretence of purpose of marriage, before their parents have given way and allowance in that respect; And whereas it is a common practice in diverse places, for young men irregularly and disorderly to watch all advantages for their evil purposes, to insinuate into the affections of young maidens, by coming to them in places and seasons unknown to their parents for such ends, whereby much evil hath grown amongst us, to the dishonor of God and damage of parties; For prevention whereof for time to come; It is further Ordered, That whatsoever person from henceforth, shall endeavor directly or indirectly, to draw away the affection of any maid in this jurisdiction under pretence of marriage, before he hath obtained liberty and allowance from her parents or governors (or in absence of such) of the nearest magistrate, he shall forfeit for the first offence £5; for the second towards the party £10 and be bound to forbear any further attempt and proceedings in that unlawful design; And for the third offence he shall be committed to prison and upon hearing and conviction by the next Court shall be adjudged to continue in prison until the Court of Assistants shall see cause to release him."

Sewall himself always pays great respect to this law in managing matrimonial affairs for his children and others; and undoubtedly it was a law of good effect, however much it might sometimes interfere with the raw or senseless imaginings of lovers and idle youth above described. It seems to have been the custom for the elders intending a match, especially on the man's side, to send a suitable present to the lady's parents, as a preliminary to his approaches. If the match was to be refused, the present was probably returned. This custom perhaps explains a rather blind letter of Sewall's, with no address, but dated: —

BOSTON, Jan. 13, 1701.

MADAM;

The inclosed piece of silver, by its bowing, humble form bespeaks your favor for a certain young man in town. The name (Real) the motto (*Plus ultra*) seem to plead its suitableness for a present of this nature. Neither need you accept against the quantity; for you have the mends in your own hands; and by your generous acceptance you may make both it and the giver great. Madam I am

Your affect friend

S. S

It was also ordered, in 1646, that no one should be married by any one except a magistrate or one appointed by the authorities. This law was due to the reaction against the Church of England, where the clergyman always marries; and some still regard the rite as a sacrament. However, this law must have soon fallen into disuse; for we find in Sewall's time that marriage was solemnized by the minister Yet under this law, as Winthrop tells us (Journal II., 43), Governor Richard Bellingham, the last survivor of the patentees named in the charter, performed a marriage service for himself and his new bride: —

"His last wife was ready to be contracted to a friend of his who lodged in his house and by his consent had proceeded so far with her when on the sudden the Governor treated with her and obtained her for himself. He was fifty and the lady twenty and Bellingham also solemnized the marriage himself."

An event such as this, and others like, scattered not plentifully through the Puritan annals, remind us that the Puritan in his love affairs could be as remorseless and as enterprising as when smiting at a Cavalier with his long sword, or hunting an Indian trail with a tribe of savages hid somewhere in the wild before his handful of white men. We may assume, in history, that in all those vital affairs, of which lovemaking is by no means the least, mankind constitutes one brotherhood. The ashes of all Puritan lovers are cold enough, but Sewall's Diary shows the blood to have been very warm which throbbed under Puritan bodice and doublet. Nor is evidence altogether lacking in Sewall's Diary that the Hester Prynne of Hawthorne's "Scarlet Letter" must have had her kin at hand, — cousins at least in blood.

Cold and stern, on a surface congested by most forbidding social customs, our fore fathers and mothers loved mightily as they wrought. The fine ladies of our old Boston life, as we see them in their portraits, seem to wear a veil of reserve thicker than those of their sisters of the East, and to seclude themselves from the ordinary weaknesses and passions of us mortals. But the eyes look straight and open, the head sets firm and steady, and it is often a sweet mouth that might easily vibrate with almost boundless contempt or anger, or grow set and pale in a crisis; and altogether they impress us as women of large reserved powers, — as many show themselves to be, — worthy mothers of a stalwart and able race.

Comedy and tragedy mix themselves in men's love affairs as in no other. Here is a bit of comedy worthy Hogarth, from an early entry in Sewall's Diary: —

"Saturday Even, Aug. 12, 1676. Just as prayer ended Tim Dwight sank down in a swoon and for a good space was as if he perceived not what was done unto him; after kicked and sprawled, knocking his hands and feet upon the floor like a distracted man. Was carried pick pack to bed, there his clothes pulled off. The Sabbath following, Father went to him, asked if he would be prayed for and for what he would desire his friends to pray. He answered for more sight of sin and God's healing grace. I asked him, being alone with him whether his troubles were from outward cause or spiritual. He answered, spiritual. I asked why then he could not tell it his master, since it is the honor of any man to see sin and be sorry for it. He gave no answer as I remember. Asked him if he would go to meeting. He said 'twas in vain for him; 'his day was out.' I asked what day; he answered 'of Grace.' Notwithstanding all this semblance (and much more than is written) of compunction for sin, 'tis to be feared that his trouble arose from a maid whom he passionately loved; for that when Mr. Dwight and his master had agreed to let him go to her he eftsoons grew well."

A happy recovery to Master Tim out of all his troubles!

There was one question concerning marriages which very acutely vexed the Puritan, especially as the profoundest of human passions was often arrayed against public opinion. The matter is stated by this extract from the colony laws (1679): —

"In answer to the question, Whether it be lawful for a man who hath buried his first wife to marry with her that was his first wife's natural sister, The Court resolves it on the negative."

The following letter of Sewall puts plainly the Puritan verdict on this point; especially their aversion, founded, as they thought, on the Mosaic Law, to marriages of too near blood: —

TO COUSIN JOHN SEWALL, at Newbury, Feb. 23, 1703.

You tell me you have been advised to marry the widow of your cousin German. You say you have thought it not so near as second cousins by blood. In this you are plainly mistaken, for it is by casuists laid down as a rule in these cases, that degrees of consanguinity and affinity do equally affect marriage. For my own part it is not plain to me that it is lawful for first cousins to marry. I rather incline to think it is unlawful. . . . Learned men and councils have been against these kind of matches; yet because you ask my advice, I will not refrain to give it. Do that which is safe, which is most safe, in a matter of the greatest importance. Be sure you have the license of Heaven to produce. If one were to purchase a hundred acres of land to build and plant on; one would choose to have an undoubted and undefamed right to it; and not venture the perplexity and disappointment of a crazy title. Much more ought a man to be concerned, to choose such a woman to be his wife to whom he may have a good, clear, indisputable title without the least flaw or appearance of it. Do that which is honorable and of good report. (Phil. iv. 8, 9.) Marriage is honorable. James Printer told me the Indians call cousin Germans, brothers, as the Jews did. And he told me the Indians seldom marry so near. 'Tis pity that any English Christian should need to be put to an Indian school to learn the practice of temperance and sobriety. The generality of good people use to be displeased and grieved at these matches; and ordinarily that which grieves the Saints grieves the Holy Spirit of God. . . .

Your loving uncle,

S. S.

Elizabeth, or "Betty" Sewall as her father calls her, was his fourth child, and was born Dec. 29, 1681. Her religious experience has already been given. So far as is known to us, there is no portrait of her extant, and only such personal history as is writ by the father, of whom she seems to have been a favorite child. But in the absence of all such testimony, and from the glimpses we get of her, we imagine her to have been a demure, fresh-colored, shapely maiden, with the Saxon look the father has; not averse to beaus, but very careful whom and how she entertains; a trifle inconstant and unsteady about her heart, but, withal, as wholesome, fresh-natured, and by blood as vivacious and charming, a specimen of Puritan womanhood as throve and wed in the colony. A few glimpses like this serve to explain her:—

"1699, Jany. At night Cap. Tuthill comes to speak with Betty who hid herself all alone in the coach for several hours till he was gone, so that we sought at several houses till at last came in of herself and look'd very wild." "Jany. 9. Speaks with her in my presence. Jany. 10. At night sent Cap. Tuthill away because company was here and told him was willing to know her mind better."

"Jany. 20. Cap. Brown and Turner breakfast here; Betty came in afterward and served almonds and raisins and filled a glass of wine to us; and it fell to her to drink to Cap. Turner. She went out of the way at first after I had spoke to her to fill wine; which surprised me; and I contrived that of the raisins on purpose to mend the matter."

Sewall might mend as he liked, and carry votes in Council, but a young Puritan maiden, as much coquette as Betty Sewall, was bright enough to mend his ways, and she was now doing so. Her courtship by Mr. Grove Hirst apparently was full of vicissitudes, bred of her own fastidiousness or coquetry, though they finally married. On one occasion, returning home from his Circuit, Judge Sewall writes:—

"Find my family in health and only disturbed at Betty's denying Mr. Hirst and my wife hath a cold."

Years before he had written fondly of her:—

"Little Bettie can read and spin passing well;
things very desirable in a woman."

This passage, in its rhythm and Saxon words, reminds one of Shakespeare's Cordelia:—

"Her voice was ever soft,
Gentle and low; an excellent thing in woman."

The subjoined letter of advice to his daughter in regard to her relations with Mr. Hirst is an admirable summary of practical truths which those intending courtship might ponder with profit: —

ELIZABETH. Mr. Hirst waits on you once more to see if you can bid him welcome. It ought to be seriously considered, that your drawing back from him after all that has passed between you will be your Prejudice; and will tend to discourage persons of worth from making their Court to you. And you had need well to consider whether you be able to bear his final Leaving of you howsoever it may seem grateful to you at present. When persons come toward us, we are apt to look upon their Undesirable Circumstances mostly; and thereupon to shun them. But when persons retire from us for good and all, we are in danger of looking only on that which is desirable in them, to our woeful disquiet. Whereas it is the property of a good Balance to turn where the most weight is, though there be some also in the other scale. I do not see but the Match is well liked by judicious persons and such as are your Cordial Friends, and mine also.

Yet, notwithstanding, if you find in yourself an unmovable, incurable Aversion from him, and cannot love and honor and obey him, I shall say no more, nor give you any further trouble in this matter. It had better be off than on. So praying God to pardon us and pity our Undeserving and to direct and strengthen and settle you in making a right judgment and giving a right answer, I take leave, who am, Dear Child,

Your loving father.

Your mother remembers to you.

The upshot of the matter is as follows in the Diary: —

"Oct. 18, 1700. In the following evening Mr. Grove Hirst and Elizabeth Sewall are married by Mr. Cotton Mather."

Sewall had only four out of his fourteen children who married, most dying young; and one of these, at least, made anything but a happy marriage. Considering all things, it would be hardly true to say that the marriages of Sewall's children rivalled at all that of their parents. But eight years later another daughter was about to assume the silken ties, and here, again, the way was a trifle rough.

Sewall's daughter Mary was now about to have a beau, Mr. Gerrish of Wenham, bent on serious business. Sewall proceeds to make preparations. The elders on both sides had had probably their consultations, and Sewall now proceeded to prayer.

"Jany. 24, 1709. I propound to Joseph to pray with his mother and me for his sister Mary; he declines it and I pray and was assisted with considerable agony and importunity with many tears. The Lord hear and help." "Jany. 31. Mr. Spencer calls here and I enquire of him about Mr. Gerrish of Wenham, what he should say. He answered not directly; but said his cousin would come, if he might have admittance. I told him I heard he went to Mr. Coney's daughter. He said he knew nothing of that. I desired him to enquire and tell me. I understood he undertook it; but he came no more."

Here was *finesse* somewhere; but Sewall was a hard man to beat, looking out for his own, and besides, was one of the richest of Puritan papas.

"Feby. 4. Nurse Smith buried. Coming from the grave I asked Mr. Pemberton [the parson] whether S. Gerrish courted Mr. Coney's daughter. He said no: not now. Mr. Coney thought his daughter young." "Feby. 7. I delivered a letter to S. Gerrish to inclose and send to his father which he promised to do. Feby. 17. I receive Mr. Gerrish's letter just at night

Feb. 18. I leave word at Mr. Gerrish's [S. G.] shop that I would speak with him after Mr. Bromfield's meeting was over. He came and I bid him welcome to my house as to what his father writ about. So late, hardly fit then to see my daughter, appointed him to come on Tuesday, invited him to supper. I observe he drunk to Mary in the third place. Feb. 23. When I came from the meeting at Mr. Stevens, I found him in the chamber, Mr. Hirst and wife [Betty Sewall] here. It seems he asked to speak with Mary below; her mother was afraid because the fire was newly made: and Mr. Hirst brought him up. This I knew not of: He asked me below, whether it were best to frequent my house before his father came to town. I said that were the best introduction; but he was welcome to come before and bid him come on Friday night." "Feb 24. Mr. Hirst tells me Mr. Gerrish courted Mr. Coney's daughter. I told him I knew it and was uneasy. Friday Feb. 25. In the evening S. Gerrish comes not; we expected him, Mary dressed herself: it was a painful disgraceful disappointment." "Saturday. Sam Gerrish goes to Wenham unknown to me, till Lord's Day night Capt Greenleaf told me of it. He was not seen by us till Wedns March 2."

The course of true love was not just then running smooth in the Sewall family; but on March 14:—

"The Revd Mr. Joseph Gerrish [*père*] comes to our house in the evening and dines with us the next day. At night his son comes and Mary goes to him. Comes the next night also." "Friday night. S. Gerrish comes. Tells Mary except Saturday and Lord's Day night intends to wait on her every night; unless something extraordinary happens."

This is the first time in the Diary, so far as has been noted, when Sewall applies the term "reverend" to a minister.

"June 3. Mary returns well from Wenham. *Laus Deo.*" [She had been out to see her lover's family, all which promises well for a wedding. Midweek, Aug. 24. The wedding comes.] "In the evening Mr. Pemberton marries Mr. Samuel Gerrish and my daughter Mary. He began with prayer and Mr. Gerrish, the bridegroom's father concluded."

Next day Mr. Cotton Mather and Mr. Pemberton and wife, with others, dined with Sewall, who invited the governor and Council, with about twenty others, to drink a glass of wine with him in the evening. The house was well filled with the Boston fashion.

"Gave them variety of good drink and at going away a large piece of cake wrapped in paper. They very heartily wished me joy of my daughter's marriage."

Mary Sewall's married life was short. She died in her father's house Nov. 16, 1710, a little more than a year after her nuptials.

CHAPTER XIV.

ANNE BRADSTREET AND OUR PURITAN LITERATURE.

"How doth his warmth refresh thy frozen back,
And trim thee brave in green, after thy black.
Both man and beast rejoice at his approach,
And birds do sing to see his glittering coach."

ANNE BRADSTREET on "The Sun and Earth."

FOR reasons evident to every student of that period, our early Puritan literature is scant and a trifle starved. Letters require leisure, and leisure presupposes a more or less comfortable estate; while our forefathers were among the busiest of mortals, and fortunes, for the most part, lay in a not near future. Besides, literature for the Puritan was more than a trifle aside from his mission and his temper. What had he to do with sonnets, epigrams, idyls, or verses to a lady's eyes? — he who was always confronting the Judgment Day, and agonizing with all his English energy, on land or sea, to attain, if haply he might find it, to the reward of the just made perfect. Besides, had not the emissaries of the Evil One been busy with their pens against God and his saints? Were there not Hudibras Butler, Congreve, and Wycherley, Vanbrugh, and a host of others to fling mud at him and to asperse his holy cause?

Had not even that gentle daughter of Israel, Mrs. Lucy Hutchinson written: "Every stage and every table and every puppet play belched forth profane scoffs upon them [the Puritans]; the drunkards made their songs and all fiddlers and mimics learned to abuse them as finding it the most gainful way of fooling"? So polite literature came very close, in the Puritan consciousness, to a profanity. It is quite possible that there were not five copies, perhaps not one, of Shakespeare's plays in Massachusetts Bay for nigh the first hundred years. And even these five very likely were brought in by people not Puritans. Judge Sewall notes in his Diary that he found and perused at a certain place on his circuit a copy of Ben Jonson; but that place was in Rhode Island. It was true that in England John Milton, both in prose and verse, had written books which the world will not willingly let die; but these books were either on Puritan politics or religion, and gave themselves little concern with the mere æsthetics or forms of literary art. The Puritan painted no pictures and wrote no plays. But if this be a true record, it should be at once added that this same Puritan spent his life in creating those substances out of which literature enriches itself. The world has not yet recognized the rich stores of romance and tragedy which are unappropriated in the history of the New England Puritans. Hawthorne has done his part generously, but there are more to come. The disturbances of home-life among the Puritan clergy in Old England, when they were driven from their rectories, and their sons and daughters, with broken social ties that had run, may be, into the circle of House and Castle, made wanderers and with a social brand; men separated from their wives in the long, uncertain Atlantic voyage, and wives at home in the passive but mighty heroism of those who wait and must be still; letters out of those same homes with names of the new-born, or a sad wail sounding across seas for the first-born of the defenceless flock; all the blood, the plot, the violence of Indian wars; all the ravages of pirate ships along the coast some of whose sailors were prodigals out of pious families, born of the very blood they spoiled, and whose punishment, when taken, was the gallows at the hands of kindred; all the plannings, craft, uncertainties of politics, over which friends broke from each other, and plighted sons and daughters were forced to face broken vows, in a strife which ran through British governors and patriot deputies, from Andros and the elder Dudley to Gage and Samuel Adams; all distances of abode and an ever-changing estate of men and women whose passions of love or hate were not cooled, but rather made intense, by the strange, exacting, but tonic life of the New England land — all these are still unexhausted storehouses from which genius one day will bring forth riches in triumph.

There are exceptions to this statement of the actual poverty of our early New England literature, provided we make the word elastic enough. If sermons and religious controversies are to be counted in, there is plenty of that sort; indeed, a singular fecundity. Cotton Mather is a wonder in composition, — unique in quantity, and the reverse in quality; cultivating, as a wit puts it, his memory till he lost his mind. There are others who approach him in these respects. There are two mysteries in the old New England civilization which demand solving by some one. (1) Exactly why and where did that composite holy day and fast day all in one, the Puritan Sabbath, come from? (2) Why and where did the New England Puritan sermon come from? To some men who have looked at these problems, and seen the difficulty of the analysis and the curious precipitate liable to remain if the analysis succeed, the bewilderment is a little like what must have been the mind of the ancient Job when asked, "Out of whose womb came the ice? And the hoary frost of heaven, who hath gendered it?" How men could ever write, or other men listen to, or read, such lucubrations, is, like the wisdom of God, past finding out. Yet there are libraries of such books hid away from this judicious generation by dust and neglect. And except as warnings to the coming generations of scribes, or to furnish an occasional tint or antithesis to the historian, it is difficult to see what further use is in them.

There are also many crude and shapeless histories and narratives of travels, voyages, and current events in the New England commonwealth which will always have a certain interest to the antiquarian and the philosopher of men. They, too, sleep under their shroud of dust, and give little bread to the hungry.

There are two marked exceptions to the general drift of old New England literature. In brief, these are John Winthrop's Journal and the Winthrop papers in general, and Judge Sewall's Diary. The respect of this book for the Winthrop character and agency in moulding New England is elsewhere in its pages; and Sewall's Diary must speak for itself.

There are also another class of writings; substantially, histories or travels which, though in general in bad form, have a certain archaic value liable to last. The brave, heroic Daniel Gookin, Sewall's friend for the Indians, who stood so bolt upright for the good ones in King Philip's War, and became so unpopular that the very "small boys" hooted him in his house, and who after stood equally straight against English emissaries like Randolph, until he became the most popular man in the colony, was said to have written a valuable history of his times, especially touching the red men and Christianity, the manuscript of which was destroyed by fire. But Wm. Wood in his "New England Prospect" shows marked literary skill, and the naturalist Josselyn has somewhat to be read. The political and theological tracts are numerous.

One man, and he the strongest writer, may be taken to represent Puritan authorship here of the second class, — Nathaniel Ward of Agawam, now Ipswich. He graduated at Emmanuel College, Cambridge, 1603, and resided at the university as one of its learned writers and scholars. He was the literary friend of men like Sir Francis Bacon, Archbishop Usher, and the divine, Parens of Heidelberg. First he studied and practised law; travelled several years on the Continent, and then took orders in the Anglican Church. For ten years he was a country parson in Essex, where he was excommunicated for his Puritanism (and probably his tongue) by Archbishop Laud in 1633. Then with all this wealth of learning and experience, he came here, and settled as pastor in the wilderness at Ipswich, where, nevertheless, he sometimes had several university men in his congregation, Simon Bradstreet among them. While on the Continent, somehow he made the intimate acquaintance of the family of the unfortunate but beautiful Princess Elizabeth, daughter of James I., and so sister of Charles I., but now married to the Elector Palatine of Germany (with her ruined but ivy-clad tower in Heidelberg Castle still standing), and appears to have been attached to her court. Anyway, he seems to have dandled her infant son,—after, the famous Prince Rupert. For when, years after, Prince Rupert had become the profane, brave soldier he was, "swearing like a trooper," Rev. Nathaniel Ward wrote from across seas into England:—

"I have had him in my arms. . . . I wish I had him there now. If I mistake not he promised then to be a good prince; but I doubt he hath forgot it. If I thought he would not be angry with me I would pray hard to his Maker to make him a right Roundhead, a wise-hearted Palatine, a thankful man to the English: to forgive all his sins, and at length to save his soul notwithstanding all his God-damme's."

In 1647, with the strife between king and parliament running swiftly towards the king's scaffold, Ward, this long-brained, cultured man, as Professor Tyler so felicitously says, with a radical brain and a conservative heart, wrote his "Simple Cobbler of Agawam," an "oaky," rambling book, a prose satire on the mental chaos of the times, New England varieties, and English politics.

The title-page runs curiously thus:—

> "The Simple Cobbler of Agawam in America; willing to help mend his native country, lamentably tattered both in the upper leather and sole,—with all the honest stitches he can take; and as willing never to be paid for his work by old English wonted pay. It is his trade to patch all the year long, gratis. Therefore I pray gentlemen keep your purses. By THEODORE DE LA GUARD. IN REBUS ARDUIS AC TENUI SPE ORTISSIMA QUAEQUE CONSILIA TUTISSIMA SUNT. CIC. In English:
>
> When boots and shoes are torn up to the lefts
> Cobblers must thrust their awls up to the hefts;
> This is no time to fear Apelles gram;
> '*Ne sutor quidem ultra crepidam.*'"

The keynote is in the opening sentence:—

> "Either I am in an apoplexy or that man is in a lethargy who doth not now sensibly feel God shaking the heavens over his head and the earth under his feet. . . . The truths of God are the pillars of the world, whereon states and churches may stand quiet if they will; if they will not he can easily shake them off into delusions and destractions enough."

In mere felicity of phrase Roger Williams is perhaps entitled to carry off the palm from all his New

England contemporaries. He often appears in these pages; and the reader will often remark a delicacy in the phrase or turn of his sentence which is rare now, as it certainly was then. Never with the balanced and able mind of a man like John Winthrop, and by nature not even a good wreckmaster of the very things which he would have destroyed; yet no wise man will willingly affront his memory, even when pointing out his weaknesses. The fact is that Roger Williams was made up after a polyglot pattern. He was a sort of Oriental caravan, bearing all sorts of balm, myrrh, and frankincense for delight and use; but he wandered often from the track, brought little bread, though a few pearls of great price, and, to say truth, had not great store of anything to feed the hungry into mastery in the land to which he fared.

Yet his spices are still fragrant. Here are a few:—

"Alas, Sir, in calm midnight thoughts what are these leaves and flowers and smoke and shadows and dreams of earthly nothings about which we poor fools and children, as David saith, disquiet ourselves in vain."

"We are born to trouble as the sparks are to fly upward. Above the sun is our rest in the Alpha and Omega of all blessedness, unto whose arms of everlasting mercy, I commend you, desirous to be yours, even in Him."

"Your worships, sorry that I am not more yours and neither of us more the Lord's." ROGER WILLIAMS.

Speaking of a hard winter, with deep snows, he writes:—

"It hath pleased the Most High to besiege us all with his white legions." "Prince Rupert was one whose name in these parts sounds as a north-east snowstorm." "Better an honorable death than a slave's life."

Here is an epigram worthy of being written on the senate house of any free people.

"I fear not so much iron and steel as the cutting of our throats with golden knives."

By some standards none of these books would be ranked as literature; though there was not one of these men who had not in him the power of literature, both as to form and substance. Sewall's Diary may be only reckoned a storehouse in which literature may find its riches; yet the man who could write in as good form as this, had he set about it, could have written what would stand the brunt of most modern criticism: —

"Communion with God is the centre which rests the motions of a weary soul; 'tis the rest and refreshment of a man's spirit. (Psalm 116. 7) 'Return unto thy rest O my soul.' When we attain perfect communion with God in heaven, we attain to perfect rest; and all the rest the spirit of man finds on earth is found in communion with God."

Composed by S. S. in London while on his visit to England.

Perhaps (to indulge in the pleasantry of a conscious bull) the one real literary man of these old days in New England was a woman, — Anne Bradstreet. If so, the honor, justly given, derives itself not more from her performance than from the fact that she seems to have given herself more to writing as a serious business than any New England man of affairs (her own father and husband, for instance) had leisure.

Anne Bradstreet was born in England (1612), probably at Northampton. Her father, Thomas Dudley, after associate with Winthrop in the Puritan Exodus of 1630, and later governor of the colony, was the son of Captain Roger Dudley, killed in battle about 1586. He himself had been a soldier, and of later years steward to the Earl of Lincoln, whose estates he rescued from their embarrassments, proving himself an able business man, and raising Simon Bradstreet, son of a Nonconformist minister to be his coadjutor in the task. At a very early age Anne Bradstreet, from her father's official position, was much at the castle, and was there educated by the magnificence and culture common to a nobleman's house of that era. At the age of sixteen, in 1628, she married Simon Bradstreet, nine years her senior, with whom she lived till her death at sixty (1672). They emigrated to New England, where the husband became colonial secretary, judge, legislator, governor, ambassador, royal ambassador, and soldier in turn, dying at the age of ninety-four. After several changes in abode, the family finally settled near Andover, Mass., where she reared eight children, although of a delicate constitution; and in this quiet country home most of her literary work was done, before thirty, — from 1630 to 1642. It will surprise some to read that her writings were enough to fill a royal octavo volume of some four hundred pages. She herself writes of her earlier life: —

"After a short time I changed my condition and was married and came into this country where I found a new world and new manners at which my heart rose. But after I was convinced it was the way of God I submitted to it."

No wonder that a lady, raised almost in an earl's family, should feel her heart rise against the almost sordid, certainly the low, estate, especially of the Lord's maidens, who were also wives, set to rear families in the New England wild.

It is not intended here either to catalogue or analyze Anne Bradstreet's literary work, or, indeed, to give much more than significant extracts from her writings. Any one who would study the subject thoroughly, is respectfully referred to a charming life of her written in the most crystal English by the late John Harvard Ellis, who evidently himself died too early not to bequeath a loss to American historical literature. But one point should be looked at beforehand. It will surprise very many to hear that the Puritans of New England were almost universally addicted to verse-making, very much in the same fashion as led the Lady Mary Montagu to say that in her time "verse-making had become as common as taking snuff." Rather poor verses they no doubt were in both cases; but men and women made them all the same, and in case of the Puritans, probably for two reasons. Assuming the fact to be substantially as stated, — and it must be remembered that the Puritans as English folk had inherited from their Saxon, Norse, and Celtic ancestry about as much folklore in the shape of jingling rhymes and saws in verse full of an earthy, robust common-sense, as any people on the face of the globe, — these rhymes and saws in their almost universal currency would make some sort of rough rhyme-making and versification a natural avocation for our forefathers. Governor Dudley, her father, died with a copy of some verses in his pocket; and Anne Bradstreet, evidently a sensitive and imaginative child, must have heard the like, and no doubt better, from her youth up. Besides, it should never be forgot that the honest Puritans, both men and women, lived in a sort of religious ecstasy which was bred even more from a quivering heart than their strong head. As is well known, all strong emotion tends to express itself rhythmically, and takes on the form of poetry, as is often seen in very young and sensitive children, who, when led away from a death-bed, or the spot where a favorite dog or bird has just been buried, proceed to make a poem on the sad event, in all sincerity of grief. So far, we may be sure that Anne Bradstreet was reared in such an atmosphere, where poetical feeling, as it does everywhere to-day, far outruns all or any artistic forms of poetical expressions. Yet, on the other hand, a comparison of dates will show that Anne Bradstreet's era is one of poetical expression and performance, hardly excelled before or since in England.

Here are a few extracts from poems addressed to relatives; this first to her father, Governor Thomas Dudley, whom she elsewhere calls a magazine of history, her guide and instructor in her love of books: —

"Most truly honored and as truly dear
If worth in me or aught I do appear
Who can of right better demand the same
Than may your worthy self from whom it came."

A. B.

Next, an epitaph on "my dear and ever-honored mother," Mrs. Dorothy Dudley, who died 1643, Æ. 61:—

MRS. DOROTHY DUDLEY.

ANNE BRADSTEET'S MOTHER.

A worthy matron of unspotted life
A loving mother and obedient wife
A friendly neighbor, pitiful to poor
Whom oft she fed and clothed with her store.
To servants wisely aweful, but yet kind,
And as they did, so they reward did find;
A true instructor of her family
The which she ordered with dexterity.
The public meetings ever did frequent,
And in her Closet constant hours she spent;
Religious in all her words and ways
Preparing still for death, till end of days;
Of all her children, children lived to see
Then dying left a blessed memory.

Next, a quaint conceit on her own children:—

"I had eight birds hatched in one nest
Four cocks there were, and hens the rest
I nurst them up with pain and care
Nor cost nor labor did I spare,
'Till at the last they felt their wing
Mounted the trees and learned to sing." A. B.

"Upon my son Samuel [her eldest son] going for England, Nov. 6, 1657":—

"Thou mighty God of sea and land
I here resign into thy hand
The son of prayers, of vowes, of tears
The child I stayed for many years.
Thou heard'st me then and gav'st him me.
Hear me again I give him Thee.
He's mine but more O Lord thine own,
For sure thy grace on him is shown
No friend I have like Thee to trust
For mortal helps are brittle dust
Preserve, O Lord from storms and wrack
Protect him there and bring him back:
And if thou shalt spare me a space
That I again may see his face
Then shall I celebrate thy praise
And bless Thee for't even all my days.
If otherwise I go to rest
Thy will be done, for that is best
Persuade my heart I shall him see
Forever happefy'd with Thee."

The true Puritan rage against the English Church and Crown is very vividly expressed in these lines, addressed, apparently, to her native land, considered somehow as existing apart from both:—

"Dear Mother cease complaints and wipe your eyes
Shake off your dust, cheer up and now arise,
You are my mother nurse and I your flesh. . . .
Blest be the nobles of thy noble land
With ventur'd lives for Truth's defence that stand.
Blest be thy commons who, for common good
And the infringed Laws, have boldly stood.
Blest be thy counties who did aid thee still
With hearts and states to testify their will.
Blest be thy preachers who do cheer thee on.
O, cry the sword of God and Gideon: [Judges vii. 18–20.]
And shall I not on them with Mero's curse
That help thee not with prayers, arms and purse?

And for myself let miseries abound
If mindless of thy state I e'er be found.
These are the days the church's foes to crush
To root out Popelings, head, tail, branch, and nesh;
Let's bring Baal's vestments forth to make a fire
Their Myrtires, Surplices, and all their tire
Capes, rotchets, crosiers and such empty trash
And let their names consume, but let the flash
Light Christendome and all the world to see
We hate ROME'S whore with all her trumpery.
Go on brave *Essex* with a loyal heart
Not false to King nor to the better part;
But those that hurt his people and his crown
As duty binds, expel and tread them down."

But undoubtedly the most remarkable of all the literary performances of Anne Bradstreet is her "Meditations," which she dedicates to her son in the letter subjoined:—

FOR MY DEAR SON SIMON BRADSTREET.

Parents perpetuate their lives in their posterity and their manners in their imitation. Children do naturally follow the failings than the virtues of their predecessors, but I am persuaded better things of you. You once desired me to leave something for you in writing that you might look upon when you should see me no more. I could think of nothing more fit for you, nor of more ease to myself than these short Meditations following. Such as they are I bequeathe to you; small legacies are accepted by true friends, much more by dutiful children. . . . The Lord bless you with grace here and crown you with glory hereafter that I may meet you with rejoicing at that great day of appearing which is the continual prayer of

Your affectionate mother

A. B.

March 20, 1664.

MEDITATIONS.

There is no object that we see; no action that we do; no good that we enjoy; no evil that we feel or fear but we may make some spiritual advantage of all; and he that makes such improvement is wise as well as pious.

Many can speak well but few can do well. We are better scholars in the theory than in the practical part; but he is a true Christian who is a proficient in both.

Youth is the time of getting; middle age of improving and old age of spending; a negligent youth is usually attended by an ignorant middle age and both by an empty old age. He that hath nothing to feed on but vanity and lies must needs lie down in the bed of Sorrow.

The finest bread hath the least bran; the purest honey, the least wax; and the sincerest Christian the least selflove.

Downy beds make drowsy persons but hard lodging keeps the eyes open. A prosperous state makes a secure Christian but adversity makes him consider.

Sweet words are like honey — a little may refresh but too much gluts the stomach.

Authority without wisdom is like a heavy axe without an edge, fitter to bruise than polish.

The reason why Christians are so loath to exchange this world for a better, is because they have more sense than faith; they *see* what they enjoy they do but *hope* for that which is to come.

If we had no winter the spring would not be so pleasant; if we did not sometimes taste of adversity, prosperity would not be so welcome.

That house which is not often swept, makes the cleanly inhabitant soon loathe it, and that heart which is not continually purifying itself, is no fit temple for the Spirit of God to dwell in.

Corn till it have past through the mill and been ground to powder, is not fit for bread. God so deals with his servants; he grinds them with grief and pain till they turn to dust and then are they fit bread for his Mansion.

He that walks among briers and thorns will be very careful where he sets his foot. And he that passes through the wilderness of this world had need ponder all his steps.

An aching head requires a soft pillow and a drooping heart a strong support.

Dim eyes are the concomitants of old age; and short sightedness in those that are eyes of a republic foretells a declining state.

Sore laborers have hard hands and old sinners have brawny consciences.

Wickedness comes to its height by degrees. He that dares say of a less sin, "Is it not a little one?" will ere long say of a greater, "Tush! God regards it not!"

Fire hath its force abated by water, not by wind; and anger must be allayed by cold words and not by blustering threats.

As the brands of a fire, if once severed, will of themselves go out, although you use no other means to extinguish them — so distance of place together with length of time (if there be no intercourse) will cool the affections of intimate friends, though there should be no displeasance between them.

Since Anne Bradstreet's day, many of her New England sisters of Puritan stock, in the name of the Puritan ideas of liberty and piety in literature, have fairly won fame before the world as philanthropists and artists, while others are surely approaching the gates of the great temple. By that same beautiful river of the lordly elms, intent on marshalling its tides, have dwelt and will, women who make this world purer and the next nearer for the poetry (sometimes in prose) which they have written and lived out. It is they, at least, and women like them of Massachusetts Bay, who will keep in honor the memory of their eldest New England sister in their great Guild of Letters, — Anne Bradstreet.

CHAPTER XV.

SEWALL AND THE CHURCH OF ENGLAND.

It is hardly to the honor of that part of the human race called Christians, that they have been so seldom able either to understand or withstand human opinions adverse to their own, with charity. For charity, as time shows, is not only the first of Christian virtues, but it is also the youngest and most difficult. The British race, in managing its religious affairs, reveals this defective habit of man. The agnostic, of course, regards all this with wonder or contempt. For men to quarrel over a guess, and spend lives and gold over a remote hypothesis; to die, self-exiled, in some far-off clime among savages, forsaking home and fatherland, for a delusion from which that common-sense which is all men's birthright should have saved them,—is to him acutely absurd. Yet men, and those, too, of no base degree, have done this a thousand times. But British Christians have never been of the agnostic type. No men ever held more dogmatically and unswervingly to their religion than those children of the English Reformation called Puritans. What for them was true in Christianity was true in all time and space. What was contrary thereto was equally false in duration and extension. Since, then, their religion was, in their mind, man's salvation, its opposite must work man's perdition; and he who upheld that opposite must be logically the enemy of the human race. It makes naught to say that the Puritan, having rejected the old church as false authority, made himself a new and more vulgar one, which lacked even the dignity of antiquity. Such are ever the necessities and limits of the human mind in religion, that it will find what it thinks solid ground somewhere to stand on, and will allow no one to meddle with its foundations. Neither modesty nor timidity will cause it, when the gauntlet of its adversary is thrown down, to hesitate to pick it up.

For the Puritan, his new religion was both an ecstasy and a fanaticism. His strong, sturdy English nature, inflamed with his new love, became revolt and bitterness against its enemies. "It was the Puritan pulpit," as Dr. South said, "that supplied the field with swordsmen and the parliament house with incendiaries."

It resulted, hence, that Puritan zeal evoked a counter flame in its enemies often quite as consuming as its own. This was in measure true as regards the opponents of the Reformation everywhere. That mediæval church, which had reposed in the serenity of its unquestioned creeds for a thousand years and more, giving the Holy Bread and the Kiss of Peace to its laity, with only an occasional firestroke at sporadic men like Huss and Savonarola, roused itself at the new danger, to preach death to the heretics, and to argue that as heresy destroyed the soul, while other murder only destroyed the body, heresy should be erased with fire and sword as the greatest of crimes. Hence Alva, the Spanish Armada, the Thirty Years' War in Germany, and the untold misery of man. It hardly avails to say that we, heirs of a privilege which the men of old purchased with their sorrow, are wiser. Wiser we may be, but better only with a limit. The Puritan religion may have been an evil, but is no religion a good? Liberty of conscience may be a good, but if it be followed by the lack, what then? The reformers and their enemies hated each other in a circle, but each loved somewhat which was and is true and fruitful of good. As we pass, two quotations may serve to cast a sidelight upon the earnestness and bitterness of the Reformation age, as between the old and the new.

One Romanist, to show his absolute faith in Transubstantiation, said that he believed Christ not only to be present in the Sacrament, but that he was there booted and spurred as he rode to Jerusalem.

The underlying bitterness of the Reformation age against Rome and her mysteries is perhaps exposed as well as in any other way in a carved group in Strasbourg Cathedral, where was represented a boar carrying the holy waterpot and sprinkling-brush; a wolf, the cross; a hare, the taper; a pig and a goat, a box of relics in which lay a sleeping fox; and an ass reading mass, whilst a cat served as reading-desk.

All this was to a degree true of the controversy between the Puritan and the Church of England. Neither side was indifferently Christian. Both were Protestant, and advocates of reform. Both agreed to withstand the claims of Rome, and had withstood together the Jesuits and the Armada. The question at issue between the two was as to more or less in reform, and the Puritan stood stoutly for more. Error and wrong were on both sides; only the Church of England, being in power, imposed, by now historic public acts, through its ally, the Crown, its judgments upon the Puritan; and these were sometimes wrong. The Puritan had his way under Cromwell and the Commonwealth. That he was always right, few would hardly care to affirm; especially in the face of the fact that in the Restoration of Charles II. the English nation declared that it would brook Puritanism, as a governing force, no longer. Yet the bitterness was there, and corroded. Before remarking on Sewall's attitude, as a representative man, towards the Church of England, it is only fair to place as a background the current church attitude towards the Puritan, as seen in a very spicy correspondence between Roger Williams and Mrs. Sadlier, daughter of the famous lawyer, Sir Edward Coke, a lady apparently of much spirit and mental acumen, but a Church-of-England woman. Williams had been a *protégé* of Sir Edward, and on his visit to England, in 1653, addressed the daughter a characteristic letter, accompanied by some of his own books as a present. The letter begins: —

LONDON, 1652.

"MY MUCH HONORED FRIEND, MRS. SADLIER,—

"The never-dying honor and respect which I owe to that dear honorable root and his branches, and among the rest to your much honored self, have emboldened me once more to enquire after your dear husband's and your life and health and welfare."

He then proceeds to magnify his own travails in the wilderness, and to give the lady a round dose of the current Puritan piety. She replies: —

MR. WILLIAMS;

Since it hath pleased God to make the prophet David's complaint ours. (Psalm lxxix.) O God the heathen have come into our inheritance [the Puritans were now in power], I have given over reading many books and therefore with thanks have returned yours. Those that I now read, besides the Bible, are first, the late King's book [Charles I., lately beheaded by Williams's friends]; Hooker's Ecclesiastical Polity; Rev. Bishop Andrew's Sermons with his other divine meditations; Dr. Jeremy Taylor's works; and Dr. Thomas Jackson upon the Creed. Some of these, my dear father was a great admirer of and would often call them the glorious lights of the Church of England. These lights shall be my guide. I wish they may be yours; for your new lights that are so much cried up, I believe, in the conclusion they will prove but dark lanterns; therefore I dare not meddle with them.

Your friend in the old way,

ANNE SADLIER.

Not a whit discouraged by this rather tart reply, Williams returns to his point with: —

"MY MUCH HONORED KIND FRIEND, MRS. SADLIER;

"Your last letter, my honored friend, I received as a bitter sweeting — [a kind of well-known English apple] — as all that is under the sun is — sweet in that I hear from you and that you continue striving for life eternal; bitter in that we differ about the way, in the midst of the dangers and distresses. You were pleased to direct me to divers books for my satisfaction. I have carefully endeavored to get them and some I have gotten; and upon my reading, I purpose with God's help, to render you an ingenious and candid account of my thoughts, results &c. At present I am humbly bold to pray your judicious and loving eye to one of mine.

"'Tis true I cannot but expect your distaste of it; and yet my cordial desire of your soul's peace here, and eternal, and of contributing the least mite to it, and my humble respects to that blessed root of which you spring, force me to tender my acknowledgments, which if received or rejected, my cries shall never cease that one eternal life shall give us meeting, since this present minute hath such bitter partings."

"The one of mine" turns out to be a controversial tract against Rev. John Cotton, asserting that "in soul-matters no weapons but soul-weapons are reaching and effectual." Cotton, it appears, had controverted a former tract of Williams's, entitled "The Bloody Tenent of Persecution for Cause of Conscience." He signs himself:—

"I am your most unworthy servant, yet unfeignedly respective,

"ROGER WILLIAMS."

To which Mrs. Sadlier replies:—

SIR; I thank God my blessed parents bred me up in the old and best religion and it is my glory that I am a member of the Church of England, as it was when all the reformed Churches gave her the right hand. When I cast my eye on the frontispiece of your book and saw it entitled "The Bloody Tenent" I durst not venture to look into it, for fear it should bring into my memory the much blood that has of late been shed and which I would fain forget; therefore I do with thanks return it. I cannot call to mind any blood shed for conscience: — some few that went about to make a rent in our once well governed Church were punished, but none suffered death. But this I know that since it has been left to every man's conscience to fancy what religion he list, there has more Christian blood been shed than was in the ten persecutions. And some of that blood will, I fear, cry till the day of judgment. But you know what the Scripture says, that when there was no King in Israel, every man did that which was right in his own eyes — but what became of that, the sacred story will tell you.

Thus Entreating you to trouble me no more in this kind, and wishing you a good journey to your charge in New Providence I rest,

Your friend in the old and best way.

[No signature.]

But the man who always insisted that that sturdiest fighter of all England, George Fox, the Quaker, ran away from a discussion with him at Newport, R.I., was not to be denied this way, even by a lady. He proceeds with a long letter, in which he thrusts the Puritan knife into the old sores, and speaks plain words of King Charles I. Yet both the opening and the close are colored with a chaste Christian charity very amiable, after two centuries, to the reader: —

(WINTER OF 1652–3.)

MY HONORED, KIND FRIEND, MRS. SADLIER;

I greatly rejoice to hear from you, although now an opposite to me, even in the highest points of heaven and eternity. . . . This I humbly pray for your precious soul, of the God and Father of mercies, even your eternal joy and salvation Earnestly desirous to be in the old way, which is the narrow way which leads to life, which few find.

Your most humble, though most unworthy servant,

ROGER WILLIAMS.

Mrs. Sadlier, as is customary, had the last word, and it was a bitter one:—

MR. WILLIAMS;

I thought my first letter would have given you so much satisfaction, that, in that kind I should never have heard of you any more; but it seems you have a face of brass, so that you cannot blush. . . . For the foul and false aspersions that you have cast upon that King of ever blessed memory, Charles the martyr, I protest I trembled when I read them, and none but such a villain as yourself would have wrote them. . . . For Milton's book that you desire I should read, if I be not mistaken, that is he that hath wrote a book of the lawfulness of divorce; and if report says true, he had at that time two or three wives living. This, perhaps, were good doctrine in New England; but it is most abominable in Old England. For his book that he wrote against the late King, that you would have me read, you should have taken notice of God's judgment upon him, who stroke him with blindness, and, as I have heard, he was fain to have the help of one Andrew Marvell, or else he could not have finished that most accursed libel. God has begun his judgment upon him here — his punishment will be hereafter in hell. But have you seen the answer to it? If you can get it, I assure you it is worth the reading. [From all which it is plain that the Puritans were not the only privy councillors of God who knew exactly what he did with his poor creatures in the other world.] . . . Bishop Laud's book against Fisher I have read long since; which if you have not done, let me tell you he has deeply wounded the pope; and I believe, howsoever he be slighted, he will rise a saint, when many seeming ones, as you are, will rise devils.

I cannot conclude without putting you in mind how dear a lover and great an admirer my father was of the liturgy of the Church of England and would often say, no reform church had the like. He was constant to it, both in his life and at his death. I mean to walk in his steps.

By what I have now writ you know how I stand affected. I will walk as directly to heaven as I can, in which place, if you will turn from being a rebel and fear God and obey the King, here is hope I may meet you there; howsoever trouble me no more with your letters for they are very troublesome to her that wishes you in the place from whence you came.

ANNE SADLIER.

On the outside of Williams's first letter to her is a note of hers upon him, which in style and temper sounds very much like a description for the police. It concludes thus: —

"I leave his letters, that, if ever he has the face to return into his native country, Tyburn may give him welcome."

Sewall himself inherited the Puritan bitterness, and he shows it. Though born in England, his whole makeup, except his blood in heredity, was as a son of New England. He came on the stage after Cromwell and the Commonwealth, when the Puritans were embittered by defeat and severe laws of repression and hardship. Puritanism had grown sullen, sore, and expectant, biding its time, which came in the American Revolution. Sewall was in full sympathy with it; and the one thing from which he is altogether averse, even at the expense sometimes of his heart and breeding, is the Church of England. This extends to almost everything belonging to it, — its liturgy, customs, holy days, symbols, and ministers; though, as he aged, and the church came in under a semi-court patronage, he found it both safe and in the way of good breeding to keep terms with its clergy, with a grave reserve which had behind it a very limited good will.

As a member of the Old South Church, he had a taste of his old enemy when Sir Edmund Andros insisted on occupying it, in the absence of his own, for the worship of the Church of England.

The question, "What right had the Church of England to establish itself in Boston?" creates for fair-minded men examining it a very difficult dilemma in ethics. To say that a national church should not go where the nation went; that where his soldiers might come in defence, the king's church should not come in worship; or that the king's worship should be forbidden to any of his loyal subjects in any of his domains; or that a church vindicated by the favorable verdict of a nation after a long war and much bloodshed, and set up again as an indisputable fact in that people's life, should be repudiated and forbidden by a province of that nation, peopled by those very Puritans who had gone to the wall in the late struggle, would seem to be plain, flat treason to the realm and king. The Puritans, of course, never undertook all this in plain act, but they and Sewall wrought for it all they could, and perhaps it is not too much to say, all they dared. On the Puritan side, it might be said that their charter gave them very generous powers to regulate their own affairs; that they had borne at their own charges the burden and heat of the day in subduing the wild, and giving a new and valuable colony to the Crown; that they had come three thousand miles across seas to be rid of this very church and enjoy their own; that the two had been and were antagonists; and that it was aside from reason, justice, and common humanity to now propose or impose a religion here which they and their fathers had refused everywhere; that, in short, it was cruelty and slavery both to admit, much less nurture, among Puritan exiles in Massachusetts Colony, the church of Archbishop Laud and of Charles I. Nor could the Church of England fairly claim entrance here because it was the better way. That all might be. But so long as the Puritans thought theirs the better way, it is hard to see why the Church of England here was not an intrusion as against the prince of virtues, Christian charity, — an intrusion both ungracious and lacking mercy. The church came, of course, and went on its comfortable mission till now. Happily this book is not called on to decide the ethics of its coming.

The General Court in 1659 passed an Act: —

> "For preventing disorders arising in several places within this jurisdiction, by reason of some still observing such festivals as were superstitiously kept in other Countries to the great dishonor of God and offence of others; It is therefore ordered by this Court and the authority thereof, that whosoever shall be found observing any such day as Christmas and the like, either by forbearing labor, feasting, or any other way upon any such account as aforesaid, every such person so offending shall pay for every such offence, five shillings as a fine to the Country."

The inclusion here of both the active and passive observance of Christmas is truly remarkable. It was lucky that the fine was not fixed at £100, and it probably would have been if it had been thought that so extreme a penalty would have killed Christmas. This law in the Record Book is sandwiched in between laws against gaming and dancing, and is followed by this preamble of a law against cards and dice: "And whereas not only at such times [Christmas, etc.] it is a custom too frequent in many places, to expend time in unlawful games as cards, dice, &c." There is a wise economy here in refraining from the mention of the fact that Christmas was kept according to English law from time immemorial, and that by their own charter the dates of holding their own law courts were fixed by church days. Nor is it quite possible to imagine a more unmitigated offence against a pious Churchman than thus to involve in a public law one of his most cherished festivals with the vulgar sports of dice and cards. It is surprising, considering the nature of the earlier Puritan legislation, that the Massachusetts Colony kept its charter as long as it did. Had it not been for the home troubles in England, it is safe to say that the charter would have been voided long before.

Sewall kept a keen Puritan eye on Christmas, as indeed he did on all other festivals of the old religion. As his Diary shows, he remarks with pleasure when Christmas is treated like any other day; and his alarm is acute when any new church custom begins to make headway. This is Sewall's general way of noticing its recurrence: —

"Decr 25, 1685. Friday. Carts come to town and shops open as is usual. Some somehow observe the day; but are vexed I believe that the body of the people profane it, and blessed be God no authority yet to compel them to keep it."

The trouble with the whole Puritan system, so far as it attempted to control human nature, was that it was a system "in the air," — too transcendental for ordinary mortals, and crossing the trend of human instincts, so that as time went on the Puritan *régime* grew outlaw and superannuate, with new floods coming in; but Sewall never heartily modified himself, and, as he aged, seems to have gained small comfort from the waning fortunes of a losing fashion.

"Oct. 1, 1702. The Governor and Council agree that Thursday Oct. 22 be a fast day. Governor moved that it might be Friday, saying Let us be Englishmen. [But they were first of all Puritans, as Sewall's Diary proves.] I spake against making any distinction in the days of the week. Desired that the same day of the week might be for fasts and thanksgiving."

This is the temper of aversion to old church customs which avoided Friday, the day of the cross, and especially Good Friday, almost until this day no governor of this State ever daring to change the order. We used to fast, obedient to the yearly proclamation, by making merry.

"Nov. 26, 1703. When mention was made of putting them to their oath [these men were before the governor and Council] Harrison said he was ready to swear, but then it must be by laying his hand on the Bible. Governor said 'So he ought,' and ordered Mr. Secretary to fetch the Bible. Mr. Paine also slipped on his hand. Mr. Harrison first looked into it to see that 'twas the Bible. When he had sworn, seemed to applaud himself and said he would have this forwarded and upheld. When questions were asked him he answered 'By that Booke it is true.'"

Mention has been already made of Sewall's silence in the matter of Lady Andros's funeral. He lapses into the same ungracious silence, and even worse, in the face of any disaster to any man identified with the Church of England, as one who, before some terrible calamity fallen on his bitter enemy, is too well bred to aggravate the other's sorrow with a sneer, and too sincere to lament. Take an instance or two: —

"Oct. 26, 1711. A man falls from a scaffold at the Church of England [King's Chapel] into the street and is stricken dead."

"Aug. 20, 1720. 'Tis said Mr. Lucas, the Church of England minister, cut his own throat at Newbury. However the minister of Marblehead set a good face on it, had the corpse carried into the church, preached a funeral sermon and buried him therein; a rueful consecration of the chapel."

"Tuesday, April 23d, 1706. Governor comes to town guarded by the troops with their swords drawn; dines at the Dragon, from thence proceeds to the town house. Illuminations at night. [This was probably St. George's Day.] Capt Pelham tells me several wore crosses in their hats; which makes me resolve to stay at home. Because to drinking healths now the keeping of a day to fictitious St George is plainly set on foot. It seems Capt Dudley's men wore crosses. Somebody had fastened a cross to a dog's head. Capt Dudley's boatswain seeing him struck the dog and then went into the shop, next where the dog was and struck down the carpenter, one Davis, as he was at work, not thinking anything. Boatswain and the other with him were fined 10s each for breach of the peace, by Jer. Dummer, Esq.: pretty much blood was shed by means of this bloody cross and the poor dog a sufferer."

Probably the poor dog was a sufferer, as Sewall's sympathetic nature notes; and Sewall's sympathy for that particular dog was perhaps sincere. But so was the other dog killed at Andover for the misery of being bewitched. But among the people called Christians, both then and now, it is merely impossible to find words to express what lies open in Sewall's entry here. It does not merely shock, it repels far; for, whatever be allowed to these Puritan times, it comes from a man who in most other ways seems so amiable.

"To Jere Dummer, 1710.

"Barter away none, nothing of our religious privileges though you might have millions in lieu of them. Be watchful and diligent for their preservation."

About Deacon Brown and the Church-of-England people at Newburyport, who petitioned to be erected into a parish, Sewall writes to Colonel Thomas Noyes, March 3, 1712:—

"Notwithstanding their aprons of fig leaves they walk naked and their neighbors see their shame; yet I apprehend it will be most advisable for those of the West Precinct not to meddle with them or forcibly take anything of them towards defraying any of the charges of the Precinct. This seems to me best for the Precinct, and best for Newbury and for the Province. And most for the interest of religion. And we should stick at nothing for Christ."

March 12, same year, he writes to Mr. John Webster of the same town concerning Brown:—

"I desire you to go to him in your own name and mine; but especially in the name of God. Give him Mr. Higginson's sermon; tell him I have sent it to him as a token of my love. Demand of him whether that which Mr. Higginson and the New England worthies accounted the Cause of God, he does advisedly to account it the Cause of the Evil one and to desert it accordingly? Ask him whether he be persuaded that Mr. Bridger doth more earnestly desire and seek his good than you do who have lived by him and loved him above these fifty years? Enquire of your friend Joshua Brown whether what he is now about, be a justifiable Keeping of the Fifth Commandment; and whether he be now denying himself and taking up his Cross and following Jesus Christ? Ask him whether it be best to have the Apocrypha and the Canonical Scriptures yoked up together? Whether it be best to have the Sign of the Cross in baptism? Whether it be best to have a great number of days in the year, placed as high as the Lord's day, if not above it? I shall not enlarge, hoping that by the good spirit of God you will be assisted to speak beyond what I can write."

In August, 1708, Sewall addressed a letter to Mr. Henry Flint, tutor in Harvard College, which shows the anxious eye about any sort of approach to the Church of England, and is therefore here quoted: —

"I thank you for your good sermon yesterday. The subject is excellent and always seasonable. Upon this occasion you will allow me the freedom of speaking what I have lately been often thinking. According to the simplicity of the Gospel the saying *Saint* Luke and *Saint* John has been disused in New England. And to take it up again is distasteful to me because it is a change for the worse: I have heard it from several; but to hear it from the senior fellow of Harvard College is more surprising; lest by his example he should seem to countenance and authorize inconvenient innovations. Thus I reckon; but if reckoning without my host I reckon wrong; your adjusting the account will gratify,

"Sir, your humble Servant;

"SAMUEL SEWALL."

In Sewall's Diary, under date of Aug. 26, 1708, there is an account of a subsequent interview between these parties: —

"Mr. Henry Flint in the way from Lecture came to me and mentioned my letter and would have discoursed about it in the street. I prevailed with him to come and dine with me and after that I and he discoursed alone. He argued that saying *Saint* Luke was an indifferent thing; and 'twas commonly used; and therefore he might use it. Mr. Brattle used it. I argued that it was not Scriptural; that 'twas absurd and partial to *Saint* Matthew &c., and not to say *Saint* Moses, *Saint* Samuel &c. And if we said *Saint* we must go thorough and keep the holy days appointed for them and turned to the order in the Common Prayer Book."

A single fact will serve to show the trend of the Puritan temper. The Jane Hirst referred to in the preface was Betty Sewall's daughter, and therefore Sewall's grandchild. Yet it is she who Sewall agrees, as guardian, shall be courted by the rector of Trinity Church, a minister of the Church of England.

CHAPTER XVI.

CURRENT NEW ENGLAND LIFE FROM 1714 to OCT. 13, 1729.

"MAY 12, 1714. In a piece of a Gazette mentioned a large Dromedary seven foot high and twelve foot long, taken from the Turks at the siege of Vienna, to be sold."

"June 3. This Court the Deputies send in a bill to complain of a duty laid on boards brought from Kittery and Berwick [Maine] by the government of New Hampshire."

A TARIFF tax between two provinces forsooth! The court proposed as a remedy a duty on wines from New Hampshire! It was thought that the board tax would amount to £500 against the Bay State. The deputies seem to have contented themselves with voting, June 25th, that the tax "is a great grievance and abuse to her Majesty's good subjects of this Province, highly injurious to the government and a breach of the good correspondence between the Provinces." So the matter, without much more ado, ended. Yet there is a smack of Puritan stubbornness in the refusal of the deputies to send a messenger north to confer about the matter, because, they said, "it imported our inability to help ourselves."

"July 13. P.M. I lay a brick in Mr. Colman's house building near his meeting house [Brattle Square]; gave Hill the mason 3s.; Coffee [negro] called him from above. This Coffee tells me he gives Mr. Pemberton £40 for his time that he might be with his wife. I gave him 5s. to help him."

"Aug. 31. About 4 P.M. visited Mr. [Rev.] Peter Thatcher, Milton. He was very glad to see me, said 'twas a cordial. Carried him two China Oranges."

"Sept. 17. News was brought to us of the Queen's death [Anne] as we sat on the bench. Chapman told it Mr. Corwin, and he standing up with a very sad countenance said to me, 'Sad news.' I was afraid Boston was burnt again."

Here, again, Sewall's silence is significant. Queen Anne was a High Churchwoman, and had given much aid to the Church of England here. It was not the crown that Sewall so much abhorred, but the mitre behind the crown. Not a word of eulogy, regret, or meditation over a dead queen, though he can sometimes pity a dog.

"Sept. 20. At Milton heard the Proclamation of George I. was to be on Wednesday."

So midweek George I. was proclaimed with oaths, and a state dinner at the Green Dragon, when one divine craved a blessing and another gave thanks. The new king was not a great theologian, nor did he or his strain meddle much with the Church of England, which ought to have made them more acceptable in Puritan Boston than Queen Anne, Mary's sister, and daughter of James II.

"Octr 8th. I visit Mr. William Homes, Mr. Thomas Craighead, ministers, in order to know what was best to be done as to the ships coming up. [Probably missionaries to the Indians, detained down the harbor by some infectious disease on shipboard.] Carried them a bushel turnips, cost me 5*s*. and a cabbage cost half a crown. [To keep down scurvy?] Dined at the Castle. Mr. Stanton, the chaplain, gone a gunning."

"Decr 10. The king is styled the Supreme Lord of the Massachusetts."

This entry may fairly lead us to suppose that at penning it Sewall was jealous for the Lord Jehovah, whom all Puritans fondly hoped was and was to be "the Supreme Lord of the Massachusetts."

Lord's Day, Dec. 26, Sewall leaves his own meeting, and goes to communion at another, noting: —

"I did it to hold communion with that Church; and, so far as in me lay, to put respect upon that affronted, despised Lord's Day. For the Church of England had the Lord's Supper yesterday, [Christmas], the last day of the week; but will not have it to-day, the day that the Lord has made. [But according to the Bible it was the seventh day of the week which the Lord made a Sabbath. The first day was made a Sunday merely by church authority.] And Genl Nicholson who kept Saturday was this Lord's Day rummaging and chittering with wheelbarrows to get aboard at the Long wharf and firing guns at setting sail. I thank God, I heard not, saw not anything of it, but was quiet at the New North."

"July 6, 1715. This day it is fifty four years since I first was brought ashore to Boston near where Scarlett's wharf now is; the Lord help me to redeem the time which passes so swiftly. I was then a poor little schoolboy of nine years and ¼ old."

May, 1716. About this time an anonymous letter was published, reflecting on the government. This was attributed to Wm. Dummer, a relative of Sewall: —

"In the Council Lieut. Governor spake very coarsely of cousin Wm. Dummer; — '*this fellow*' and I think worse. I said he was a gentleman and his father and grandfather, which calmed him and brought him to better language. I said at the same time [speaking probably of politicians] There are some men in the world are so mortally sick of the plague of selfishness, that except they might be charioteers, they wished the chariot burnt or off the wheels, I was for upholding government whether in or out of it."

Very possibly, but within limitations. Sewall was a Conformist, and his blood tended to a middle course of compromise. But too sharp a challenge to his conscience, as, for instance, if the government had proposed to set a cross on the Old South Meeting-House, would likely have driven him to become a very stout and unsparing rebel; at least in his Diary.

Here is a bit of personal gossip which, considering the very grave person involved in it, is not a trifle grotesque: —

"Now about Aug. 15 Dr. C. Mather fishing at Spy Pond, falls into the water, the boat being ticklish, but receives no hurt."

"Novr 7, 1717. Last night died the excellent Waitstill Winthrop Esq., for parentage, piety, prudence, philosophy, love to New England ways and people very eminent. Help Lord!"

"Decr 22. Lord's Day we had great lightning and three claps of loud thunder, the last very sharp and startling. This was a little before the rising of the sun. Two houses in Boston were stricken with it."

"Lord's Day Feby 23, 1718. I set York tune and the congregation went out of it into St. David's in the very 2^d^ going over. They did the same 3 weeks before. This is the 2^d^ sign. This seems to me an intimation and a call for me to resign the precentor's place to a better voice. I have through the Divine long suffering and favor done it for 24 years, and now God by his providence seems to call me off; my voice being enfeebled. I spake to Mr. White earnestly, to set it in the afternoon; but he declined it. I then went to the two pastors, my son Sewall and Prince, and laid this matter before them, told them how long I had set the tune; Mr. Prince said 'Do it six years longer.' I persisted and said that Mr. White or Franklin [Benjamin Franklin's father] might do it very well."

"March 2. I told Mr. White the Elders desired him, he must set the tune, he disabled himself as if he had a cold. But when the psalm was appointed I forebore to do it, and rose up and turned to him and he set York tune to a very good key. I thanked him for restoring York tune to its station with so much authority and honor. I was glad. I saw 'twas convenient that I had resigned, being for the benefit of the congregation. (P.M. Madam Winthrop's Essex is baptized, she undertaking for the child's education)."

"March 24. Had much business in the probate office. In proving Gaul's will one of the witnesses held up his left hand. I bid him hold up his right hand. He told me he had none."

"March 31. Madam Rebecca Brown comes to town." [Undoubtedly an eligible match lately recommended to him by President Leverett.]

"April 16. I was nominated for Chief Justice," [etc.].

"Jany 23, 1719. A notorious counterfeiter of the new twenty shilling bill, is apprehended; had his plate made in London and came over in Clark. He went to England on purpose to get it done."

"March 31. This day a ship arrives from Lisbon, 6 weeks' passage; brings news that war is declared by France against Spain; and also by England against Spain. The King of Sweden [Charles XII.] is dead, being shot in the trenches before place in Norway he was besieging."

"April 1. In the morning I dehorted Sam Hirst and Grindal Rawson from playing idle tricks because 'twas first of April. They were the greatest fools that did so. New England men came hither to avoid anniversary days, the keeping of them, such as the 25th of December. How displeasing must it be to

God, the giver of our time, to keep anniversary days to play the fool with ourselves and others."

"April 4. Planted buttonwood trees."

It is surprising how many fruit trees and shade trees of English stock the New Englanders set out, and in how short a time.

"I have received 4 presents lately; 4 oranges, 2 pieces of salmon, Madam Foxcroft's wedding cake; and this (a very good pair of white kid gloves and a gold ring with the motto, *Lex et Libertas*) which is a very fair present indeed. I have hardly any to compare with it. The Good Lord help me to serve faithfully the Supreme Donor."

"May 12, 1720. In the evening I join the Revd Mr. William Cooper and Mrs. Judith Sewall in marriage. [This young lady, as the Diary shows, had been sought by no less a personage than Colonel William Dudley, the governor's son, and there had been negotiations between the families accordingly, who were already intermarried; but the young Puritan parson carried off the prize, as we see.] I said to Mr. Simeon Stoddard and his wife, Sir — Madam — The great honor you have conferred on the bridegroom and bride, by being present at this solemnity, does very conveniently supersede any further inquiry after your consent. And the part I am desired to take in this wedding renders the way of my giving my consent very compendious. There's no manner of room left for that previous question 'Who giveth this woman to be married to this man?' Dear child — you give me your hand for one moment and the Bridegroom forever. Spouse — You accept and receive this woman now given you &c. Mr. Sewall prayed before the wedding and Mr. Colman after. Sung the 115 Psalm from the 9th verse to the end. Then we had our cake and sack posset."

There is one entry worth quoting in this connection, as a glimpse into the future of these two:—

TUESDAY, Sept. 15, 1724.

HON^D SIR;

Our dear babe quietly departed a few minutes after 5, P.M. I humbly trust the Good Shepherd who laid down his life for the lambs as well as the sheep has gathered it into his bosom. Asking prayers

I am, your afflicted Son,

WILLIAM COOPER.

"Lord's Day, April 3, 1726. My son [Joseph Sewall] preached in the forenoon from Gen. i. 26. Read the whole chapter and commented pithily and well upon it; and after that spoke to the 26th verse. I desire with humble thankfulness to bless God who has favored me with such an excellent discourse to begin my 75th year, withal delivered by my own son, making him as a parent to his father."

The last entry in the Diary is Oct. 13, 1729. Speaks of a request made to Judge Sewall for permission "for a young man to wait upon Jane Hirst, now at my house, in the way of courtship. I gave him my hand at going away and acknowledged his respect to me, and granted his desire. The Lt Governor commended the young man and reckoned it a very good match."

Two brief entries may serve to show the political epoch at which Sewall passed off the stage of affairs, on which he had been so long a conspicuous actor: —

"Midweek, Aug. 16, 1727. King George, the Second is proclaimed at Boston at 2 P.M. Aug. 17. The Revd Mr. Joseph Sewall preaches King George's funeral sermon. 'Twas his turn and the Council also desired him."

July 10, 1716, Mrs. Hirst (Betty Sewall) died. She suffered from a long languishment, probably consumption. Sewall seems to have been proud of her, for some reasons his favorite daughter. At the death-bed Sewall said, "When my flesh and my heart faileth me, God is the strength of my heart and my portion forever. Thus," he adds, "I have parted with a very desirable child, not full thirty-five years old. She lived desired and died lamented. The Lord fit me to follow and help me to prepare my wife and children for a dying hour."

On his circuit in western Massachusetts he notes: "Eating our Deerfield bread and drinking of the river out of David's bottle." Next morning he breakfasted on "roast fowls." The same night he lodged where there was no glass in the house.

"Oct. 5, 1716. Governor and Lt Governor laid their hands on the Bible and kissed it very industriously."

"Decr 25, 1716. Shops are open and sleds come to town as at other times."

"April 16, 1716. This day I first saw the swallows. I think I had heard some chipper before."

"April 17. I see plenty of them."

"April 27, 1716. Mr. Bromfield has prayer at his house respecting his son Edward, troubled in mind; and Henry, student of Harvard College, having a dangerous swelling on his back."

"June 8, 1716. This day I received a letter full of vile reproaches which I desire to spread before the Lord."

"1715, Feby 6. Tuesday I set Winsor tune and the people at the 2^d going over run into Oxford, do what I could."

Going to the gate with a departing guest, from the founding of Boston at least to the middle of the eighteenth century, was in general a courtesy of obligation.

"Aug. 18, 1715. Mr. Pemberton appears in a flaxen wigg."

After the governor and Council had arranged some perplexing affairs of state at the expected coming of Governor Burgess, Sewall writes: —

"I acquainted Mr. Pemberton with this transaction that he might know how to pray."

This management between the Council board and the pulpit appears again and again in the Diary.

"Oct. 18. Now about Dr. Mather shows me a copy of Govr Dudley's signing a petition for a bishop as the only means to promote religion here."

Sewall was now on his circuit.

"May 12, 1714. Not being able to get hay, sent our horses to pasture on the Kittery side."

Courts were often held in houses; oftener in meeting-houses. The old New Englanders had the same happy faculty of adjusting themselves to their circumstance that our Western emigrants have, and their posterity have not forgotten the craft.

"July 17, 1714. Benjamin Larnell [Indian] appears to have a fever by being delirious. Lord's Day, 18^{h}. I put up a note. 20th. My son comes to our house and prays for Larnell in his mother's bed chamber. I, his mother and sister Hannah present. July 22^{d}. Benj. Larnell expired last night about midnight. Was delirious to the last as far as I can perceive. I left him about 11. Buried this day. Bearers, students of Harvard College. They had white scarfs and gloves. I and the President went next the corpse. The note that I put up at Lecture was Prayers are desired that God would graciously grant a suitable improvement of the death of Benj. Larnell, student of Harvard College. I spake to Mr. Wadsworth of his death betime in the morning. He prayed very well about this article."

Sewall mellows as he ages, as good fruit always does. Here was a poor Indian youth, gone dead in Sewall's house, and buried and mourned with all the decorum which sincere sorrow could take on.

"Sun^{y}, Jany. 15, 1716. An extraordinary cold storm of wind and snow. Bread was frozen at the Lord's Table; though 'twas so cold, yet John Tuckerman was baptized. At six a clock my ink freezes so I can hardly write by a good fire in my wife's chamber."

"Feby 8. Sloop run away with by a whale out of a good harbor at the Cape. How suprisingly uncertain our enjoyments in this world are!"

This pious reflection, it should be noted, apparently does not refer to the loss of the sloop.

CHAPTER XVII.

JUDGE SEWALL'S COURTSHIP OF MADAM WINTHROP, *ALIARUMQUE.*

JUDGE SEWALL'S wife Hannah, mint-master John Hull's daughter, died Oct. 19, 1717. She had been for some time in a decline, aggravated, probably, by some sort of malarial fever; and as far back as July 3 her husband notes that he has been kept from Commencement by his wife's being taken very sick the night before. "This is the second year of my absence from that solemnity." So with the usual Puritan solemnities of prayer and fast, her household waited on this exemplary wife and mother, making her exit.

"About a quarter of an hour past four, my dear wife expired in the afternoon, whereby the chamber was filled with a flood of tears. God is teaching me a new lesson — to lead a widower's life. Lord help me to learn and be a sun and shield to me, now so much of my comfort and defence are taken away."

Next day he writes: —

"I go to the public worship forenoon and afternoon. My son has much adoe to read the note I put up, being overwhelmed with tears."

Sewall was sincere with all his great loving heart

in his sorrow, and kept, as his Diary shows, her memory in love till his death's day. So much it is right should be said as we enter upon the series of very remarkable courtships which he has recorded in his Diary. Whether it was wise in him to make the entries, or quite gracious in posterity to print the same, is a question with two plain sides to it. Men who write diaries as picturesque and vivid as Sewall's must run their own risk; and it is highly improbable that he would have taken so much pains in record, if he had not had an eye to posterity as his readers. Only, in justice to so good a man, we must recollect his new circumstance and danger. Hannah Sewall, like every good and competent wife, had been the balance-wheel, the conservative element, in the Sewall family. When she died, the better half of him gone, it was not strange if he reeled away from his ordinary good sense into marital vagaries bordering on absurdity. A man under a heavy burden staggers. They who do not see the burden as he goes down the street, may reasonably suppose that he is drunk. To say so much is simple justice; and if any reader wishes to be generous, he can be so by ignoring the dates that are to follow. Besides, it was expected, with the rigor of a society law, in the Puritan land, that widows and widowers should remarry. They all did it, and not to do it was a social offence. Apparently they all helped each other to do it, and for a man in Judge Sewall's social station there was no way of escape. Nor, truth to say, did Sewall try to find one.

All this and more appears in the Diary. Boston seems to have been rich in marriageable widows, and those of Sewall's social station were well known to him; and to them he turned both for advice and sympathy. After the feminine way and measure, they apparently gave both.

"Decr 1, 1717. Madam Winthrop comes not to meeting in the afternoon. I enquire of Mr. Winthrop. He saith she was not well at noon; but was better."

"Decr 2. I visit Madam Winthrop at her own house. Tell her of my sending Hannah to Salem to-morrow; ask her advice as to selling Mr. Hirst's goods; she advises to sell all but plate and linen. I ask her to give and take condolence. She thanks me for my kindness; I tell her she is beforehand with me. When I came away I prayed God to dwell with her, counsel and comfort her. She desired my prayers."

"Jany. 18, 1718. Inquired of Jno Walley how Madam Winthrop and her family did."

"Feby 6. This morning wandering in my mind whether to live a single or a married life, I had a sweet and very affectionate meditation concerning the Lord Jesus. Nothing was to be objected against his person, parentage, relations, estate, house, home. Why did I not presently close with him. And I cried mightily to God that he would help me so to do."

"Feby. 10. I receive a letter from Mr. Winthrop, having one inclosed to his mother which I carry to her. She tells me Mr. Eyre married her May 20, 1680. Lived together above 20 years."

"March 10. In Madam Usher's absence Madam Henchman took occasion highly to commend Madam Winthrop, the Major General's widow. March 14. Deacon Marion comes to me, sits with me a great while in the evening; after a great deal of discourse about his courtship — he told me the Olivers said they wished I would court their aunt [Madam Winthrop]. I said 'twas not five months since I buried my dear wife. Said little, but said before 'twas hard to know whether best to marry again or no; whom to marry. Dr. Mather [Increase] sends me his Marah in a letter in which is this expression, 'But your honor will allow me now at length to offer you my opinion that all the regards are not yet paid which you owe unto the *Widow*, and which are expected from you.'"

This *Marah* was probably one of the elder Mather's books, with the title, "An Essay to do Good unto the Widow," and the grave badinage here of the Puritan divine at the expense of the Puritan judge is characteristic.

"March 19. Mr. Leverett, when he and I alone, told me his wife and he had laid out Madam Brown for me and yet took occasion to say that Madam Winthrop had done very generously by the Major General's family in giving up her dower. I said if Madam Brown should leave her fair accommodations at Salem, she might be apt to repent it."

But this time, either because fate was unpropitious, or Sewall's discretion had the upper hand, he turned for comfort to the Widow Denison, whose story is told in the Diary, — "an autumnal matron," as Hawthorne would phrase it, but withal a business woman, not wasting property on sentiment.

"March 19. I write Mr. W^{m}. Denison's will, being desired by a messenger from Roxbury with minutes."

March 26, Sewall, with other Puritan notables, attended Mr. Denison's funeral at Roxbury, where his pastor, Mr. Walter, said, "he was a man of truth and of trust, a man of prayer, integrity and piety."

"Govr Dudley and I went next the mourners. Went back to the house in a coach. At coming away I prayed God to keep house with the widow." "Mr. Danforth gives the widow Denison a high commendation for her piety, prudence, diligence, humility." "April 7. I prove Mr. Denison's will. Her brother Edmund Weld brought the widow to town and gave me notice beforehand. I gave her 10s to give her sister Weld for her Indian Bible. Mr. Dorr took occasion in her absence to say she was one of the most dutiful wives in the world. Her cousin, the widow Hayden, accidentally came in with her. April 8. Mr. Boydell, when I was at his office and signed the papers, smiling said Mr. Denison's will looked as if it was written by me. I told him, 'Yes, but there was not a tittle of it mine, but the form.'"

"June 3d. Go to Roxbury, talk with Mr. Walter about Mrs. Denison. He advises me not to see her then, lest should surprise her undressed. Told him I came on purpose; yet finally submitted to his advice; he spake of her coming to town on Thursday. June 5. Nobody came — I writ to Mr. Walter. June 9. Note. Mrs. D. came in the morning about 9 o'clock, and I took her up into my chamber and discoursed thoroughly with her. She desired me to procure another and a better nurse.

"I gave her the two last *News Letters* — told her I intended to visit her at her own house next lecture day. She said 'twould be talked of. I answered in such cases persons must run the gantlet. Gave her Mr. Whiting's oration for Abijah Walter who brought her on horseback to town. I think little or no notice was taken of it."

"June 17. Went to Roxbury Lecture. Visited Govr Dudley, Mrs. Denison; gave her Dr. Mather's sermons very well bound; told her we were in it invited to a wedding. She gave me very good curds. July 2. I give Mrs. Denison her oath to the inventory [of her husband's goods]. At night when all were gone to bed, Cousin Moodey went with me into the new hall, read the history of Rebecca's Courtship and prayed with me respecting my widowed condition. July 16. Went and visited Mrs. Denison. Gave her King George's effigies in copper; and an English crown of King Charles II., 1677. Eat curds with her; I craved a blessing and returned thanks; came home after it."

"July 25. I go in the hackney coach to Roxbury. Call at Mr. Walter's who is not at home; nor Govr Dudley nor his lady. Visit Mrs. Denison; she invites me to eat. I give her two cases with a knife and fork in each; one, turtle shell tackling; the other long with ivory handles, squared, cost 4^s 6^d; pound of raisins with proportionable almonds. Visited her brother and sister Weld."

"Aug. 6. Visited Mrs. Denison, carried her sister Weld, the widow and Mrs. Weld to her brother, where we were courteously entertained. Brought Mr. Edmund Weld's wife home with me in the coach; she is in much darkness. Gave Mrs. Denison a psalm-book neatly bound in England with Turkey leather. 27th. I ride and visit Mrs. Denison, leave my horse at the Grey Hound. She mentions her discouragements by reason of discourses she heard; I prayed God to direct her and me."

In fact, Sewall visits this lady upon almost every opportunity; but as his duties as circuit judge took him away, Mrs. Denison disappears from the Diary while he is on his travels. The next significant entry is Oct. 15:—

"Visit Mrs. Denison on horseback; present her with a pair of shoe buckles cost 5*s*. 3*d*." "Nov. 1. My son from Brookline being here I took his horse and visited Mrs. Denison. I told her 'twas time now to finish our business. Asked her what I should allow her, she not speaking. I told her I was willing to give her £250 p^r annum during her life, if it should please God to take me out of the world before her. She answered she had better keep as she was than to give a certainty for an uncertainty. She should pay dear for dwelling at Boston. I desired her to make proposals but she made none. I had thought of publishment next Thursday. But now I seem to be far from it. May God who has the pity of a father, direct and help me!"

Her late husband, as Sewall well knew, had left her a life interest in all his estates. The trouble seems to have been that Mrs. Denison declined to alienate any of her interests to him if she married. In fact, all through his latter courtships Sewall shines more as a sharp business man than a man either of tact or sentiment.

"Novr 28, 1718. I went this day in the coach; had a fire made in the chamber where I spake with her before. I enquired how she had done these three or four weeks. Afterwards I told her our conversation had been such when I was with her last that it seemed to be a direction in Providence not to proceed any further; she said it must be what I pleased, or to that purpose."

Then there apparently proceeded one of those interminable wrangles, not peculiar to Puritan courtships, and in this case carried on with due Puritan decorum, which, as usual with persons in such relations, came to nothing, she holding to her own. The close only shows plain colors of human interest: —

"She asked me if I would drink; I told her Yes. She gave me cider, apples and a glass of wine; gathered together the little things I had given her and offered them to me; but I would take none of them. Told her I wished her well, should be glad to hear of her welfare. She seemed to say she should not take in hand a thing of this nature. Thanked me for what I had given her and desired my prayers. I gave Abijah Weld an Angel. Got home about 9 at night My bowels yearn towards Mrs. Denison; but I think God directs me in his Providence to desist."

We catch one more glimpse of the lady, Lord's Day, Nov. 30, when, in the evening, while Sewall was at family prayers: —

"She came in, preceded by her cousin Weld, saying she wished to speak to me in private. I was very much startled that she should come so far afoot in that exceeding cold season. She asked pardon if she had affronted me. Seemed inclined the match should not break off, since I had kept her company so long. I fetched a tankard of cider and drank to her. She desired that nobody might know of her being here. I told her they should not. She went away in the bitter cold, no moon being up, to my great pain. I saluted her at parting."

The last glimpse of Mrs. Denison in the Diary is this: —

"Dec. 22. Mrs. Dorothy Denison brings an additional inventory. I gave her her oath; asked her brother Brewer and her to dine with me; she said she needed not to eat; caused her to sit by the fire and went with her to the door at her going away. She said nothing to me nor her brother Brewer."

This lady remarried in 1720.
Next comes Mrs. Tilly.

"Sept. 2, 1719. Visit Mrs. Tilly and speak with her in her chamber; ask her to come and dwell at my house. She expresses her unworthiness of such a thing with much respect. I tell her of my going to Bristol [on his circuit probably]. I would have her consider of, she answered she would have me consider of it. Sept. 21. I gave Mrs. Tilly a little book entitled 'Ornaments for the daughters of Sion.' I gave it to my dear wife Aug. 28, 1702." "23^d. Eat almonds and reasons [raisins] with Mrs. Tilly and Mrs. Armitage. Discoursed with Mrs. Armitage, who spake very agreeably and said Mrs. Tilly had been a great blessing to them and hoped God would make her so to me and my family."

Oct. 29, 1719, they were married, with the usual Puritan festivities, by the judge's son, Mr. Joseph

Sewall. Not to make further mention of a lady who, though his wife, seems to us to have been hardly more than a shadow in Sewall's real life, albeit she was an exemplary woman, it may be noted that she died suddenly May 26, 1720.

Sewall's opinion of this wife is in a letter:—

"She, my wife carries it very tenderly and is very helpful to me, my children and grandchildren."

After Mrs. Tilly's funeral there is no record of any marital movement on Sewall's part until Oct. 1, when he writes:—

"Saturday I dine at Mr. Stoddard's; from thence I went to Madam Winthrop's just at 3. Spake to her saying, my loving wife died so soon and suddenly, 'twas hardly convenient for me to think of marrying again; however I came to this resolution that I would not make my court to any person without first consulting with her. Had a pleasant discourse about seven single persons sitting in the Fore Seat Sept. 29 [the Sunday before], viz. Madam Rebecca Dudley, Catharine Winthrop [the lady before him], Bridget Usher, Deliverance Legg, Rebecca Loyd, Lydia Colman, Elizabeth Bellingham. She propounded one and another for me; but none would do, said Mrs. Loyd was about her age."

As before noted, Sewall had never forgotten madam. He notes:—

"Feby. 3, 1718. Sent Madam Winthrop, 'Smoking Flax inflamed,' 'The Jewish Children of Berlin,' and my 'Small Vial of Tears' by Mr. Gerrish, with my service. She thanks me and returns her service to me."

Sewall, *prepense*, had now evidently gone to Madam Winthrop for a match, and he was to find his match, but not exactly in the way he hoped. He was now sixty-nine, and the lady fifty-six, twice married before, and with grown-up children.

"Octr. 2. Evening. Waited on Madam Winthrop again; 'twas a little while before she came in. Her daughter Noyes being there alone with me, I said I hoped my waiting on her mother would not be disagreeable to her. She answered she should not be against that that might be for her comfort. By and by came in Mr. Airs, chaplain of the Castle and hanged up his hat, which I was a little startled at, it seeming as if he was to lodge there. At last Madam Winthrop came too. After a considerable time I went up to her and said, if it might not be inconvenient I desired to speak with her. She assented and spake of going into another room; but Mr. Airs and Mrs. Noyes presently rose up and went out, leaving us there alone. Then I ushered in discourse from the names in the Fore Seat; at last I prayed that Katharine [Madam Winthrop] might be the person assigned for me. She instantly took it up in the way of denial, as if she had catched at an opportunity to do it, saying, she could not do it before she was asked. Said that was her mind unless she should change it, which she believed she should not — could not leave her children. I expressed my sorrow that she should do it so speedily, prayed her consideration, and asked her when I should wait on her agen. She setting no time, I mentioned that day Sennight. Gave her Mr. Willard's 'Fountain Opened,' with the little print and verses; saying I hoped if we did well read that book, we should meet together hereafter, if we did not now. She took the book and put it in her pocket. Took leave. Oct. 5. Midweek. Although I had appointed to wait upon her, Madam Winthrop, next Monday, yet I went from my cousin Sewall's thither about 3. The nurse told me Madam dined abroad at her daughter Noyes, they were to go out together. Gave Katee a penny and a kiss and came away."

"Oct. 6. A little after six P.M. I went to Madam Winthrop's. She was not within. I gave the maid 2*s.*; Juno, who brought in wood, 1*s*. After the nurse came in I gave her 18*d*., having no other small bill. After a while Dr. Noyes came in with his mother, and quickly after his wife. They sat talking, I think, till eight o'clock. I said I feared I might be some interruption to their business. Dr. Noyes replied pleasantly, they feared they might be some interruption to *my* business, and went away. Madam seemed to harp upon the same string, must take care of her children, could not leave that house and neighborhood, etc. I gave her a piece of Mr. Belcher's cake and gingerbread wrapped up in a clean sheet of paper. My daughter Judith I said was gone from me and I was more lonesome — might help to forward one another in our journey to Canaan. I took leave about nine o'clock."

"October 11th. I write a few lines to Madam Winthrop to this purpose. Madam: These wait on you with Mr. Mayhew's sermon and an account of the state of the Indians of Martha's Vineyard. I thank you for your unmerited favors of yesterday [she had given him wine marmalade, etc.], and hope to have the happiness of waiting on you to-morrow before eight o'clock after noon. I pray God to keep you and give you a joyful entrance upon the 229th year of Christopher Columbus, his discovery, and take leave, who am, madam, your humble serv't.

S. S.

"Sent this by Deacon Green, &c."

"Oct. 12. In the little room Madam Winthrop was full of work behind a stand. Mrs. Cotton came in and stood. Madam pointed to her to set me a chair. Her countenance looked dark and lowering. At last the work [black stuff or silk] was taken away. I got my chair in place, had some converse, but very cold and indifferent to what 'twas before. Asked her to acquit me of rudeness if I drew off her glove. Enquiring the reason I told her 'twas great odds between handling a dead goat and a living lady. Got it off! I told her I had one petition to ask of her to wit, to change her answer. She insisted on her negative. I gave her Dr. Preston's 'The Churche's Marriage and the Churche's Carriage,' which cost me 6*s*. Sarah filled a glass of wine, she drank to me, I to her. She sent Juno home with me with a good lantern. I gave her 6*d*., and bade her thank her mistress. In some of our discourse I told her the reason why I came every other night was lest I should drink too deep draughts of pleasure. She had talked of Canary, her kisses were to me better than the best Canary. Explained the expression concerning Columbus. [In the name of two worlds, what might it be in a love letter!]"

"Oct. 17. In the evening I visited Madam Winthrop, who treated me courteously, but not in clean linen as sometimes. She said she did not know whether I would come again or no. I asked her how she could impute inconstancy to me. Gave her this day's *Gazette*. Heard David Jeffries [her little grandson] say the Lord's Prayer and some other portions of the Scriptures. Juno came home with me."

"Oct. 18. Visited Madam Mico who came to me in a splendid dress. I said, It may be you have heard of my visiting Madam Winthrop, her sister. [Probably.] She answered, Her sister had told her of it. If her sister were for it, she should not hinder it. I gave her Mr. Homes's sermon. She gave me a glass of Canary, entertained me with good discourse and a respectful remembrance of my first wife. I took leave."

This is the lady who some suggest would have listened to Sewall's suit more patiently than her sister. "The splendid dress" in which Sewall notes she came to him, certainly squints just a trifle that way.

"Oct. 19. Visited Madam Winthrop. Sarah told me she was at Mrs. Walley's, would not come home till late. Was ready to go home, but said if I knew she was there, I would go thither. I went and found her with Mr. Walley and his wife in the little room below. At seven o'clock I mentioned going home; at eight I put on my coat and quickly waited on her home. Was courteous to me, but took occasion to speak pretty earnestly about my keeping a coach. I said 'twould cost £100 per annum. She said 'twould cost but £46."

"Oct. 20. Madam Winthrop not being at lecture, I went thither first; found her very serene with her daughter Noyes, etc. She drank to me, and I to Mrs. Noyes. After a while prayed the favor to speak with her. She took one of the candles and went into the best room, closed the shutters, and sat down upon the couch. She spoke something of my needing a wigg. I took leave."

"Oct. 21. My Son [the parson] and I pray for one another in the old chamber, more especially respecting my courtship. At six o'clock I go to Madam Winthrop's. Sarah told me her mistress had gone out, but did not tell me whither she went. She presently ordered me a fire; so I went in, having Dr. Sibb's 'Bowells' with me to read. [This was a book on "The Discovery of the Union between Christ and the Church."] A while after nine, madam came in. I mentioned something of the lateness: she bantered me and said I was later. I asked her when our proceedings should be made public. She said they were like to be no more public than they were already. Offered me no wine that I remember. I rose up at eleven o'clock to come away, saying I would put on my coat. She offered not to help me. I prayed that Juno might light me home, she opened the shutter and said was pretty light abroad; Juno was weary and gone to bed. So I came home by starlight as well as I could. Jehovah Jireh. The Lord reigneth."

"Oct. 24. As to my periwig, I told her my best and greatest Friend (I could not possibly have a greater) began to find me with hair before I was born and had continued to do so ever since, and I could not find it in my heart to go to another. She gave me a dram of black cherry brandy and a lump of the sugar that was in it."

"Nov. 4. I asked madam what fashioned necklace I should present her with. She said none at all. I asked her whereabouts we left off last time; mentioned what I had offered to give her; asked her what she would give me. She said she could not change her condition, and had said so from the beginning."

"Nov. 7. I went to Madam Winthrop; found her rocking her little Katie in the cradle. She set me an armed chair and a cushion. Gave her the remnants of my almonds. She did not eat of them as before, but laid them away. Asked if she remained of the same mind still. She said thereabouts. I told her I loved her, and was so fond as to think that she loved me.

The fire was come to one short brand besides the block, which brand was set up on end; at last it fell to pieces, and no recruit was made. She gave me a glass of wine. I did not bid her draw off her glove, as sometime I had done. Her dress was not so clean as sometime it had been. The Lord reigneth."

And so with the one black brand on a fireless hearth the curtain falls on Sewall's courtship of Madam Winthrop. Soon after he married Mrs. Gibbs.

The rocks on which Sewall's matrimonial venture here split apparently were several. He would not agree to set up a coach, claiming he could not afford it, nor wear a periwig, as madam wished; he had tried to drive a close-fisted bargain in the marriage settlement, and perhaps had tried to meddle with the status of her slaves; and, above all, she was, as she said, averse to separation from her kin and grandchildren, though she was hardly ingenuous in assigning as one reason, that the Apostle Paul had affirmed that a single life was better than a married one, inasmuch as she had married twice already. So this courtship lapsed, apparently with no ill will on either side. There are entries in the Diary later on which look like willingness on Madam Winthrop's part to leave the door just a trifle ajar; but Sewall went another way. There is one entry, however, of the very few concerning her, made on the Lord's Day, Dec. 6, 1724, which quaintly illustrates the man and the times:—

"At the Lord's Supper Deacon Checkly delivered the cup first to Madam Winthrop and then gave me a tankard. 'Twas humiliation to me and I think put me to the blush to have this injustice done me by a Justice. May all be sanctified."

In this precedency of the cup to Madam Winthrop, Sewall evidently saw a slight to his magistracy.

"June 15, 1725. I accompanied my son [the minister] to Madam Winthrop. She was abed about 10, morning. [She was evidently in her last sickness.] I told her I found my son coming to her and took the opportunity to come with him. She thanked me kindly and enquired how Madam Sewall did. Asked my son to go to prayer. At coming I said, I kiss your hand, Madam (her hand felt very dry). She desired me to pray that God would lift up upon her the light of his countenance."

The last entries are these: —

"Monday, Aug. 2d, Mrs. Katharine Winthrop, relict of the Hono Waitstill Winthrop, Esq., died, Æ 61."

She was born in September, 1664. Aug. 5, Sewall was one of her bearers. "Will be much missed." After the funeral Sewall notes he made a wedding call, and "had good bride cake, good wine, Burgundy and Canary, good beer, oranges and pears."

March 29, 1722, Sewall married the widow Mary Gibbs, who outlived him. There were certain events in the precedent negotiations leading up to this third marriage thoroughly characteristic of Sewall, which, lacking current interest, are here passed by. They can all, of course, be found in the Diary.

Sewall himself died Jan. 1, 1730.

In the *Weekly News Letter*, Jan. 8, 1730, appears a notice of Sewall's death, and a careful but friendly analysis of his life and character: —

"On the first of this instant, at half an hour past five in the morning, after about a month's languishment, died at his house here, the Honorable Samuel Sewall Esq., in the 78th year of his age; who has for above forty years appeared a great ornament of this town and country. In 1684 he was chosen a magistrate of the Massachusetts Colony; in 1692 he was appointed by King William and Queen Mary one of the first Council for their Majesties in this Province, into which he was annvally chosen and sat till 1725 when he resigned his election. In 1692 he was made one of the Judges and in 1718 Chief Justice of our Superior Courts of Judicature through the Province in which he sat till 1728 when his infirmities growing on him, he resigned that place also. In 1715 he was made Judge of Probates for this County of Suffolk, and continued in that office till 1728 when he laid it down; it being the last public post wherein he served and honored his country.

"He was universally and greatly reverenced, esteemed and beloved among us for his eminent piety, learning and wisdom; his grave and venerable aspect and carriage; his instructive, affable and cheerful conversation; his strict integrity and regard to justice; his extraordinary tender and compassionate heart; his neglect of the world; his abundant liberality; his catholic and public spirit; his critical acquaintance with the Holy Scriptures in their inspired originals; his zeal for the purity of instituted worship; his constant diligent and reverent attendance on it, both in the church and family; his love for the churches, people and ministers, the civil and religious interests of this country; his tender concern for the aboriginal natives; and as the crown of all, his moderation, peaceableness and humility rendered him one of the most shining lights and honors of the age and land wherein he lived and worthy of a very distinguishing regard in the New English histories.

"By his first wife he had seven sons and seven daughters; two of the former and one of the latter only survive him. His understanding continued with him to his last hours. He died in peace and was yesterday honorably interred."

CHAPTER XVIII.

SEWALL AND SUNDRIES.

SOMETIMES a clerk itemizing a bill grows tired, and masses the rest of the account under the head of sundries. In our examination of the old New England life, and Sewall as its expositor, many interesting facts in and out of his Diary have failed to connect themselves with the story. In this chapter it is intended to gather several of these stray items of interest.

Sewall cannot fairly be called either a wit or a humorist. Few Puritans ever were; and such a trifling with "the words of soberness" as a pun, would make against the punster, especially if he were in public station. Hezekiah Usher, whose will we have had heretofore in these pages, made perhaps the best pun among the Puritans when, at the misbehavior of some of the Christian Indians in King Philip's War, he said that "the praying Indians ought to be called *preying* Indians." But he apparently died insane. Sewall shows often an impulse towards humor, and the turn of a sentence in a letter sometimes approaches wit. But the gait is always a trifle too elephantine for success. He only approaches wit occasionally by joining together things incongruous, as where he notes that the colony at one time was troubled with Indians, small-pox, and heresy. The only resemblance to a pun which we have noted is in the following entry referring to his devout keeping of his thirty-fifth marriage day :—

"While I was spending a little fuel in private devotion I was supplied with a great pennyworth of bast i.e. bark of the bass or lime tree, by Bastian [his negro], and a load of black oak by Nathl. Sparhawk."

Here is another ponderous endeavor, a cross between a joke and a solemnity. When writing to a correspondent, he suggests :—

"It would be well if you could set on foot the printing of the Spanish Bible in a fair octavo ; ten thousand copies : and then you might attempt the bombarding of St. Domingo, the Havana, Porto Rico and Mexico itself. I would willingly give five pounds towards the charge of it."

When a certain jury gave a half verdict, Sewall writes, "I dissented from it as too small a plaster for so great a sore."

It looks as though his piety sometimes dried up all sense of humor. The Boston boys on All Fools' Day had a habit of bewildering ancient gentlemen by pointing to their ponderous shoe-buckles, and suggesting that something had gone wrong with them. Sewall actually wrote to the Boston schoolmasters (1708) :—

"Pray gentlemen if you think it convenient, as I hope you will, insinuate unto your scholars the defiling and provoking nature of such a foolish practice ; and take them off from it."

Perhaps his most creditable attempt at wit is this. The Rev. Joseph Gerrish, a country clergyman at Wenham, had declined to preach the sermon before the Ancient and Honorable Artillery, and Sewall writes (May, 1709): —

"Your choice was free and unanimous. The commission officers present their service to you, expressing their sorrow that they fail of your assistance. The reason why they do not immediately fill your house with armed men and insult you with military importunity is because they apprehend your resolution fixed; and they desire strictly to observe John Baptist's instructions (although they have no wages) to do incivility to no man; much less to yourself for whom they maintain a just respect."

Sewall also had a bias towards superstition, — at least so it looks to modern eyes, — which he shared with many of his neighbors. But in Sewall, as an educated man, this was more inexcusable. Yet even so wise and great a man as John Winthrop could write in his Journal (1640): —

"About this time there fell out a thing worthy of observation. Mr. Winthrop the younger, one of the magistrates, having many books in a chamber where there was corn of diverse sorts, had among them one wherein the Greek testament, the psalms and the common prayer were bound together. He found the common prayer eaten with mice, every leaf of it, and not any of the two other touched, nor any other of his books, though there were above a thousand."

An examination of this passage fairly reveals the fact that the educated writer actually believed that these mice had rendered a noticeable verdict against "the Book of Common Prayer." But then they were only mice, and a friend of that ancient compendium of the prayers of Winthrop's fathers, might have retorted with an equally gross *non sequitur*, that these mice had shown admirable taste in dining. Aptly enough, the next entry in the Journal is a "Query of the Child at Cambridge Killed by a Cat." Is it any wonder that the Salem witchcraft misery came?

Yet the distinction to be made between superstition and religion is often a very large and difficult question. In general, superstition is a recognition of the supernatural, not based either on revelation or science. The agnostic, declining to accept the supernatural at all, from his premise rightly calls all recognition of it superstition. Of course that has never been the way with the people called Christians. It is difficult to conceive of any religion using words exactly, which does not recognize the supernatural. Certainly the Puritans did, and with a precision not always shown by their posterity. If they, as a chosen and covenanted people, dwelt in the hollow of God's hand, then God might reveal to them his judgments in a mouse, a hailstorm, a clap of thunder, a meteor, a ship capsized, some bad man killed by accident, as truly as in His oracles, and more visibly than in His work upon their hearts by His Holy Spirit.

Sewall was, like every other sincere Puritan, always looking out for omens, or deducing divine premonitions from events. The whole business only repeats the lesson, that any truth carried to an extreme becomes error, and in this case, absurdity, — and dangerous absurdity to boot. He is greatly afraid of

Judge Samuel Sewall of Marblehead.

thunderstorms. His Diary abounds with such entries as these: —

"March 13, 1719. Between 1 and 2 or 3 last night there was great lightning with sharp thunder. Sam and Grindall came down into my daughter's chamber. I humbly and thankfully bless God that we saw the quick and powerful fire; heard the terrible voice and yet we live."

"Much lightning in a cloud toward the Castle which many observed and talked of." "Sabbath, Decr 4, 1698. Last night lying awake, but with my eyes fast shut lightning flashed in my face, I could not tell certainly what light it should be; but presently heard a loud clap of thunder. This day between the ringing of the morning bells, it thundered several times but with a more confused and rumbling noise."

Hailstorms have their uses as his monitors in the will of Heaven: —

"Monday, April 29, 1695. The morning is very warm and sunshiny; in the afternoon there is thunder and lightning and about 2 P.M. a very extraordinary storm of hail so that the ground was made white with it, as with the blossoms when fallen; 'twas as big as pistol and musket bullets. It broke of the glass of the new house about 280 squares of the front. [He mentions also that the houses of the gentry near by, and the new meeting-house, also suffered.] Mr. Cotton Mather dined with us and was with me in the new kitchen where this was; he had just been mentioning that more ministers' houses proportionably had been smitten with lightning; enquiring what the meaning of God should be in it. Many hail stones broke through the glass and flew to the middle of the room or farther. People afterwards gazed upon the house to see its ruins. I got Mr. Mather to pray with us after this awful providence. He told God he had broken the brittle part of our house and prayed that we might be ready for the time when our Clay Tabernacles should be broken. 'Twas a sorrowful thing to me to see the house so far undone again before 'twas finished."

It seems that at Milton there was no hail.

He mentions to Mr. Mather, while they were both undoubtedly nervous over the divine omen of a hailstorm in late April, that the very time in the summer that the Duke of Monmouth invaded England, 1685, a hailstorm had cracked his south-west windows.

While in England he makes this entry : —

> "June 15, 1689. Being at Mrs. Calvin's alone in a chamber, while they were getting ready dinner, I as I walked about began to crave a blessing and when about it remembered my clothes I had bought just before and then it came into my mind that it was most material to ask a blessing on my person; so I mentally prayed God to bless my flesh, bones, blood and spirits, meat, drink, and apparel. And at dinner paring the crust of my bread, I cut my thumb and spilt some of my blood, which word [i.e., blood] I very unusually or never before have used in prayer to my present remembrance."

Under date of Oct. 25, 1713, there is an entry which shows not only the nervous excitement in which many godly Puritans lived, but also this same tendency to superstition :—

> "In the night after 12, Susan comes and knocks at our chamber door; said she could not sleep, was afraid she should die. Which amazed my wife and me. We let her in, blew up the fire, wrapt her warm and went to bed again. She sat there till near day, and then returned; and was well in the morning, *Laus deo. I was the more startled because I had spilt a whole vinegar can of water just before we went to bed; and made that reflection that our lives would shortly be spilt.*"

But "the sundries should end." A pliable and a granite man in streaks, watching for the coming of the swallows every spring, and an eclipse "until," as he writes, "the clouds eclipse it;" finding solemn lessons in a rainbow, and making his very ailments signs of the will of God; setting down all the funerals he went to, all the bearers that served, all the gloves and scarfs he got or gave, until it seems as though one of the chief industries of old Boston must have been grave-digging; at weddings frequent and at christenings; in travails oft; in quarrels sometimes; praying at an old friend's bedside; keeping many private fasts at his own or others' houses; constant in the meeting-house, and always alert to make firm bargains and collect just debts — Sewall's life was as useful as busy. He seems to have had his Boswell also in the Rev. Nehemiah Hobart, a few of whose Latin verses in Sewall's honor, translated by another, — familiarly, R. Henchman, — are here strained out into this history, to show how bad they are — and perhaps some things else, as the reader uses his wit to discover: —

> "Sewall, our Israel's judge and singer, sweet
> Abroad, (whilst busied on the judgment seat),
> His progress, church required. The Sacred Quire
> At home, their fair præcentor did desire.
>
> . . . .
>
> Impartial Judge (the glory of our thrones)
> You whom our country for their Patriot owns;
> Sing, Sir, at home or travel, (for no pains
> You grudge). Fair justice, in your circuit reigns
> Nor innocent, nor nocent here complains."

CHAPTER XIX.

A SUMMARY.

It remains to conclude Sewall's character with a brief analysis. In these pages, and chiefly by his own pen, he has substantially written himself down as he was. If in his life-time he had been appealed to to describe himself, he would probably have said, in the Puritan vernacular of his age, that he was a man in whom grace and nature had long striven together for the mastery, and that each had had several falls. He who stands nearest his own age is apt to serve it best, however the future misses such a man's forecast and preparation for its own. Sewall was in the current of his own times by choice, and whatever enthusiasm of nature he had, did not fray itself out against his environment, but accepted it cordially. Had he been very other than this, and gone on such transcendental escapades, for instance, as Roger Williams did, he might have filled several pages of amazing history; but in his necessary alienation from current affairs, the world would certainly have missed his Diary. Puritanism itself was a revolution, and its enterprises satisfied his zeal. The key to his character, even to its defects, is handed the reader, when he is told that Sewall, as fully as any other man, was a man of his age. Puritanism may be looked at under two aspects, — as formal and as personal. Formal Puritanism is that movement in its creeds, politics, manners, and its other visible on-goings. Personal Puritanism is these same things as they are found in the individual, as elements of character, but colored by that man's personality. Winthrop's personal Puritanism differed from Endicott's, and both from Sewall's. Take the three portraits of Winthrop, Endicott, and Sir Richard Saltonstall, as they hang on the walls of the Historical Society, — three undoubted Puritans in form, and of the same generation. All three look straight, with sincere, open, honest eyes, as into the future; but Winthrop's are a trifle suffused, as with a hint of approaching tears, while the poise of the head is submitted, as if the man felt the weight of a thousand years of feudalism, from which it was the mission of men like him to release posterity. Saltonstall's eyes have also the clear light of honor, and are even rounder, as if in wonder, which almost approaches timidity, as to what he sees, and yet with a poise and face-lines which tell us he will confront gallantly for his religion Prince Rupert's wildest charge of cavalry, or, with a smile to last till the final pallor, endure the wild and its lack, so remorseless to a man of breeding; being worthy, so far as his face goes, at least, to be cousin to Milton in his culture, and the peer of worthier men than those who have only six hundred years of heraldry to back their station. Endicott differs from the other two in that he has not only reached fixed Puritan conclusions, but has flung to the winds every tradition and history of antiquity that contradicts them, — a man ready to carry Puritan logic into law or battle. The mustache he wears shows like the edge of a scimitar. Those merciless, unswerving eyes, the entire pose, denote a man who, if he thought God bade, would batter his head against any rock-ledge in Salem fields, and die so in an obedience dangerously near to Oriental fatalism, — this ancient man of ours, who shows, so far as the portrait goes, the very type of that always masterful revolution which bases itself on religion. These men have but one form of Puritanism; yet are there three persons here to color it.

In form, Sewall is an exact Puritan; no man of his day more so. Everywhere — in the college, in the council, in the meeting-house, in social life — he maintains it, in all its grave, granite temper, even when the form itself is softening, and the children show defection. But by nature Sewall was not a Puritan (he weighed too much for that), but something very else, — a Saxon, an earthborn, robust Englishman; led of his blood towards good dinners, merry wassail out of deep, silver-rimmed horns, as Saxons had done long before Harold had died at Hastings; fond of merrymakings; a snatched kiss under the holly; a lover of little children gleesome in the Twelfth Night dances; and, had he been ecclesiastic, and come to church preferment, an abbot with the merriest, friendliest house and brotherhood of any between Land's

End and the Fore Land. This trend of Sewall's human nature is seen in his portrait, and in his Diary to boot.

Here is intended no apology for Sewall. The man who paints his own portrait has, so to speak, his face in his own hands, and cannot complain if the picture shows some adverse features. The Diary is in print to read, and Sewall stands in it a very plain, emphatic portrait. It is said sometimes that he was commonplace, mercenary, selfish, sordid, especially in marriage matches, — his own and others. The man who wrote the one ancient diary of New England which is bound to live, did a rather uncommon work in that, and so this charge may pass. He was no more mercenary in a love of money than most people round him, or, indeed, most of us after him; and if he saved, he gave, and with an open and kind hand. Most of his New England associates and peers were obliged to be frugal, and Sewall was, whether bond or free. That he was selfish in such sense as to entitle him to wear that epithet more than other men ought only to be allowed when it can be shown that he sought his own, careless of the rights of others. It ought to be graven into literature, and especially all literature like La Rochefoucauld's "Maxims," by some one with a chisel of everlasting steel, that seeking one's own, careful of the rights of others, is never selfishness. He undoubtedly insisted in marrying upon a marriage settlement, and said what he judged. He also married rich, being rich. Both were customs of the times; and to have courted or married otherwise would have been considered by his contemporaries both as bad form and a mismatch.

The man who wrought better or more loyally for New England than Sewall did will come late in our history; and any man who can show anywhere a life as fruitful, gracious, helpful, kind, and wise as Sewall's was, should certainly have the justice of being held in lasting honor.

On Sewall's tombstone might fitly be inscribed the words written, as directed, by that other pious diarist, and of another church, John Evelyn, of blessed memory: —

HE FELL ASLEEP IN FULL HOPE OF A
GLORIOUS RESURRECTION THROUGH FAITH IN JESUS CHRIST.
LIVING IN AN AGE
OF EXTRAORDINARY EVENTS AND REVOLUTIONS,
HE LEARNT THIS TRUTH,
THAT ALL IS VANITY WHICH IS NOT HONEST,
AND THAT THERE IS NO SOLID WISDOM
BUT IN REAL PIETY.

One final word as to the New England Puritans who made up the world that Sewall lived in. The writer of these pages, differing, as he does, *toto cœlo*, from Puritanism as a system of applied religion, is yet aware that, after all its temporalities of form have disappeared, its residuum will still knead itself into the bread upon which nations who aspire to greatness must always feed. That residuum has gone into, and is in, this nation's life infallibly, exactly. That other elements of power, and from other sources, are also here makes nothing against the statement.

The very transcendentalism of this Puritanism must ever be held in honor by just history, as at the least a losing of life to find it, according to the ancient oracle. In the heyday of its resolute youth, the Puritans, too, said, "We will climb the hills and look at the stars." They, too, or at least their sages, regarding the trend of this world's affairs, even in their own age, as away from the Puritan form, would be fain to also confess, "We are old; we have climbed the hills, and the stars are as far off as ever." Yet, at least, the same stars of our human destiny are still there to be looked into; and some day some generation of man will reach them. To that achievement, whatever else it be, the old New England Puritanism remains in time as an encouragement.

Vita ſine literis eſt Mortis Imago ; At
Vita ſine Chriſto eſt Morte pejor.

Si CHRISTUM diſcis, nihil eſt ſi cætera neſcis.
Si CHRISTUM neſcis, nihil eſt ſi cætera diſcis.

SAMUELIS SEWALL

Liber.

Anno Domini.

BOOK-PLATE OF SAMUEL SEWALL.

APPENDIX.

NOTE A.

"JULY 11, 1699. I went with Mr. Willard to Pulling Point to Mr. Dean Winthrop's (77 *annorum*). Between one and two Mr. Willard married Atherton Haugh and Mercy Winthrop: said Mr. Atherton Haugh, Mrs. Mercy Winthrop; forbade all unlawful communion with other women, and *vice versa*. Gave very good advice and exhortation; especially most solemnly charged them never to neglect family prayer. . . . When Mr. Willard asked Mr. Winthrop's consent, he also complimented me respecting Atherton Haugh [Sewall's ward]. I said I was glad that had found so good a family and so good a wife. And after, when saw the bridegroom and bride together after the wedding I prayed God to bless them and give them such an offspring wherein the name of Haugh and Winthrop might flourish."

NOTE B.

IT IS the aim of this note to show that neither the Puritans of New England nor their descendants are responsible for the gradual extinction of the New England Indians. This purpose in a New England man, full of respect for his ancestors, is to be carried out by exposing a curious world-wide fact in the ethnology of the race. This exposition may be made by a quotation from Charles Darwin's "Voyage of the Beagle" (London Ed., pp. 410–411): "Wherever the European has trod, death seems to pursue the aboriginal. We may look to the wide extent of the Americas, Polynesia, the Cape of Good Hope, and Australia, and we find the same result. Nor is it the white man alone that thus acts the destroyer; the Polynesian of Malay extraction has, in parts of the East Indian Archipelago, thus driven before him the dark-colored native.

" . . . The Rev. J. Williams, in his interesting work (" Narrative of Missionary Enterprise," p. 282), says that the first intercourse between natives and Europeans 'is invariably attended with the introduction of fever, dysentery, or some other disease which carries off numbers of the people. It is certainly a fact which cannot be controverted that most of the diseases which raged in the islands during my residence there have been introduced by ships;' and what renders this fact remarkable is, there might be no appearance of disease among the crew of the ship which conveyed this destructive importation."

It is the belief in all heathen lands visited by the whites that the ships bring with them dangerous outbreaks of diseases, even though there should be no sickness on shipboard. Darwin says: "It is impossible that such a belief should have become universal in the northern hemisphere, at the Antipodes and in the Pacific, without some good foundation." And he adds, "Humboldt says that the great epidemics at Panama and Callao are 'marked' by the arrival of ships from Chile, because the people from that temperate region first experience the fatal effects of the torrid zones." It seems further to appear that on all such occasions, all diseases, both native and foreign, assume a more virulent and dangerous intensity than usual. So far forth it is submitted to the candid reader that the decay of our New England Indians was due to this well-nigh universal law which Darwin points out. And since Koch's discovery of microbes, and their exploration by other scientists, it must be an interesting inquiry how far and how the importation of civilized microbes into heathen lands throws new light upon the facts of diseases which Darwin has noted, and on which he bases a far-reaching conclusion.

NOTE C.

It is the purpose of this note to identify the spot where this meeting-house was built by Sewall. First of all, it is plain that it was somewhere in Sandwich. But exactly where? Since the eye-witnesses are gone, the weight of the evidence must be incidental and cumulative. The ancient town of Sandwich, until lately divided, was about ten miles square, not including Mashpee Plantation, which at a very early date ceased to belong to the town. Most of the territory of the town, then and now, consists of a central wood ridge or plateau, where at no time since 1620 were there any Indian villages, because the Indians' food, gained largely from the sea, was to be found along the sea-shores of Massachusetts and Buzzard's Bays. And there we find they actually were. Beginning, then, east, near the Barnstable line, we find that there were a few Indians at Scorton, but not enough to form a congregation. And if there had been, from their locality these Indians would have been more likely to have been taken in hand by the West Barnstable parish adjoining, than by the more distant Sandwich Christians. There is no tradition of any Indian meeting-house here. Moving west along the Massachusetts Bay some five miles to the town centre, we find a Puritan meeting-house from about 1640, adequate to hold both Indians and white men, and no tradition of any other place of worship. This was the usual parish meeting-house for the town; and, within the memory of some living, taxes were paid by the whole town for the support of its ministers. Two miles west of the town centre, at Scussett, there was for a short time, and at a much later date, a small meeting-house created by some obscure parish wrangle, which was for the white malecontents — not Indians. On the Buzzard's-Bay shore, though Indians abounded, there is no tradition nor knowledge of any Indian meeting-house, except some eight miles south, at Cataumet, where there was an Indian and white congregation some time before 1700 A.D. But midway between these two bays, at Herring River village (now Bournedale), on a sporadic hill, thrust out onto the plateau which forms the watershed between the two bays, with the Herring River at its west base, flowing from the Plymouth ponds, south and west into Buzzard's Bay, is, first of all, an ancient Indian graveyard, many of the graves still showing their form in rows, which shows that there was Christian or white man's burial; while elsewhere on the same hill, in all quarters, Indian skeletons have been dug up, buried in the more heathen fashion. In other words, here was an Indian burying-ground before the coming of the whites. Midway on the south front of this round hill, half-way up, is a small shelf or tableland of a few rods square; and here the tradition of both whites and blacks, preserved in all their families, declares was once, and at a very early date, an Indian meeting-house. This meeting-house must have been central for the Indians on both bays; and not two miles from this spot, northward, there now stands a modern meeting-house for the remnant of the Herring Pond Indians who live here, — the undoubted centre of the ancient Indians round about, and whose war-path, still visible in spots, must have run near the base of this hill.

But why, of necessity, must this have been Sewall's meeting-house? There were two missionaries to the upper Cape Indians, — Richard Bourne and Captain Thomas Tupper, both names still remaining in this locality; two English gentlemen, early settled here, who began, apparently without ordinary ordination, the work of Christianizing their Indian neighbors.

It has long seemed to the writer that when the labors of these two men, especially Richard Bourne, are weighed in the scales of exact and comparative history, these laborers, whether we regard the scope, the success, or the personal sacrifice, of their work, will be found entitled to a niche of honor beside John Eliot and Daniel Gookin. But Bourne's work was specially at Mashpee, where he was ordained pastor in 1670, and where he tells us in 1674 he had about five hundred parishioners, with four Indian assistants statedly employed. On the other hand, it is recorded that "Mr. Tupper's attention was toward the northward and westward of Sandwich, where he founded a church near Herring River, which was supplied by a succession of ministers of his name, the last pastor being his grandson, who died in 1787. His congregation was one hundred and eighty" (Hist. Coll., iii., 188, 189). It is this "Mr." or Captain Tupper who appears in Sewall's letters as evidently in charge of the meeting-house, and is so addressed by the judge.

But the report of the commissioners employed by the Society for Propagating the Gospel among the Indians in 1698, based on an inspection made by Rev. Grindal Rawson of Mendon and

Rev. Samuel Danforth of Taunton, men of high character, and versed in the language of the Indians, furnishes cumulate testimony. Their record of Sandwich is this: "Here we find two assemblies of Indians, Herring River and Cataumet, to one whereof Capt. Thomas Tupper, an Englishman, preaches every Sabbath Day. Here are likewise Indian preachers, whose abilities in prayer were tried; viz., Ralph Jones, a person well reputed of for sobriety [were the Indian converts usually otherwise ?], and Jacob Hedge. There are in number 348 persons, men, women, and children, generally well clothed. Preaching among these, *in a small meeting-house built for them after the English fashion*, we experienced their good attention and had their thankful acknowledgments."

What this "English fashion" was may be known from the directions given by Sewall for the building, as recorded in his Diary. Nor was there at the time of building any other meeting-house in Barnstable County for whites or Indians built in that fashion.

The spring at the foot of this hill is still called "Meeting-House spring" by its neighbors. The writer was told by an ancient red woman of this village that she had heard from her grandmother of a relative who used to tell of having walked from Manomet village with a shawl over her head in Indian fashion, and actually attended service in the meeting-house on this hill. What seemed to be the west line of Sewall's meeting-house on the plateau, when measured in the grass by the writer some years ago, was found to agree in length with that given by Sewall in his Diary.

A careful weighing of the whole testimony therefore leads to the reasonable conclusion that the site of Sewall's meeting-house for the Indians is at Herring River (Bournedale), on the hillside among the graves, as heretofore in this note described.

NOTE D.

THE fortunes of the three regicides, Walley, Goffe, and Dixwell, in New England, where they hid themselves, with a high price set on their heads, throw a flood of light upon the temper of our colonial politics. It was the temper of men who abhorred the Restoration in church and state, and clung to the memories of the Commonwealth and Cromwell's mastery. Here were three well-known men doomed and searched for by a powerful government in one of its own little provinces professing obedience to English laws. These men had been repeatedly seen and recognized here, kept up a long correspondence with their friends and families in England, and had been searched for by the king's officers among thinly peopled and not widely scattered communities, where every man was inquisitive and knew all his neighbors; and yet these men managed to live for years unreached by the king, and to die quietly in their beds.

It is simply impossible that their whereabouts were unknown to the leading Puritans of the two colonies of Connecticut and Massachusetts Bay. They were concealed in the houses of Puritan ministers; and these ministers had their professional and family connections from Hadley and New Haven, as far east as Barnstable.

The clergy especially were their friends and protectors — Increase and Cotton Mather among the foremost. Sewall's Diary has indeed no mention of them; as condemned and outlawed by the Crown they were dangerous men to meddle with, even in a private diary. Yet it is incredible that Sewall, moving in the social circles he did, should not have been in their secret. The treatment of these three men by our forefathers furnishes an indirect and therefore powerful evidence of their latent but chronic animosity against the British Crown.

In some ways the story of these three regicides is unique, in its pathos and tragedy, in our American annals. Walley was Cromwell's cousin, a major-general, and had turned the tide in Naseby battle; had been in military charge of Charles I. and a force in England. Goffe was his son by marriage of his daughter. Hunted, concealed in the wild, shut off from family and the stir of civilized life, living with folded arms, as it were, while a new England had risen upon the wreck of their own endeavor, and liberated only by that death which seemed so slow in coming, their fate was to endure long and in solitude a mental hardship seldom falling into our human lot.

A letter of Goffe's wife from England, addressed to him in his concealment, will at least hint at the pathos of the situation. There is no real address; the letter was probably enclosed in one to a New England sympathizer, and the wife addresses him as her son: —

[LETTER.]

13th OCTOBER, 1671.

For My Dear Friend Walter Goldsmith These:

DEAR CHILD, —

I have been abundantly refreshed by thy choice letter of the 10th of August as also by the book you took the pains to write for me. . . . We are all in health and do experience much of the love and care of our good God, in supporting and providing for us in such a day of trial as this is. . . . The Lord make us truly thankful and give us hearts to be willing to be without what he will not have us to enjoy, though never so much desired by us, we are to be at the disposal of our Heavenly Father, and though he exercise us here with hard things, Heaven will make amends for all, it will not be long before we shall see him as he is and be made like unto him who suffered for us that through his righteousness we may be made righteous. I know not whether this may come to you safe and therefore shall be the briefer, but I am willing to take all opportunities to let you know how it is with us, and how dear you are to me and your three sisters [his daughters], longing greatly to see you, if the Lord see it good for us, he will bring it to pass in his own time. The Lord help us to submit to his will and to keep our hearts close to himself. . . . O that all that fear the Lord would cry mightily to God for poor Ingland for the sins of his own people are great and my sins in particular, but I trust the Lord will pacify himself upon his dear Son. I bless the Lord your sisters [his daughters] are not taken with the vanities of the times.

I beg your prayers and promise mine and with my endeared love to thyself and duty and service to all friends, committing you and them to the safe protection of the Almighty I take my leave and till death remain

Your dear and loving Mother
to my poor Fra Goldsmith.

NOTE E.

It may throw a side light upon the Sewall stock in England to copy an inscription from an old brass in S[t]. Michael's Church, Coventry. On the top of the brass is engraved the figure of a female kneeling.

Her jealous Care, To serve her God
Her Constant Love to Husband Deare,
Her harmless heart To everie one
Doth live although her Corps lie here.
God Grante us all while Glass doth run
To live in Christ as she hath done.

ANN SEWELL
Y[E] WIFE OF WILLM SEW[ELL] OF THIS CITY,
VINTNER,
DEPARTED THIS LIFE 20TH DECEM[R] 1609
OF THE AGE OF 46 YEARS;
AN HUMBLE FOLLOWER OF HER SAVIOR CHRIST AN A WORTHY
STIRROR UP OF OTHERS TO ALL HOLY VERTUES.

NOTE F.

THE following summary of the main events in Sewall's life is taken bodily from the published address of Dr. George E. Ellis on Chief-Justice Sewall before the Old South Church, Boston, 1884: —

Samuel Sewall, born at Bishopstoke, England, March 28, 1652.
Arrived in Boston July 16, 1661.
Graduated at Harvard College, 1671.
Resident fellow and librarian.
Married by Governor Bradstreet to Hannah Hull Feb. 28, 1678.
Joined in covenant with South Church March 30, 1677.
Made a freeman May, 1678.
Undertook the management of the printing-press, Boston, Oct. 12, 1681. Resigned the office Sept. 12, 1684.
Followed mercantile business for some years.
Chosen deputy or representative to the General Court from Westfield, Hampden County, Nov. 7, 1683.

GRAVESTONE OF DEANE WINTHROP.

Commissioned on the Council June 11, 1686.

Sailed for England Nov. 22, 1688. Landed on return Nov. 29, 1689.

1692. One of the Royal Council of the Province.

Appointed by Governor Phipps, June 13, 1692, as one of the seven judges, by special commission of oyer and terminer, for trial of cases of witchcraft.

From 1697 to 1703, selectman, moderator, overseer of the poor.

July 25, 1699. Commissioned by Governor Lord Bellomont a judge of the Superior Court.

Oct. 14, 1699. Made a commissioner of the Society for Propagating the Gospel among the Indians.

June 24, 1700. Published the first anti-slavery tract, "The Selling of Joseph."

June 2, 1701. Elected captain of the Ancient and Honorable Artillery Company.

Sept. 16, 1713. Attends the ordination of his son Joseph, as colleague pastor of the South Church.

June 19, 1717. Appointed by Governor Shute, judge of probate of Suffolk.

Oct. 19, 1717. His wife Hannah (Hull) Sewall, dies.

Feb. 11, 1718. Appointed by the governor, chief-justice.

Oct. 29, 1719. Married the Widow Tilly.

May 26, 1720. She dies suddenly.

March 29, 1722. Married the Widow Gibbs.

June 4, 1725. Declined re-election to the Council after thirty-three years' service.

July 29, 1728. Resigns the offices of chief-justice and judge of probate.

Jan. 1, 1730. Dies in his seventy-eighth year, and buried in the Hull tomb in the Granary Burial Ground.

NOTE G.

"MARCH 16, 1703. Mr. Dean Winthrop of Pulling Point dies upon his birthday, just about the breaking of it. He was taken at eight o'clock the evening before. Hardly spake anything after his being in bed. 81 years old. March 20 is buried at Pulling Point by his son and three daughters. Scutcheons on the pall. I helped to lower the Corpse into the grave."